Democratic Incongruities

Democratic Incongruities

Representative Democracy in Britain

David Judge
Emeritus Professor of Politics, University of Strathclyde

First published 2014 by
PALGRAVE MACMILLAN

Palgrave Macmillan in the UK is an imprint of Macmillan Publishers Limited, registered in England, company number 785998, of Houndmills, Basingstoke, Hampshire RG21 6XS.

Palgrave Macmillan in the US is a division of St Martin's Press LLC, 175 Fifth Avenue, New York, NY 10010.

Palgrave Macmillan is the global academic imprint of the above companies and has companies and representatives throughout the world.

Palgrave® and Macmillan® are registered trademarks in the United States, the United Kingdom, Europe and other countries.

ISBN 978–0–230–31446–7

This book is printed on paper suitable for recycling and made from fully managed and sustained forest sources. Logging, pulping and manufacturing processes are expected to conform to the environmental regulations of the country of origin.

A catalogue record for this book is available from the British Library.

A catalog record for this book is available from the Library of Congress.

Typeset by MPS Limited, Chennai, India.

Contents

v

Preface and Acknowledgements

'Know your audience' should be the guiding dictum for all authors. In the case of this book the audience is known and apparent: it is me. Or, to avoid accusations of being self-indulgent, I should make it clear that the audience is 'people like me' who want to understand how representative democracy works in Britain. There are already a multitude of books and articles that tell us how it works, most of which are intensely critical of the 'democratic deficit' or the degree of 'democratic drift' observable in Britain; and most of which point to a fundamental mismatch, an incongruity, between democratic theory and political practice. In essence, British democracy does not work as a standard account of representative democracy stipulates that it should. Even in its own terms there is a series of mismatches between the prescriptions of that account and routine political practice: citizens would be expected, as the essence of democratic engagement, to participate in elections, in contrast to the actual propensity of significant numbers of the British citizenry not to engage even in this minimal level of participation; political parties would serve as representational transmitters of power from voters to governors rather than the other way round; representative institutions would represent the 'shared experiences' of the various peoples of the political nation and internalise the values of political equality, instead of institutionalising limited representativeness and sustaining representational inequalities; governments would be authorised by, and held accountable to, elected representatives (and ultimately to the electorate) rather than being enmeshed in governance networks insulated from electoral representative processes.

If the starting point for understanding is thus taken to be a 'standard model' of representative democracy, then that model does not get us very far, as there is a distinct lack of fit between such an account and political practice in Britain. (The focus of attention in this book is Britain and its constituent countries of England, Scotland, and Wales. Given the differences and complexities of politics in Northern Ireland the following analysis only mentions Northern Ireland when it is specifically appropriate to do so in the context of the United Kingdom state (UK). In turn, the term UK is used, rather than Britain, when the legal and constitutional entity of 'the state' is being referred to). Yet one of the incongruities to be analysed in this book is why, in spite of evidence

vi

to the contrary, UK governments continue to propound such a standard account as 'the official model' of representative democracy in Britain. Clearly, alternative models have been available. For most of the period since the acceptance of representative democracy as a viable mode of government in Western Europe, political theorists have illuminated the democratic deficiencies of that state-form. However, in recent years there have been significant developments of democratic theory, with political theorists pursuing, vigorously and productively, a 'representative turn' in the conceptualisation of democracy. In particular, theories of legitimate representative democracy have been developed out of a conceptual separation of democracy from representation, and representation from election. The former separation leads towards participatory and deliberative forms of citizen engagement beyond formal representative institutions; the latter separation points in the direction of non-electoral modes of representation beyond electoral representation. In each direction new theories have helped to locate complex ecologies of representation in the broader ecosystem of democracy. Moreover, several of these theories have inspired 'democratic innovations' designed as practical enhancements of representative democracy. And, despite continuing to subscribe to the 'standard account' of representative democracy, successive British governments have sought to incorporate some of these innovations into the practice of British governance. To what effect, and how incongruously, will be examined in later chapters.

But if the target audience of this book is those political scientists, political theorists, political practitioners, and students of politics more generally, who want to know how representative democracy works in Britain, then what is the 'distinctive selling point' of this book? There are a host of empirical analyses that show that democracy in Britain is deficient, there are a plethora of contending analytical models – of network governance, multi-level governance, differentiated polity, asymmetric power, post-parliamentary governance – that claim to provide more compelling explanations of how it actually works, and there are many elaborate theories – based on deliberative or participatory premises – as to how it should work. So: why yet another book tramping over familiar terrain?

My answer is short: there are a number of outstanding concerns left untouched or unresolved in many existing analyses of British representative democracy and which are worthy of attention. I use 'concern' here in two senses: first, as a matter of importance and interest, and second as a matter of anxiety or unease.

In the first sense, my concern is with the conjunction of two discrete concepts – 'representation' and 'democracy' – into 'representative democracy'. This is a matter of importance and interest, not least because representative democracy is often treated as an oxymoron. Whereas 'democracy' privileges popular participation and inclusion in decision-making processes, 'representation' posits the absence and exclusion of 'the people' from decision-making in conceiving of *re*-presentation as 'mak[ing] present again ... *in some sense* something which is nevertheless *not* present literally or in fact' (Pitkin 1967:8–9 original emphasis). This inclusion–exclusion paradox is at the core of representative democracy and has been of concern to me throughout my academic career and has surfaced in some of my earlier books. More importantly, it has also become of importance for new waves of democratic theorists in their 'reconceptualisations' of representation and their recognition that political representation is, indeed, as much about exclusion as inclusion, and that electoral representation simultaneously separates and links representatives from the represented. Yet, even if direct popular inclusion is episodic, and confined to the moment of election, the intervals between elections nonetheless provide political spaces which allow for exclusion to be mitigated in continuing processes of mediated representation. In this sense, political representation can be conceived as systemic, encompassing not only electoral processes and institutions but also non-electoral processes, and 'informal' or 'self-authorised representation'. At the point of intersection between mediated and unmediated participatory processes, and between electoral and non-electoral representation, the fundamental question is posed of the compatibility – both ideationally and practically – of representation *with* democracy.

This question provides an organising thread throughout the book. It is commonplace to treat this question rhetorically and to answer affirmatively that unmediated participation and non-electoral representation are simple complements and supplements for the mediated participation and electoral representation of representative democracy. In the analysis that follows in this book, however, a more sceptical approach is taken in the discussion of the democratic enhancement of representative democracy. What particularly concerns me (in terms of interest and importance) is how notions of, and schemes for, the democratic enhancement of representation serve to alter the legitimating frame provided by elections in representative democracy, and do so by inhering discordant legitimation claims into a reconceived conjunction of representation *and* democracy. In this process, electoral claims come to be destabilised while non-electoral participatory claims are simultaneously defused. A mismatch, an incongruity, is thus to be found at the theoretical core of reconceptualisations of representative democracy.

My other concern, in the second sense of unease, is that these theoretical incongruities come to find reflection in the mismatched practice of 'democratic innovations'. This concern links to an extensive audience that has already been assembled to voice anxiety about citizens' distrust, disconnect, disengagement, and disappointment with the processes and institutions of representative democracy in Britain. While these anxieties are not exclusive to Britain, they are more pronounced and more stridently expressed in reflecting the deeper levels of disenchantment with formal politics in Britain than in many other European representative democracies. One powerful explanation of this negativity is that it arises from a profound sense of popular frustration with, and disempowerment within, the existing system of representative democracy. In seeking to redress the perceived deficiencies of representative democracy, a number of 'democratic innovations' – rooted in deliberative democracy, or direct democracy, or increasingly e-democracy – have been implemented by successive British governments. The concern examined within this book is that the democratic potential of these innovations becomes transmuted in their accommodation within a legitimating frame provided by electoral representation. Theories of unmediated citizen engagement become entangled in mediated processes and institutions of representative democracy. My concern is with the assumption that 'democratic innovations' simply complement and supplement, and so enhance, representative democracy. However, the interaction between mediated and unmediated forms of citizen engagement also holds the alternative negative potential that, in the process of enhancement, both participation and representation may be altered and diminished in incongruous ways.

Before reaching this end-point in the analysis, however, other more immediately pressing concerns need to be investigated. As noted above, there are many observable mismatches and incompatibilities between theory and practice. In part, this 'jarring effect' reflects incongruities within a standard account of representative democracy itself. Whereas the standard model is predicated upon a simple principal–agent relationship between individual representatives and individual citizens; such an unmediated relationship comes to depend upon mediated relationships for its institutional realisation – through 'constituencies' designed to organise individual voters into collectivities (based upon territory, or social class, or gender, or ethnicity), and political organisations formed around those collectivities (political parties, organised groups, and social movements). How those constituencies are constituted and how they are mediated becomes of prime concern both in terms of interest and of unease. Equally, a standard account, while adhering to the value of political equality, in the notion of equally weighted votes in elections, has no intrinsic requirement of representational equality for all citizens. Yet the search for greater representational equality, through strategies to promote descriptive representation and to link substantive representation to the outcomes of those strategies, brings with it further incongruities.

No book on representative democracy in Britain could avoid raising concerns about the 'Westminster model'. This is a model that has come to provide a short-hand descriptor for a distinctive institutional structure which captures the representative and responsible elements of representative democracy yet transmutes those elements into a particular 'power-concentrating' form of government. In itself this transmutation is of concern. Yet a further concern has attracted the attention of a broad and critical audience of political scientists, constitutional lawyers, and political practitioners – who are all keen to point out the extent of divergence between the ideational foundations of the Westminster model and the practice of modern British governance. The point of intersection between this orthodox and longstanding concern and the specific concerns of this book is to be found, however, in the incongruous proposition that a model of transmuted democratic representation that no longer fits political practice nonetheless still provides a legitimating frame for state decision-makers. This stacking of incongruity upon incongruity is sufficient to attract concern, in terms of both interest and unease, but it is the stacking of a further incongruity onto this already teetering analytical construction that elevates 'concern' to academic 'disorientation': the legitimating framework deployed by decision makers to authorise their actions is derived from the 'standard' account – the pre-mutated version – of democratic representation rather than the mutated version in the Westminster model that contemporary governments seek to defend. When critics of the Westminster model call upon governments to provide a new narrative or theory of government beyond the existing legitimating frame they are, therefore, asking either for an alternative to representative democracy, as conceived in the standard model, or for the acceptance of 'reconceptualisations' of democracy which still, in their various representative forms, presume a frame of electoral representation. Incongruous solutions thus come to be posited for incongruous 'problems'.

Having stacked incongruity upon incongruity, we find that the audience for this book now extends well beyond 'me'. There are, however, several audiences that will remain beyond reach. A (vast) number of people undoubtedly will not read this book or share my academic concerns, and in the past have not read a word that I have written nor made a contribution to my academic thoughts. In the front row of this lost audience is Lorraine, whose achievement in not having read any of my books (while providing the constant love and support that enabled me to write them) in the 40 years that we have been married is truly worthy of mention. Equally, Ben and Hannah have proved to be a credit to their mother in following her example. Right behind this family audience in terms of achievement is Fiona Macintyre, who, in her capacity as Manager of the Department/School of Government at Strathclyde University, read every word of my administrative and managerial outpourings during my ten-year tenure as Head of Department/ School, but resolutely refused to read any of my academic writings.

There are, however, more receptive audiences that deserve mention. These are, of course, those colleagues who have helped me over the years in shaping the ideas in this book. They have been many. Many of their contributions have been unwitting. And many would not necessarily agree with what I have written. In these circumstances it is probably diplomatic simply to record my gratitude to those who recognise their contribution with the words 'you know who you are'.

I am not brave enough, however, not to mention by name the people responsible for bringing this book before its reading audience. So I offer my thanks to the editorial team at Palgrave Macmillan, especially to Amber Stone-Galilee and Andrew Baird, who have tracked my progress and offered encouragement at appropriate times (and might even have read some of the words in this book!).

1
Democratic Incongruities:
Old Models and New Perspectives

Representative democracy in the United Kingdom:
the official version

Official descriptions of the United Kingdom's (UK) system of government, to be found in official publications and on parliamentary and government websites, present a consistent and unambiguous 'standard account' of representative democracy. The key elements of this 'standard account' are: 'the UK is a Parliamentary democracy'; 'people vote in elections for MPs who will represent them in Parliament'; 'every adult has the right to vote – known as "universal suffrage"'; 'government is voted into power by the people, to act in the interests of the people'; there is 'an Executive drawn from and accountable to Parliament' and 'a sovereign Parliament, which is supreme to all other government institutions' (Cabinet Office 2011a; Home Office 2013; UK Parliament 2013).

This official 'standard account' is clearly premised upon parliamentary democracy as a variant of representative democracy, and so deems state decision-makers to be both representative of and responsible to 'the people' through the process of elections. More particularly, in this UK variant, parliament, as the state's primary representative institution, is also deemed to exercise legal sovereignty. Out of this conjunction of electoral democracy, representative and responsible government, and parliamentary sovereignty emerged the shorthand descriptor 'the Westminster model'. Although often conceived simply as an empirical description of governing practice (and an inaccurate one at that), the Westminster model is in fact infused with normative theories about representation and accountability, as well as legal theories about the sources of legislative supremacy and constitutional theories about the interactions of political institutions. In which case, if 'clearly the

1

Westminster model presupposes representative democracy' (Bevir 2010: 124), then it is advisable to identify the defining characteristics of this representative form of democracy before examining the incongruities of theory and practice associated with contemporary UK representative democracy.

Representative democracy: 'standard account'

Contemporary analyses of representative democracy often outline a 'standard account' (Urbinati and Warren 2008: 389), or a 'conventional view', or 'an orthodox understanding' (Hayward 2009: 111) in preface to subsequent theoretical and empirical dismantling of these accounts. As with any summary account, therefore, such general views and understandings sketch at best a delimiting analytical frame rather than nuanced conceptualisation of the variegations of representative democracy. Nonetheless, a 'standard account' provides a baseline model against which competing, often critical, democratic and representative claims can be assessed and the resilience of the original model tested.

The starting assumption of representative democracy is that the decision outputs of such a system are legitimate because the representatives taking those decisions are themselves deemed to be legitimate. A comprehensive account of democratic legitimacy has to explain, therefore, why some individuals (in the absence of all other individuals) have the right to make decisions on behalf of those who are not present. Under a 'standard account', what provides political representation with legitimacy is a set of procedural standards of authorisation and accountability associated with free and fair elections (Rehfeld 2006: 3).

Threaded through 'standard accounts' of representative democracy, therefore, are normative assumptions about legitimacy, authorisation, accountability, and control. These assumptions can be seen in two recent examples of a 'standard account', provided respectively by Urbinati and Warren (2008) and Alonso *et al.* (2011). Urbinati and Warren (2008: 389) ascribe four main features to their 'standard account'. First, there is a principal–agent conception of representation, in which the elected representatives serve as the agents of their constituents, organised in territorial constituencies, and in which there is a separation of 'the sources of legitimate power from those who exercise that power'. Second, electoral representation 'identifies a space within which the sovereignty of the people is identified with state power'. Third, electoral processes ensure some degree of responsiveness to 'the people' by representatives and political parties who speak and act in the name of 'the people'. Fourth, the notion of political equality is incorporated into electoral representation through the universal franchise.

Similarly, Alonso *et al.* (2011: 2) identify the characteristics of representative democracy as 'a type of government in which people, in their role as voters faced with a genuine choice between at least two alternatives, are free to elect others who then ... represent them by deciding matters on their behalf'. Democratic representation is thus a process of making present the interests and views of citizens who are not physically present at the point of decision. It is a dialectic process of authorisation and accountability: 'it is an ongoing tussle between representatives who make political judgements and the represented, who themselves also make political judgements' (Alonso *et al.* 2011: 5). In this sense it is not merely a process of delegating decision-making to representatives, but also of holding the elected responsible for their actions. Every election, therefore, is 'as much a beginning as it is an ending' (Alonso *et al.* 2011: 6). Elections enable electors to make prospective estimations of the potential performance of their representatives as well as retrospective assessments of actual performance. The election of representatives in this account is 'a dynamic process subject to what can be called the disappointment principle' (Alonso *et al.* 2011: 6). The 'disappointment principle', as enunciated by Keane (2008: 32), is simple and powerful:

> 'the people' make their periodic appearance in elections in order to judge, sometimes harshly, the performance of their representatives. That is the whole point of elections, which are a means of disciplining representatives who have disappointed their electors, who are then entitled to throw harsh words and paper rocks at them ... [to] throw scoundrels out from office.

Representative democracy in this view allows for – indeed encourages – the rotation of leadership. It embeds at the core of the democratic system a contingency and temporality of decision-making authority. As Kateb (1981: 358) argued: 'representative democracy signifies a radical chastening of political authority ... political authority is, at every moment, a temporary and conditional grant, regularly revocable'. Through this periodic chastening, a standard account of representative democracy identifies a 'distinctive form of government that simultaneously distinguishes and links together the source of political power – the people or *demos* – and the use made of political power by representatives' (Alonso *et al.* 2011: 5). The process of representation thus serves both to include 'the people' in decision-making – indirectly and periodically through elections – yet at the same time to exclude them from direct and continuous participation in the decision-making process. Hence embedded in a 'standard account' of representative democracy is a fundamental inclusion–exclusion paradox (see Judge 1999: 9–12; Urbinati 2011: 24). Yet out of this elemental paradox the standard model offers, in terms of democratic legitimacy, a 'holistic framework' within which to analyse processes of democratic authorisation, accountability and control.

The notion of a 'holistic framework' is of some significance in a standard model because there is 'a presumption of generality' (Urbinati 2010: 83) built into representative democracy. This presumption is essential to the processes of legitimation in this form of democracy. In essence, representative democracy presupposes that decisions – public policies – will be collective in the manner of their formulation and implementation. This does not mean that decisions will be made unanimously or accepted uniformly, but rather that decisions are framed as collective decisions and received as such by winners and losers (as defined in relation to the consequences of those decisions). In this view the systemic nature of political representation is of some importance. Political representation is not confined to a micro-level interaction between individual constituent and individual representative, but encompasses systemic level democratic representation, which Saward (2010: 163) characterises as a 'complex, mixed bag of election, acceptance, acclamation and proposition'. In this sense, as Pitkin (1967: 221) argues, '[w]hat makes it representation is not any single action by any one participant, but the over-all structure and functioning of the system' (1967: 221). This is a view to which Mansbridge (2011: 628) and Rehfeld (2011: 640) also subscribe, as they both agree that 'representation at its broadest is systematic, in the sense of involving many different parts interacting with one another in interesting and complex ways' (Rehfeld 2011: 640). As a process of adjudicating amongst, and reconciling, conflicting claims, representative democracy assumes the articulation of some common interest and provides, through electoral processes and representative institutions, a capacity for communal judgement of that articulation (Manin 1997: 192). In fact, as Rehfeld (2005: 149; emphasis in original) notes: 'There is simply no plausible justification for establishing a national representative legislature *without* some reference to the resulting good of all, whatever the good may turn out to be'.

From this systemic 'generality' emerges the paradox that 'although a representative is supposed to deliberate about things that affect *all members* of the polity, she is also supposed to have a sympathetic relation to *a part* (the part that votes for her)' (Urbinati 2006: 44; original emphasis). More fundamentally, 'partial or partisan aggregations such as political groups or parties ... are not optional or accidental in a representative democracy ... *political* representation breaks with the logic of homogeneity and identification although it is a process of unity, not fragmentation' (Urbinati 2006: 134). Representative democracy does not assume a homogeneous *demos* or a pre-given 'general will'; instead it assumes permanent contestation and the representation of diverse social interests and opinions (Alonso *et al.* 2011: 5). Ultimately what the 'democratic bargain' at the heart of representative democracy seeks to fashion, out of this diversity and contestation, are 'winners who are willing to ensure that losers are not too unhappy and for losers, in exchange, to extend their consent to the winners' right to rule' (Anderson *et al.* 2005: 190).

Problems of the standard account

Having presented a standard account of representative democracy, Urbinati and Warren (2008: 390) are quick to point out that 'the standard account has been stretched to the breaking point'. Equally, Hayward's (2009: 111) purpose in sketching 'the conventional view', is to 'make trouble' for this view by rethinking the orthodox understanding of the democratic value of representation. And Alonso *et al.* (2011: 8) recognise that there 'has always been a gap between the bold ideals of representative democracy and its complex, multi-layered and defective real world forms'. Their purpose, therefore, is not only to reconsider the standard account, or what they prefer to call the 'core founding principles', of representative democracy, but also to use those principles to assess current forms of democratic representation which 'defy textbook accounts of representative democracy' (Alonso *et al.* 2011: 9).

While it would be easy to dismiss the specification of a standard account as simply the creation of an analytical straw man, such an account serves three related purposes for the present study. First, a standard account provides a distillation of the essential characteristics of representative democracy from which theoretical complexities can be unpicked and analytical ambiguities and incongruities identified. Second, a standard account provides a checklist against which the 'rethinking' of representative democracy can be set and the distance of travel from the core principles to 'representation in practice' can be measured. Third, it reflects almost exactly the official description of representative democracy in the UK, as noted in the opening paragraph of this chapter. As such, both its inherent conceptual problems and its contemporary practical dysfunctions are also those of UK representative democracy.

Inherent conceptual problems

Elections and participation

Elections are the key institutions of representative democracy, as they serve as a tensile link between representatives and represented. Indeed, as Bühlmann and Kriesi (2013: 46) point out, elections 'establish a double linkage between the political input (the citizens' preferences) and the political output (public policies adopted by the elected representatives) by allowing for a combination of responsiveness and accountability'. Some 'thin' accounts of representative democracy focus almost exclusively upon elections as the essence of democratic participation in decision-making, with popular participation being limited to periodic selection or deselection of decision makers (Alonso *et al.* 2011: 5–6; Bellamy and Castiglione 2013: 211). Indeed, as Coppedge *et al.* (2011: 256) contend, 'If one were interested in a thin concept of electoral democracy ... then elective government, free elections, and regular elections would probably suffice'. But few theorists beyond Schumpeterians (who conceived of democracy in terms of the electoral competition of elites (see Schumpeter [1943] 1976: 269)) would maintain that a mere electoral account of representative democracy is sufficient to capture either the democratic or representative dimensions of this form of 'rule by the people'.

Before examining thicker conceptions of representative democracy, however, the genetic problem of elections as a core element of representative democracy needs to be addressed. Stated starkly 'elections simultaneously separate and link citizens and government' (Urbinati 2011: 24). In terms of participation:

> The [aim of the] electoral procedure ... is actually to make people's direct participation inessential to the performance of deliberative institutions. The deterrent power of elections lies in their ability to stimulate decisional activism in those who can be held accountable: the representatives, not the people. Elections make apathy, not agency, the main quality of popular sovereignty ... they make citizens' participation during the period between elections superfluous. (Urbinati 2006: 14)

Representative democracy thus institutionalises the self-exclusion of the bulk of the population from systematic involvement in decision-making through their punctuated participation in the electoral process

(Judge 1999: 9). The 'central paradox of modern democratic government' is that political representation is 'necessarily about exclusion' (Rehfeld 2005: 6). From this meta-conceptual problem stems the further empirical incongruity that, even when given the periodic opportunity to participate in elections, significant segments of 'the people' do not avail themselves of the opportunity to do so. As a result, they doubly self-exclude themselves from participation: both directly in the act of voting and indirectly in their dyadic relationship of authorisation/accountability with elected decision makers.

Elections, representation and equality

In 'the standard account' representative democracy is endowed with a basic formal political equality in the universal franchise (see Urbinati and Warren 2008: 389). The norm of political equality is incorporated in the principle of one person, one vote, one value. Robert Dahl (2005: 195) insisted, for instance, that if the desirability of political equality is accepted:

> then every citizen must have an equal and effective opportunity to vote, and all votes must be counted as equal. If equality in voting is to be implemented, then clearly, elections must be free and fair. To be free means that citizens can go to the polls without fear of reprisal; and if they are to be fair, then all votes must be counted as equal.

A standard account also assumes that individuals, for the purposes of elections, are grouped in territorial constituencies. Historically, as Urbinati and Warren (2008: 389) point out, territorial representation has had an important relationship to political equality in so far as 'the bare fact of residence [became] a sufficient condition for equal power sharing'. Yet, increasingly, modern theorists have broadened the political equality requirement to factor other notions of equality (for instance, socio-economic, ethnic, gender) into the representational relationship. Saward (2003: 164), for example, while not dismissing the reasonableness of efforts to identify a 'single, superior meaning' for political equality, such as equality of voting power, maintains that political equality has as its corollary 'inclusion', because 'it is difficult to see how anything other than an inclusive, involving form of institutionalising political equality can be acceptable democratically' (2003: 162).

Closely linked to this contention is the view that political equality is dependent for its realisation not simply on the legal status of voting but also in relation to social and economic resource distribution. Once resource distribution is factored into the democratic equation, then 'structural inequalities' – defined as 'asymmetries in access to resources and opportunities and in the social capacity to act' and which are institutionalised in 'deep and enduring social hierarchies' (Hayward 2009: 112–13) – pose a problem for the standard account of representative democracy. This is because the structurally disadvantaged 'often cannot, by virtue of their positions in the hierarchies structural inequalities define, authorize representatives and/or hold them to account' (Hayward 2009: 113). This inability is tantamount to exclusion from the representative process:

> If the disadvantaged cannot constrain such representatives to 'act for' them, or if such representatives do not understand the needs, experiences, and/or perspectives of the disadvantaged (the worry is) representative institutions will fail the test of democratic legitimacy. (Hayward 2009: 113)

By this view a principal–agent conception of representation, where the votes of formally equal individuals in territorial constituencies are aggregated, simply serves to justify and perpetuate existing patterns of exclusion. To mitigate this variant problem of representational exclusion, strategies of inclusion have been constructed around notions of 'descriptive representation' (Pitkin 1967: 60–91) or the 'politics of presence' (Phillips 1995: 5–26). However, these strategies are not founded on political equality *per se*, but are rooted more specifically in the ideas of 'equality of presence' and 'equality of recognition' (Phillips 1995: 34, 40). In privileging these equalities, the focus of attention is redirected away from territorial constituencies as the constituted group for the purposes of political representation to social constituencies and rules of selection for representatives. In so doing, the incongruity emerges: to secure these specific representational equalities requires political strategies – of equality promotion and equality guarantees – that infringe the 'simple political egalitarianism on which the institutions and mechanisms of modern representative democracy were established' (Castiglione and Warren 2006: 2).

Representational transmission of power: political parties and beyond

The standard account of representative democracy, as presented by Urbinati and Warren above, starts from the premise of a principal–agent relationship between individual voters and individual representatives cohered within a territorial constituency, but simultaneously acknowledges collective principal–agent relationships between electors and representatives cohered around political associations – most distinctly around political parties in the electoral process (but also interest groups, civil society organisations, and social movements at the interstices between electoral and non-electoral representation). Representation becomes mediated: political associations serve to modulate the authorisation and accountability of representatives and serve as institutions for the 'representational transmission of power' (Sartori 1987: 30). As a result, '[r]ather than individual legislators serving as the linking mechanism between public opinion and policymaking, parties provide this linking mechanism' (Dalton 1985: 271; Dalton *et al.* 2011: 3–5). In this process a 'chain of democratic linkage' with five main forms of voter–party linkage can be identified (see Dalton *et al.* 2011: 7–9). First, 'campaign linkage' identifies the centrality of parties in the recruitment of representatives and in defining the agenda and the nature of political discourse of elections. Second, parties mobilise citizens to vote and chase citizens' votes as part of 'participation linkage'. Third, parties aggregate voter interests into party choices. This 'ideological linkage' assumes that voters have informed preferences and policy choices, that they are capable of making judgements about which party best represents their preferences and that these judgements guide their voting behaviour (Dalton *et al.* 2011: 8). Fourth, 'representation linkage' specifies congruence between citizens' policy preferences and the policies of parties in parliament and government. Fifth, parties in government implement the policies promulgated during the election process. This form of 'policy linkage' is a corollary of 'ideological linkage'.

The ubiquity of political parties in western representative politics is such that they have been described as endemic to, and an unavoidable part of, representative democracy (Stokes 1999: 245, 263). And for many analysts, the term 'party government' has been taken as a synonym for representative democracy (see Dalton *et al.* 2011: 3). Yet, as mediating institutions between citizens and government, political parties occupy problematic spaces both in theory and practice. In representative theory they encounter the problem of being 'partial-yet-communal associations' (Urbinati 2006: 36). The aggregation of partial preferences enables parties to translate 'the many instances and particularities in a language that is general and wants to represent the general' (Urbinati 2006: 37). Yet this requires a dialectic interaction between the process of partial or partisan aggregation and the formulation of public/general policies dependent upon the articulation of an idea of 'the general'. In representative practice, parties occupy a problematic space in acting simultaneously as representative institutions and as governmental institutions. In Mair's (2009: 5) words: '[t]he same organization that governed the citizenry also gave that citizenry voice, and the same organization that channeled representation also managed the institutions of the polity. This was the key to the legitimation of representative government in democratic political systems'. The problem arises, however, when this synchronicity is fractured, either when the voices of the citizenry and the party are discordant or when the governmental role is privileged over the representative role. At those points the incongruities of the idea and the practice of party government become manifest.

Moving beyond the limitations of a standard account of democratic representation

Non-electoral representation

Although the standard account of representative democracy focuses upon conjoined electoral processes and institutions and representative processes and institutions, it has been widely acknowledged that 'there are limitations to a purely electoral rendering of democracy and representation' (Urbinati and Warren 2008: 402). These limitations are apparent in the 'problems', associated in both theory and practice with electoral democracy, identified above. Recognition of these problems has led to sustained arguments that a theory of legitimate representative government requires the conceptual separation of democracy from representation, and representation from election (Näsström 2011: 508). The former separation looks towards participatory and deliberative forms of citizen engagement beyond formal representative institutions; the latter separation looks towards non-electoral modes of representation beyond electoral representation.

According to Saward (2010: 82), 'many observers' maintain that 'the elected simply are the representatives, and the unelected, though often politically important in varied ways, are something different'. To counteract this view what is needed, he argues, is recognition that the simple fact of electing a politician or political party into office does not mean that elected representatives are able to speak 'for the range of interests and identities' of citizens (Saward 2010: 84). The essence of non-electoral representation, in contrast, is that it is a claim to represent 'the *interests* of a *specified group*' (Saward 2010: 95; original emphasis). The recognition of legitimate representative claims beyond the institutional configurations of elections and representative assemblies is thus a key part of a reconceptualisation of representation (Urbinati and Warren 2008: 391). In this 'rethinking', prior assumptions – that elected representatives are the sole or '*fully* legitimate representatives' – are questioned, as is the notion that 'the unelected are automatically *illegitimate* representatives' (Saward 2010: 167; emphasis in original). It is the claiming rather than the possession of the attribute of legitimate authority that is important: 'What needs to be generated is a sense of legitimacy' (Saward 2011: 77). This allows Saward to conceive of democratic representation as a diffuse set of political practices and performances whereby democratic representation can plausibly be seen in 'many manifestations of non-statal political representation' (Saward 2011: 93). In this reformulation the essence of democratic legitimacy 'is understood as "perceived legitimacy" as reflected in the acceptance of claims over time by appropriate constituencies under certain conditions' (Saward 2010: 84).

But, as Saward acknowledges, his approach does not constitute a 'black-and-white alternative' to conventional conceptions of electoral democracy: 'My critique of electoral representation does not add up to a rejection of electoral representation' (Saward 2010: 84). In fact, he observes that those representative claims that are held to be compelling, or which have particular resonance among relevant audiences, 'will be made from "ready mades", existing terms and understanding that the would-be audiences at a given time will recognize' (Saward 2010: 84). One of the 'ready mades' of 'modern democratic constitutional design' is the 'centre-staging' of electoral representation, which is 'often now taken to be the paradigm of democracy'. Indeed, it is worth reiterating here that elections underpin the 'perceived legitimacy' of electoral representation, and provide recurring opportunities where the represented assent to being represented – whether assent is based upon prospective or retrospective judgements of representatives' performance, or both (see Rehfeld 2006: 188). In other words, electoral representation is identified as 'the received (and adaptable) frame within which we understand and interpret politics' (Saward 2010: 178). If this is the case, then this poses a problem for self-authorised representatives (such as interest groups, social movements, civil society organisations, or international non-governmental organisations) in terms of the 'perceived legitimacy' of their representative claims. If an alternative case is hypothesised, and the perceived legitimacy of non-elected representation coalesces with the 'negative power' of citizens to the extent that the complex process of 'unifying-and-disconnecting citizens' at the heart of electoral representation (Urbinati 2006: 228) becomes dislocated, then the problem is one of the challenge posed to the perceived legitimacy of electoral representation itself. In seeking to question orthodox views of democratic representation and to 'enhance recognition of the complex ecology of representation' (Saward 2010: 168), the intention is to 'add to', 'to extend', and 'to make democracy more representative' (Saward 2010: 167–8).

Yet to argue that non-electoral representation supplements and enhances electoral representation somehow generates the incongruity that in the process of supplementation the latter would become less distinct. To paraphrase Dubnik's (2011: 712) statement on accountability: 'Any effort to enhance representation also alters representation'.

Democratic innovations

'Enhancement' of representative democracy has been evident in the proliferation of 'democratic innovations', such as citizens' juries, citizens' surveys, deliberative polling, deliberative forums, and minipublics. Such innovations represent a departure from political representation conceived primarily in relation to electoral institutions and processes, and are 'specifically designed to increase and deepen citizen participation in the political decision-making process' (Smith 2009: 1). They are particularly noteworthy because they are 'more than ideas and theories; they are ideas in action' (Newton 2012: 5). They are 'innovative' in that they represent a departure from the institutional configurations of electoral representation and are designed to engage citizens directly in political decision-making processes. They are 'democratic' in that they are institutionalised forms of participation that occur 'beyond traditional modes of institutionalised engagement' (Smith 2009: 2), yet formally involve citizens in the making of public policy at multi-levels.

Although often presented as modes of 'participatory democracy', or 'direct democracy' or 'unmediated citizen engagement', and hence as alternatives to representative democracy, 'democratic innovations' have been situated in recent analyses within the discursive and institutional frames of 'representation'. Thus, for Urbinati and Warren (2008: 405), the more important properties of democratic innovations are that they are representative. Ultimately, 'a few citizens actively serve as representatives of other citizens' (Urbinati and Warren 2008: 405). In which case, the problem of the perceived legitimacy of innovative institutions is rooted in the dialectical relationship of the non-electoral legitimation claims of these institutions with the legitimation claims stemming from election: a directly analogous problem to that noted above in relation to non-electoral representation. For many analysts, however, this is not 'a problem'. Newton (2012: 11), for instance, resolutely maintains that democratic innovations 'are inevitably developed within and by the institutions of old forms of representative democracy'. Similarly, in the specific case of innovations occasioned by the 'deliberative turn', Goodin (2008: 7) argues:

> Inevitably, however, deliberative democracy can only supplement rather than supplant the institutional apparatus of representative democracy as we know it. Representative assemblies will not disappear, political parties will not disappear, international fora will not disappear, policy networks will not disappear. Deliberative democrats need to figure out to how to fit their particular contribution to existing institutions of representative democracy, just as practitioners of democratic politics have to figure out how to incorporate deliberative insights.

However, if deliberative innovations constitute a response to the perceived deficiencies of aggregative representative democracy and a search for a legitimate political order based upon deliberative praxis, then rooting that order in an existing electoral representative frame holds the potential to generate fundamental conceptual and practical democratic incongruities. Not the least of these is that the institutional forms taken by deliberative innovations are often restricted in size and scope and so actively engage only relatively few citizens. Their democratic claims ultimately distil, therefore, into the incongruous proposition that to address the shortcomings of the formal representative system, citizens are required to act in some sense as representatives of other citizens. Yet, when located on the conceptual terrain of representation, deliberative innovations are confronted with the same legitimation dilemmas as other forms of non-electoral representation.

In contrast, direct modes of citizen participation offer an unmediated form of legitimation. The referendum as a decision-making procedure – a direct vote, with a formally equal weighting, with simple majority decision requirements – has been found to hold a special legitimising appeal among citizens (Esaiasson *et al.* 2012: 803). Direct democracy would thus appear to constitute a clear conceptual and practical challenge to the legitimation claims of representative democracy. Yet there is a presumption among many political analysts that there is 'something wrong' with the contention that direct and representative modes of participation are incompatible (Newton 2012: 11; see also Budge 2012: 32–5; Mendelsohn and Parkin 2001: 3–4). However, in making the assertion that direct modes of participation, especially referendums, can be conceived as supplements to representative democracy, the incongruity of the need to reconcile unmediated modes of participation with the mediation of electoral representative processes and institutions is sidestepped.

Sovereignty: popular, parliamentary and problems

Popular sovereignty

In Urbinati and Warren's (2008: 389) standard model, electoral representation 'identifies a space within which the sovereignty of the people is identified with state power'. This signifies a dual identification: first, identifying sovereignty with a territorial state; and, second, identifying sovereignty with the location of ultimate political authority within a state. The first is 'a representational and ordering device which identifies discrete polities that can act in the name of an undifferentiated collective notwithstanding an internal diversity of interests, values and wills' (Walker 2013: 6). It refers simultaneously to an internal claim of monopolistic political authority within a state as a precursor to an external claim of authority in a state's relations with other sovereign states. It is a view significantly at odds, however, with modern conceptions of a 'decentred' state where the 'undifferentiated collective' is challenged from two directions: first, at a supra-state level by the 'supplementary tiers of transnationally connected legal and political authority' (Walker 2013: 12) of regional institutions (for example the European Union(EU)), or global institutions (the United Nations (UN) or the Group of Eight (G8)), or international agencies (for example the World Trade Organization (WTO) or the International Atomic Energy Agency (IAEA)); and, second, at sub-state level by nationalist/regionalist claims for greater sub-national territorial institutional differentiation.

The second 'identification' is concerned with locating the source of ultimate political authority within the state. For some constitutional lawyers popular sovereignty is manifest in 'a people's direct democratic capacity to act as the supreme source of constitutional law in foundational constitutional acts' (Tierney 2012: 14). This serves as a reminder that 'constitutional authority finds its democratic legitimacy in the consent of the people' (Tierney 2012: 13) and echoes Rousseau's ([1762] 1968) belief that the sovereignty of the people could only be retained so long as its legislative right was not transferred to another body or individual. This is often taken to mean that Rousseau, in opposing 'representation' as the alienation of the people's sovereignty, unambiguously favoured direct democracy (for an alternative view see Garsten 2009: 97–8; Marini 1967: 469). Certainly, modern proponents of direct democracy still seek to associate referendums, as acts of collective will-formation and expression, with the mobilisation of 'popular sovereignty'. Yet treating the people as a constituent authority, possessing the power of decision, requires sovereign popular will to remain general in order to retain its legitimacy (see Douglass 2013: 3; Garsten 2009: 94; Marini 1967: 457). Once called upon to decide upon specific policies, direct popular participation runs the danger that the particular interests of 'a people' would come into conflict with the general expression of the will of 'the people'. In these circumstances, even Rousseau professed a predisposition in favour of an indirect system of government rather than a more direct form of democracy (Marini 1967: 469). This leads Garsten to conclude that, although Rousseau professed his opposition to representation, his prescriptions about government 'were not so different than those at the heart of our [modern] practice of representative democracy' (Garsten 2009: 97).

Parliamentary sovereignty

The problem in the UK, however, is that although the practice of representative democracy is infused with notions of popular sovereignty, 'the official theory or dominant theory of the constitution has never located a supreme authority in the people' (Turpin and Tomkins 2011: 518). Instead, the legal doctrine of the sovereignty of parliament has served as the 'fundamental constitutional principle' (Bogdanor 2009: 14). It has also served to narrow the scope and ambition of constitutional debate in positing a simple dichotomy between popular and parliamentary sovereignty. Yet just as notions of popular sovereignty inspired by Rousseau can be accommodated within the practice of representation, so the changes in the practice of representative democracy itself have opened up a theoretical space for the seemingly incongruous positioning of political notions of popular sovereignty alongside legal principles of parliamentary sovereignty. Nowhere is this incongruity more evident than in the writings of A. V. Dicey (see for example 1915 [1982]). Dicey, the most influential populariser of the doctrine of parliamentary sovereignty, was willing to acknowledge that, although parliament was the legal sovereign, the people – or more accurately the electorate – were the political sovereign in the UK. This has prompted some analysts to conclude, therefore, that 'Dicey was not Diceyan' and that he was in fact an 'ardent supporter of popular sovereignty' (Weill 2003: 493). While this conclusion will be left hanging here, awaiting further consideration later in this book, it does point to apparent incongruities in the discourses of sovereignty in the context of representative democracy in the UK.

Westminster model

The official account of representative democracy in the UK, identified at the start of this chapter, not only adheres closely to a standard account of representative democracy but also encompasses legal conceptions of parliamentary sovereignty. This combination has been encapsulated in the shorthand term 'the Westminster model'. The immediate problem with this term is that, while it still provides the dominant image of British government it is a 'threatened' image (Bevir 2010: 123). Or, to use Flinders' (2010: 2, 289) terminology, while it remains 'the meta-constitutional orientation' of the UK state, it is subject to new, and arguably incompatible, meta-constitutional orientations which 'question' and 'contest' the meta-orientation of the Westminster model (Flinders 2010: 27–9).

This problem is exacerbated by the fact that there is no agreed definition of the Westminster model. Rhodes *et al.* (2009: 7), for instance, identify 14 key beliefs and core institutions that have been identified as essential elements of the Westminster model across various periods. Nonetheless, it is possible to identify some 'core features' (to the extent that they recur in different academic analyses): a legally sovereign parliament; parliamentary representatives who are accountable to the people through regular competitive elections; responsible government with political executives drawn from parliament and ultimately dependent upon sustaining the legislature's confidence; and an executive whose members are individually and collectively accountable to parliament (see Gamble 1990: 407; Kavanagh 2009: 29; Rhodes *et al.* 2009: 10). They are deemed to be core ideas in that they have the deepest historical roots and 'typically gravitate' around the constitutional fusion of the executive and legislature (Rhodes *et al.* 2009: 9; see also Richards 2008: 15–16; Richards and Smith 2002). Equally importantly, these core ideas serve as the prism through which state actors interpret their roles (Rhodes *et al.* 2009: 9). In this sense, the Westminster model 'survives above all as an image to which politicians and public officials orient themselves. Many political actors in Britain still use the language of the Westminster model to describe their world' (Bevir 2010: 125).

What is absent, significantly, from these core ideas is an automatic association of the Westminster model with single-party majoritarian government, a two-party system and a unitary state. Yet, Lijphart (1984, 1999, 2012), in his seminal study of *Patterns of Democracy*, identified these as defining institutional characteristics of the Westminster model (in addition to the core features identified above). In essence,

Lijphart's prime objective was to make a categorical distinction between majoritarian and consensus democracies as 'general models of democracy'; but, in so doing, he chose to use the term 'Westminster model' interchangeably with the term 'majoritarian model'. As a result, successive characterisations of the Westminster model have been inclined to include a two-party system and majority control of the executive as part of the definition of the Westminster model (Bevir 2010: 124; Flinders 2010: 20). What these later characterisations have been less inclined to do, however, is to acknowledge the original reservation made by Lijphart that, although 'British politics was in close conformity with the Westminster model' for much of the post-1945 period, before then there had been 'significant deviations from the Westminster model of majoritarian democracy with regard to almost all of the model's ... characteristics' (Lijphart 1984: 10). Stated slightly differently, if, as Flinders (2010: 24–5) maintains, the UK version of the Westminster model was confirmed in the mid-19th century and 'remained undisputed' for around 150 years, then it needs to be recognised that, even within this timeframe, there were episodes of party fluidity (in terms of electoral competition and government composition (see Bogdanor 2011: 61–71; McLean 2012: 6–7)), along with pronounced administrative devolution (see Mitchell 2009), which did not correspond to some of the key 'meta-constitutional orientations' identified in Lijphart's conception of the Westminster model. Moreover, Rhodes *et al.*'s (2009: 10) contemporary comparative study of the Westminster model 'allows for variations such as multi-party systems, different voting structures (plurality, preferential, or proportional representation), federal structures and written constitutions' without infringing the core features of the model.

It is of some importance when examining the 'distance of travel' of modern UK democratic politics from the Westminster model to be clear, therefore, upon the 'essential core' of that model and to recognise the conceptual optionality of such 'add-ons' as interest group pluralism (Lijphart 2012: 15–16), executive control of the central bank (Lijphart 2012: 20), first-past-the post electoral system (Richards and Smith 2002: 4) or non-political civil servants (Richards and Smith 2002: 4). Indeed, just to take the example of a professional, non-partisan and 'permanent' public service, there is some contestation as to whether this is a defining feature of a Westminster model (Rhodes *et al.* 2009: 10) or rather of a bureaucratic 'Whitehall model' (see Page 2010: 407–8; van Dorpe and Horton 2011: 235) or a hybrid Whitehall–Westminster model (Flinders 2002: 23).

Thus a major problem in assessing the contemporary relevance of the Westminster model is simply to determine what the constituent elements of that model are in the first instance.

Structure of the book

The preceding discussion of a 'standard account' of representative democracy has highlighted a series of 'problems' inherent within such an account. A 'problem' is used here in its literal sense as both a proposition that is questionable and hence requires further investigation, and a proposition that is difficult to reconcile with its starting premises. Such problems are treated as macro-questions and are used to construct chapter headings. The identified macro-problems, and hence chapter headings, are: the problem of the people; the problem of the representational transmission of power; the problem of representatives; the problem of representative government (and in its UK variant, the problem of the Westminster model); and the problem of citizen participation. Within this macro-frame of 'problems' a series of incongruities can be identified. Incongruity is taken to mean, again in a literal sense, something that is out of keeping with its immediate environment. In the specific case of representative democracy, incongruity is taken as a 'mismatch' in either the theory or the institutional practice of representation (or one with the other). At one extreme a basic *incompatibility* between two co-existing conceptualisations or between theory and practice may be posited. At another extreme, incongruity may simply point to a perceived *lack of fit* between ideas, or between ideas and the way institutions operate.

Phrased more colloquially, what drives the analysis of the book is a sense that 'something isn't quite right' – not only with the standard model, but also with reconceptualisations of representation designed to address the theoretical shortcomings of that model and to align theory more closely to the practice of contemporary representative democracy in the UK.

The 'problem' of 'the people' is examined in Chapter 2. Whereas theories of representative democracy tend to assume an active, participatory and knowledgeable citizenry – willing and able to contribute indirectly to decision-making when called upon to do so – the empirical incongruity is that significant sections of the UK's citizens do not participate in the minimal act of voting, or engage in any other form of institutionalised political activity, or, for that matter, possess deep resources of political knowledge or information capable of informing electoral choice. In addition, significant sections of 'the people' in the UK display deep levels of mistrust both of political representatives and of representative institutions. If there is an 'inclusion–exclusion paradox' at the centre of conceptions of representative democracy theory, then the practice of representation in the UK appears to have resolved the contradiction largely in favour of exclusion.

Yet whether low levels of electoral participation, declining political trust, weakening social capital, and widespread political illiteracy are inimical, in themselves, to representative democracy is itself an incongruous question. At a conceptual level, the arguments of 'stealth democrats', or of those who believe in the 'democratic innocence' of low levels of electoral turnout, or of those who hold the view that citizens need not be overburdened with political knowledge in order to participate, have fashioned revisionist views which sit incongruously with standard accounts of representative democracy.

Further incongruities are revealed when attention is focused upon arguments that political participation, beyond engagement in formal representative politics through voting or membership of political parties, serves as a substitute for electoral participation. While there is strong evidence that people, especially young people, are active in informal political activities, these are often displacement or replacement activities. In many respects they are seen as alternatives to, rather than supplements to, formal political engagement. In which case, they do not solve 'the problem of the people' and their disengagement from formal representative political processes. Instead, they simply underline the incongruities between formal political processes and 'informal' political activities.

Chapter 3 analyses 'the problem' of the representational transmission of power. At the heart of a standard account of representative democracy is the notion of 'linkage' between the people and their representatives. In this process of linkage representation becomes mediated, with political associations, most notably political parties and organised groups, interposed in the processes of authorising representatives and holding them accountable. The fundamental incongruity, noted above, is that of reconciling the representation of partial political interests to the formulation of general public policies. This incongruity is merely compounded in practice when parties are identified as 'damaged goods' in the performance of their linkage roles. As Chapter 3 reveals, this 'damage' is most pronounced at the electoral interface with citizens.

Whereas standard accounts of party representation identify the capacity of political parties to articulate interests, aggregate demands, formulate collective preferences into patterned policy programmes and mobilise electoral support, the practice of party representation highlights the incongruities of discordant policy preferences between parties and their electors, hazy voter perceptions of parties' positions and diminished mobilisation capacities resulting from declining membership and restricted funding. At the other end of the chain of linkage, parties serve as 'governing institutions' in translating their policy preferences into public policies. Yet if the 'unique contribution of parties' (Mair 2009: 5) to representative democracy is that they traditionally combined the roles of representing and governing, then the contemporary privileging of the latter role over the former has impacted upon how policy preferences are aggregated and how voters use government performance as a heuristic for making voting decisions.

Beyond the electoral transmission of power through parties, however, are other modes of representational linkage – in the form of organised groups and social and protest movements. The incongruities arising from the interplay of aggregative, collectively authorised, electoral representation and particularised, self-authorised, non-electoral representation are examined in Chapter 3.

Chapter 4 drills down beyond the 'collective' modes of representation examined in Chapter 3 to analyse principal–agent relationships between individual representatives and their constituencies (conceived variously in terms of territory, gender, ethnicity and social class). In this analysis, the macro-problem – of how representatives make present again something that is not present – reveals a series of micro-incongruities associated with explanations of 'what' is being made present, 'how' the 'what' is being made present, and 'who' is making the 'what' present again.

If the 'what' is taken to be a territorial constituency, then the representative is confronted with incongruities associated with contrasting principles of territorial segmentation in determining constituency boundaries; a 'perceptions gap' arising from a perceived dissonance between the expectations of constituents and the role prioritisation of their representatives; and territorial interests being taken as a proxy for other non-territorial 'communities of interest'.

If the 'who' is taken to denote the desirability of a correspondence of social characteristics between represented and representatives; then incongruities can be observed: first, between 'descriptive' and 'substantive' representation in the possibility that 'non-descriptive representatives' may be equally, or more, effective in representing the substantive interests of a group than descriptive representatives, and, second, in the conflict between practical strategies of equality promotion and broader conceptions of representative equality.

If the 'how' is taken to mean a complex multi-dimensional relationship mapped out on a continuum between 'trustee' and 'delegate' positions, then how representatives structure and receive decision-making cues from the citizenry – from individual opinions and conscience at one pole through to mandates and management by parties at the other – reveals incongruities in theory as well as in practice (in the contrasting perceptions of voters and representatives about the linearity of the relationship between electoral authorisation and policy outputs).

The 'problem of representative government' is examined in Chapter 5. The terms 'representative democracy' and 'representative government' are often used as synonyms, and clearly there is significant overlap in their meanings (see Judge 1999: 8–15). Chapter 5 makes a simple distinction, however, between 'representative democracy' as an overarching term to characterise the fundamental organising principles of a political system, and 'representative government' as primarily concerned with the issue of leadership within that broader political framework.

This distinction moves the discussion away from an assumption that representatives are equal and undifferentiated decision makers or political leaders, towards recognition of a fundamental divide between the institutions of representation (parliaments or legislatures) and the institutions of decision or leadership (political executives). In the UK the political executive is drawn from the legislature itself and has no independent source of legitimacy other than that derived from the legislature. Hence the claims of government to be democratic depend upon the wider claim of the legislature to be an electoral representative institution. In the case of the UK, a particularly executive-centric form of government developed, whereby extensions of the franchise and of the liberal state in the late 19th century led to the broader notion of 'representative democracy' subsuming within it the older, narrower notion of 'representative government'. Thereafter, the central paradox of British representative democracy was that the latter notion not only predated, but also continued to predominate over, the former (see Judge 1999: 17–19). This particular form of representative government became encapsulated in an idealised 'Westminster model', which combined a theory of legitimate decision-making (derived from authorisation and accountability accounts of representation) with a legal conception of sovereignty (derived from the constitutional experience of the Westminster parliament). The problem for representative government in Britain is that the combined precepts of the Westminster model have come under sustained criticism (both theoretically and empirically) from adherents of alternative models of 'governance' and 'popular sovereignty'.

In examining these critiques, Chapter 5 points to a profound incongruity that, although the Westminster model is deemed to be deficient empirically, nonetheless, the underpinning representational precepts of the model still provide a 'legitimating framework' within which state actors define and defend their decisions. Correspondingly, although the relevance of 'parliamentary sovereignty', as both legal principle and constitutional practice, has been subject to withering critical analysis, nonetheless, the official position of successive governments displays an absolute certainty in the location of legal sovereignty within Westminster. This incongruity is matched, in turn, by an alternative incongruous contention that parliamentary sovereignty and popular sovereignty are not incompatible, but instead may be seen to have some conceptual coexistence when nested within a frame of electoral representation.

Having identified, in Chapter 5, the challenges posed by governance perspectives and notions of popular sovereignty to the 'Westminster model', Chapter 6 addresses the further 'problem' posed to this model by direct citizen participation and deliberation in the political decision-making process. Representative democracy is premised upon a political division of labour; yet increasingly this division has been questioned in a series of 'democratic innovations', all of which, whatever their particular institutional form, 'redraw the traditional division of political labour ... by providing citizens with more influence in the political decision-making process' (Smith 2009: 3–4). The distinctiveness of these innovations is their concern to translate democratic theory into practice, whether these are deliberative theories or direct participatory theories. However, fundamental conceptual and practical incongruities emerge when, in searching for a new legitimate political order based upon deliberative and participatory praxis (as a response to the perceived deficiencies of aggregative representative democracy), that order is conceived as a supplement to, rather than a replacement of, electoral representation. Thus, in examining deliberative innovations (most particularly mini-publics and citizen-representatives) and participatory innovations (most notably referendums and 'e-democracy' initiatives), Chapter 6 reveals the incongruities between the foundational legitimation claims of these innovations and the formal legitimation claims associated with democratic authorisation and accountability afforded by election. Moreover, the experience of implementing democratic innovations in the UK reveals the incongruous constraining of unmediated deliberative participation and direct citizen participation in an attempt 'to expand' mediated citizen participation in representative democracy. The assumptions, legitimation discourses, and power structures of the latter sit uneasily with the assumptions and legitimation claims of the former.

Chapter 7 makes explicit what has been implicit in many of the preceding chapters: that the theories and practices of non-electoral representation, multi-level governance and democratic innovation (especially deliberative initiatives and e-democracy) impact upon Britain to the extent that domestic representative democracy cannot be isolated, spatially, from broader representational and democratic interactions at supra-state levels. Encapsulated within this simple, and (to many analysts) self-evident statement, however, is a basic incongruity: democratic 'input legitimacy' remains rooted primarily in electoral processes and institutions at state level while the expansion of non-majoritarian institutions and non-electoral representative processes and institutions (with other claims to legitimacy) has refocused theoretical and empirical attention beyond the nation state. Thus the concept of multi-level governance extends ideas familiar to the analysis of state-level politics to patterns of transnational institutional interconnectedness. In turn, notions of non-electoral representation underpin analyses of democratic initiatives that seek to enhance the diversity and influence of citizens beyond elections and beyond individual state borders. These developments coalesce in 'post-state' and 'post-representative' conceptions of 'post-democracy', 'post-parliamentary' and 'monitory democracy', which variously identify the marginalisation of formal representative processes and institutions whilst simultaneously, and incongruously, maintaining that these processes and institutions are neither meaningless nor redundant.

In examining this fundamental tension at the heart of analyses of the malaise of national variants of representative democracy and prospective global institutional blueprints (in the form, for example, of global stakeholder democracy or global representative assemblies) the analysis of this book returns full-circle to the affirmation of the distinctiveness of electoral representation and the continuing centrality of domestic democratic legitimation derived from British electoral representative processes and institutions. Equally, in making this reaffirmation, the discussion returns to the starting premise that these processes and institutions remain central to an understanding of contemporary British politics in a regionalising and globalising world, yet they also remain deficient in the practice of British representative democracy. This is the ultimate democratic incongruity.

2
The 'Problem' of the People

Introduction

At the core of any definition of democracy (*demokratia*) is the *demos*: 'the people'. Yet the difficulty in defining democracy adequately is in specifying the linkage between the *demos* and *kratos*: 'rule'. Nonetheless, however this linkage is conceived, a common precept of democracy is the participation of 'the people' in the making of decisions that affect them. Exactly how the people participate, and the conditions under which they participate, has provided a fundamental conceptual distinction between unmediated/direct forms of participation and mediated/indirect forms. In turn, these forms have tended to be subsumed within broader, contrasting conceptions of direct democracy and representative democracy. In the former, 'democracy mean[s] that each and every citizen ha[s] an equal and meaningful chance to take part in lawmaking' (Urbinati 2006: 2), with political legitimacy stemming directly from the people's direct engagement in public policy-making. Indeed, from this perspective, 'participation is thought of *as* democracy' (Weale 2007: 101), in which case 'the people' do not constitute a conceptual 'problem' in their relation to decision-making as there is an unmediated link: they are the decision makers.

In contrast, the participation of 'the people' becomes problematic when it is mediated through representation. Indeed, for those who treat democracy and participation as synonyms, the term 'representative democracy' is an oxymoron (Urbinati 2006: 4). This is because in a representative system popular participation is episodic. As noted in Chapter 1, some 'thin' accounts of representative democracy focus almost exclusively upon elections as the essence of democratic participation in decision-making, with popular participation being limited to periodic selection or de-selection of decision makers. In this thin version, elections provide recurring opportunities for representatives to be simultaneously authorised and held accountable by voters. Yet at the exact point of recording their vote, the democratic incongruity arises that popular political participation is neutralised 'by making the people a legitimizing force at the very instant they renounce their ruling power' (Urbinati 2006: 4). It is at this point that the inclusion–exclusion paradox at the heart of representative democracy is revealed most starkly. It is at this point also that the participation of 'the people' is unproblematic (at least conceptually), to the extent that punctuated participation in elections is decisive in legitimising the decision-making process and the policy outputs of the electoral process, *as long as 'the people' self-exclude* themselves from the representative process thereafter. This is the position adopted famously by Schumpeter ([1943] 1976: 282) in his declaration that 'voters do not decide issues'. For Schumpeter ([1943]1976: 295), voters 'must respect the division of labour between themselves and the politicians they elect'; they also should exercise 'self-control' and 'refrain' from 'political backseat-driving' in between elections.

However, the participation of the people becomes more problematic when representation is conceived not simply (or exclusively) as episodic interventions at election time, but rather as an ongoing process. This processual view of representative democracy is captured by Dalton *et al.* (2011: 22 original emphasis) in their suggestion that:

> Rather than a discrete, point-in-time choice, [representative] democracy is based on a process of ongoing, dynamic representation that occurs through a comparison of the past and future across repeated elections. In other words, elections function not simply as a method of political choice at election time, *but as a dynamic method of steering the course of government.*

In this dynamic process, representation becomes a process of continuous filtering, refining, and mediating political judgement (Urbinati 2006: 6); and 'electoral participation alone is not sufficient indication of meaningful participation' (Saffon and Urbinati 2013: 461). A conception of representation as 'a process', therefore, in moving beyond intermittent expressions of 'authorising will', extends the participatory space beyond elections to include other political institutions as the means for citizens 'to give their political presence an effective and persistent character through time' (Urbinati 2011: 26). It is in this sense that political parties and other political associations serve as institutions for the 'representational transmission of power' (see Chapter 3).

Of more immediate concern here, however, is the relationship between participation and legitimacy. It is frequently asserted that the idea of electoral democracy is the key to political legitimacy (Rothstein 2009: 314). Elections serve to enhance legitimacy through the participation of voters in the electoral process itself and in political associations of parties, groups and movements (Anderson *et al.* 2005: 22–3). A clear connection is thus posited between institutions of representation, popular participation and perceptions of political legitimacy. In this connection, citizens' attitudes – what people think about the processes and institutions of representation – are crucial to understanding systemic political support. If macro-attitudinal positions are constructed from a mix of individual judgements and calculations of political legitimacy, of trust and of consent then, in this context, 'the people' re-emerge as 'a problem' for representative democracy. The problem is that insufficient trust in the institutions of representation holds the potential for significant popular distancing from voting; reduced participation in other 'representational transmission' activities; electoral 'losers' reacting negatively to the mediated outcomes of representative processes; or, more broadly, widespread questioning of the legitimacy of those outcomes and of the very processes themselves.

In considering 'the problem of the people' the following sections of this chapter analyse the incongruities – of conceptual disjunction, theoretical misfit and incompatible empirical findings – associated with the self-exclusion of the people from electoral participation: the conjoined linkages of social trust, social capital and political trust, and of the relationship between political trust and legitimation.

Participation in elections: Incongruities of turnout

Voting in elections is still the most common form of citizen political engagement in representative democracies (Dalton and Gray 2003: 23; Whiteley 2012: 34). In most western liberal democracies, however, it is a declining form of participation as measured by 'turnout' (see Clarke *et al.* 2009: 232). Of the 34 member states of the OECD in 2011 the average decline in turnout since 1980 was 11 percentage points, with turnout in the UK falling by 10.9 per cent between the 1979 and 2010 general elections. Although the negative trend in turnout has been 'remarkably uniform' in cross-country comparisons (Blais and Rubenson 2013: 96), turnout at 21st century UK general elections has been described as 'dismal' when compared with domestic national elections in the second half of the 20th century (Clarke *et al.* 2009: 231). Even the 'dismal' turnouts at recent Westminster elections seem positively buoyant, however, when compared with turnout at other elections in the UK – for local authorities, the European Parliament, the Scottish Parliament, the Welsh Assembly, City Mayors, and local Police and Crime Commissioners.

Does turnout matter?

For those who believe that turnout is important in representative democracy, the act of voting encapsulates political participation. As Fieldhouse *et al.* (2007: 797) observe: 'turnout matters not only because it is an obvious indicator of political participation, but also because it may be regarded as a democratic health check'. The basic problem of declining turnout, therefore, is that if voting is the expression (and extent) of most people's formal engagement with the democratic process, then non-voting becomes an aggregate indicator of political 'dissatisfaction' (Stoker 2006: 32). As such, the decline of electoral turnout is to be viewed as an 'alarming' trend that 'merely emphasises the extent of the contemporary disaffection and disengagement of citizens with formal politics' (Hay 2007: 12, 20). More specifically, in the words of Harriet Harman (2006), then Leader of the House of Commons: '[o]ur democracy lacks legitimacy if, whatever the formal rules about universal suffrage and the right to vote, people don't make it a reality by turning out to vote'.

Arguments that 'turnout matters' tend to be premised on a basic assumption – that turnout is an unmitigated good and that increments in non-voting are matched by increments in loss of governing legitimacy or in increases in the levels of public political dissatisfaction. Whether there is an exact proportionality between these increments is seldom explicitly considered. What has been considered, however, is the effect of differential turnout by voters from different social groups (whether based upon differences of gender, ethnicity, religion, age or socio-economic status). Indeed, the skewed nature of turnout has raised deep concerns about how well the interests and policy preferences of non-voters are represented in the democratic process. Yet comparative empirical evidence suggests that the policy preferences of non-voters do not necessarily differ significantly from those of citizens who do vote at elections (see Godefroy and Henry 2011; Hajnal and Trounstine 2005; Highton and Wolfinger 2001). Nevertheless, there remains widespread concern in the UK that skewed participation rates in elections is associated with skewed representation of interests and preferences in public policy-making. Whereas for most UK general elections in the immediate post-war decades there were few habitual non-voters and few socio-economic differences associated with the propensity to vote, by the general elections of 2005 and 2010 there was 'a clear division in the levels of turnout between relatively well-off, well-educated professional middle classes on the one hand and less well-educated manual working class on the other' (Denver 2007: 40; 2011: 76). Not surprisingly, such individual level behaviour found reflection at constituency level, where, although turnout increased in every region across the UK in 2010, urban, working class and socially deprived areas witnessed lower turnouts than constituencies that were preponderantly suburban or rural, middle-class and relatively affluent (Denver 2010: 603).

In addition, there has been acute concern about skewed electoral participation rates by ethnic minorities in most western representative democracies. Notably, however, at the UK general election of 2010, ethnic minorities recorded practically the same levels of turnout (as a percentage of the registered population) as for white Britons as a group (Heath *et al.* 2013: 143). This finding does, however, mask the fact that ethnic minorities have a lower propensity to register to vote than the white British. Whereas 93 per cent of the white British sample were registered to vote, only 82 per cent of ethnic minorities in the Ethnic Minority British Election Study sample (and only 73 per cent of Black Africans) were registered (see Heath *et al.* 2013: 140). Manifestly, those not registered to vote boost the numbers of non-voters.

The marked decline in the proportion of young people (aged 18–24) voting at general elections over the past 20 years has also provided grounds for concern. Certainly, this decline has been notable, both in domestic terms and in comparison with other countries (Sloam 2012: 96). Youth turnout declined from an average of 75 per cent in the UK general elections of the 1980s to an average of 40 per cent in the first three elections of the 21st century. In this 20-year period the gap between youth turnout and overall turnout increased from 9 to 21 points. In 2010 it was estimated that 44 per cent of the cohort of 18–24 year olds voted, which was an improvement on the turnout of 39 per cent and 37 per cent for young people in 2001 and 2005 respectively (Electoral Commission 2010). Yet the improved turnout for 18–24 year olds in 2010 still left them trailing behind the turnout of older age cohorts: 55 per cent for the 25–34 cohort, 60 per cent for 35–44 year olds, 65 per cent for the 45–54 group, 69 per cent for 55–64 year olds, and

77 per cent for those aged over 65 (Denver 2011: 77). Indeed, over a period of nearly 30 years of British Election Study surveys, this 'turnout gap', between the 18–24 and over-65 age cohorts, had widened from 10 per cent in 1983, to 29 per cent in 2010 (and had reached 38 per cent in 2005) (Clarke *et al.* 2009: 237; Denver 2011: 77).

These significant age differences in turnout would be of little interest if they were simply 'life-cycle' events: that is, if young people are identi-fied as being at a transitional stage of life – somewhere *en route* to 'adult-hood' with its traditional connotations of 'steady work', establishing households and families, and developing community affiliations (see Flanagan *et al.* 2012: 30). The logic underpinning life-cycle explanations is that once this transition has been completed, with the assumption of adult social roles, then increased political participation is likely to follow in the wake of increased social and material stakeholding. One assumption is that those with greater 'stakes' will pay closer attention to political decisions and processes that affect those 'stakes'. Another assumption is that 'as people grow older they 'become more involved in the political process, acquire a greater sense of responsibility and are more likely to view voting as a civic responsibility' (Denver 2007: 40). One possible explanation for low levels of youth turnout at recent elec-tions is simply, therefore, that the transition to adulthood is now more protracted in the UK and most European societies, as macroeconomic changes have resulted in lengthier periods of formal education, reduced opportunities for full-time, 'continuing' employment, delayed forma-tion of family groupings and shallower roots in neighbourhoods and communities. In essence, the contention is that young people will even-tually 'grow up' and 'grow out of' electoral apathy, but that the process of assuming adult roles is now far more protracted and convoluted than only a few decades ago.

The reduced level of electoral turnout by young people assumes greater significance, however, if it can be shown that the decline in voting is a generational effect. While fluctuations may occur, there has been a marked tendency for age cohorts to continue to vote at roughly the same rate as they did when they reached the age of 18 (Clarke *et al.* 2004: 268; 2009: 239). In the UK, Clarke *et al.* (2009: 239) note a distinct generational component to the marked decrease in voting since the early 1990s. Explanations of this generational effect have coalesced around two main views. First, the generation gap in turnout reflects larger culture value change. Second, this effect reflects contextual factors where certain characteristics of electoral competition, or change to the franchise, impact differently upon generations in the electorate.

The first view holds that new generations hold different values that predispose them not to vote, whereas older generations hold a set of values which predispose them to vote. Exactly which values prompt these contrasting predispositions varies across different analyses: from a shift from materialist to post-materialist values across age cohorts, through differences in attention and interest in formal politics, to different emphases upon the value of a sense of civic duty (for an overview see Blais and Rubenson 2013: 98). In the UK, for example, it has been found that the 'Thatcher' and 'Blair' generations of new voters subscribed less to notions of civic duty than older generations (Clarke *et al.* 2004: 272–3; Denver 2011: 78). In particular, members of these younger generations were much less likely to think of non-voting as a 'serious violation of their responsibilities as citizens' (Clarke *et al.* 2004: 274).

The second view has two dimensions: first, that changed electoral arrangements can have cumulative effects – most dramatically the effect on young people of the lowering of the voting age; and, second, short-term effects of particular 'entry-stage' elections – whether these elections are closely competitive or of perceived importance – influence turnout for first-time voters and their subsequent participation as voters (Franklin and Wessels 2002: 17). The first dimension has been identified as a continuing, and cumulative, deflator of turnout (Franklin *et al.* 2004: 120). Evidence suggests that voters in any particular generation learn to become voters based upon their experiences of their first few elections, with an estimate offered that it takes about three elections for the habit of voting or non-voting to be established (see Franklin and Hobolt 2011: 69). In which case, 'many young people today are learning not to vote and, consequently, are likely to remain abstainers in the future' (Clarke *et al.* 2009: 239). The second dimension has been used to explain how successive generations of first-time voters in the UK, beginning with those who entered the electorate during Mrs Thatcher's premiership and continuing through the Blair era, experienced a different political socialisation process to preceding generations. This is in tune with broader sociological findings that 'individuals born in the same period of time may share exposure to certain socio-historical events that shape their political socialization' (Bhatti and Hansen 2012: 264). The relative non-competitiveness of Westminster elections throughout most of the 1979–2010 period (with apparent foregone conclusions in 1983 and 2001), combined with a perceived narrowing of ideological distance between the major parties and declining partisanship, may have served to depress turnout generally and youth turnout specifically. Yet a series of quantitative studies has tended to find little impact (in terms of statistical significance) of electoral competiveness upon turnout (see Smets and van Ham 2013: 355).

There is evidence, however, that generational effects do not seem to be mitigated by increased opportunities to vote (at subnational and supranational levels). If anything, if the first opportunity to vote is presented at low-salience second-order elections (see below) then not only will young voters be less likely to turnout at such elections, but they will also be less likely to vote subsequently in other first-order elections (see Franklin and Hobolt 2011: 75). In this case, more opportunities to vote in elections for different political institutions, perceived to occupy second-order, or third-order rankings, may have the incongruous effect of depressing levels of turnout in the long term. At this point, therefore, it is apposite to examine arguments about the increased 'marketplace' of voting.

Turnout and incongruities of the 'Electoral Marketplace'

A person voting for the first time in the general election of 1970 would have been part of a political generation that benefitted from the lowering of the voting age to 18, which had come into effect one year earlier in 1969. Thereafter, apart from the vagaries of random parliamentary by-elections, s/he would have had one further scheduled opportunity to vote, in local elections, before the next UK general election in February 1974. A person voting for the first time in the UK general election of 2010, depending on where s/he lived in the UK, would have had numerous opportunities to vote in elections (leaving aside voting in referendums) before the next UK general election in 2015: pilot elections for Health Boards in two regions in Scotland (June 2010), elections for the Scottish Parliament, National Assembly of Wales, and the Northern Ireland Assembly (May 2011), local elections throughout the UK (May 2012), English mayoral elections (May 2012), elections for 41 local police and crime commissioners (November 2012), elections for 35 local authorities in England and Wales and for two mayors (May 2013), and European Parliamentary Elections (June 2014).

Clearly there has been a significant expansion of the 'electoral marketplace' in the UK in recent decades. Yet this expansion is not unique to the UK. It reflects wider trends of simultaneous institutional regionalisation and Europeanisation in other EU states, which in turn have generated more voting opportunities for more elected institutions at more levels of governance (Dalton and Gray 2003: 27–35). As the 'amount of electing' has increased, admittedly asymmetrically in the UK, so too has there been an intensification of the debate about the importance of turnout.

On the one hand, the relatively low levels of turnout at elections for all institutions have been used to argue that the expansion of the 'electoral marketplace' simply reinforces the conclusion that voters remain reluctant 'electoral consumers' even in more diverse electoral markets. If anything, low turnout at more elections appears to amplify the message that there is a serious disconnect at all levels between voters and representative institutions. Paradoxically, this disconnect may increase as the demands upon voters also increase to inform themselves of the issues involved in any specific election as well as comprehending the complex institutional configurations and interactions entailed in sequential multiple elections. In short, as Dalton and Gray (2003: 38) conclude, 'the motivation to participate in any single election may decrease as the number of electoral opportunities increases'.

On the other hand, and in incongruity with the first argument, the counterargument has been advanced that the *scope* of voting has been widened, and with it aggregate levels of voting have increased within any given time period, even if the *depth* of voting at any particular election remains relatively shallow. By this argument, electors are discerning consumers capable of making decisions based upon perceptions of the institutional significance or political salience of different elections. In other words, voters assign different participation weights to what they see as first-, second- or even third-order elections (see Dalton and Gray 2003: 36; Rallings and Thrasher 2005: 587–91). This mitigates the effects of low turnout at any individual election in two different respects: first, low turnout might not matter too much if more voters are caught in the net of more elections over time; and, second, low turnout at a particular election might simply be a rough reflection of the perceived importance of that elected institution in comparison to others. The difficulty with such arguments, however, is that there is the possibility that the same people tend to vote across the range of elections, rather than different people voting at different elections, and that these people tend not to be young people. Indeed, as noted above, the logic of Franklin and Hobolt's argument is that the more second- and third-order elections there are, the more the odds increase that young 'voting generations' will fail to develop the habit of voting (see Aldrich *et al.* 2011 on turnout as habit).

Turnout: What's the problem?

Stealth politics

As the preceding discussion illustrates, for many political commentators and politicians alike, low electoral turnout is 'a problem'; and what needs to be explained is why people do not vote when given the opportunity to do so. Yet a counter proposition can be made that low turnout is not necessarily 'a problem' and that what needs to be explained is why people would be expected to vote in the first instance. Starting from the assumption that 'the people would rather not be more involved in politics' (Hibbing and Theiss Morse 2002: 233), the 'real problem' that needs to be explained is thus the motivation of citizens for voting, given that people generally do not like politics and do not want to be politically active. In the words of Hibbing and Theiss Morse (2002: 3): 'They do not like politics when they view it from afar and they certainly do not like politics when they participate in it themselves'. This disposition not to participate is based not on 'anti-politics' sentiments as such, in the sense of a debilitating disconnect or deep alienation from political processes, but rather a pervasive indifference to political activity. At its simplest: 'Most people have strong feelings on few if any issues that government needs to address and would much prefer to spend their time in nonpolitical pursuits' (Hibbing and Theiss Morse 2002: 2). This leads Hibbing and Theiss Morse (2002: 2) to argue that what 'a remarkable number of people want' is 'stealth democracy'. Just as stealth aircraft are designed to be invisible to radar, but exist, nonetheless; so too significant sections of the populace want democratic processes to exist but not to be routinely visible.

In terms of explaining turnout, therefore, 'low levels of voting participation do not automatically indicate a flawed people or a flawed procedure for voting. They indicate a people for whom politics is not a high priority' (Hibbing and Theiss Morse 2002: 215). What matters for present purposes is that the notion of stealth politics accepts that aversion to politics is a 'basic and sensible trait' (Hibbing and Theiss Morse 2002: 4). What is important, therefore, is the *opportunity* provided by elections to secure the responsiveness and accountability of elected representatives, even if many people do not wish to avail themselves routinely of such an opportunity.

Democratic values: Opportunity to vote

The basis of the explanation for non-voting from a stealth politics perspective is claimed to be empirical: aversion to politics is 'a fact'. Yet an explanation and defence of non-voting has also been made on the basis of democratic principles. Saunders (2012: 307), for example, maintains that: '[t]he mere opportunity to vote is sufficient to realise the value of democracy, whether or not people exercise it. ... A democracy in which all enfranchised turn out (or even vote) is not necessarily democratically better than one where not all do so'. This is a theoretical contention. In Saunders' (2012: 309–15) case, the contention is based upon an understanding of democracy as 'rule of the people', whereby the people, provided with a universal *opportunity* to vote, participate indirectly in decision-making through representatives elected at periodic elections. Thus it is the opportunity to vote rather than the actual act of voting that has primacy in Saunders' conception of democracy. In which case, '[l]ow turnout is not itself necessarily a problem. Nor is high turnout always democratically better' (2012: 318). Ultimately, in this view, it is possible for low turnout to be 'democratically innocent' (2012: 318). Low turnout may, for example, simply be a reflection of popular contentedness.

Indeed, there has been a recurring explanation of non-voting in terms of citizens with 'no serious grievances to air, and feeling no great threat of change' having no pressing motivation to vote (Cole 2006: 150). Indeed, after the precipitous drop in turnout at the 2001 UK general election, Jack Straw, then Home Secretary, argued that such a low turnout may well have reflected the 'politics of contentment' (BBC 2001). This echoed the statements of Straw's cabinet colleague, John Prescott, who had earlier sought to explain the results of the inaugural elections to the new devolved institutions and elections to local authorities in May 1999, as being: 'Overall ... a good result for Labour ... particularly with the low turnout, but that's the politics of contentment' (BBC 1999).

The problem with such an argument is that, in light of the evidence presented above, it is essentially counterintuitive. As Cole (2006: 150) notes, with more than a hint of sarcasm, there is a basic incongruity with this argument: 'if low turnout signifies satisfaction with the way public affairs are managed, then it is by and large the most deprived constituencies which have the most contented populations'. Indeed, Saunders (2012: 318), in invoking 'contentment' and non-affectedness by 'the decision' as reasons for low turnout, obscures his own case, as it does not matter what reasons are adduced for non-voting. All that matters by his logic is that people had the opportunity to vote and, for whatever reason, chose not to avail themselves of that opportunity.

Political trust

Turnout at elections has also been associated with levels of political trust. At an individual level what is posited is a link between political trust and voting participation. In particular, a negative association has been posited whereby: 'The most straightforward way of expressing distrust is not to vote at all' (Hooghe *et al.* 2011: 261). Beyond the act of voting, political trust is also linked to political participation more generally. In one direction it is assumed that individuals need to exhibit a basic form of trust in the political system, particularly confidence in political institutions, to underpin their own political participation. As Norris (2011: 16) notes there is a widely held assumption that 'positive feelings of political trust, internal efficacy, and institutional confidence in parties, legislatures and the government ... strengthen conventional activism such as voting participation, party membership, and belonging to voluntary associations'. Indeed, Marien and Hooghe (2011: 5) pose the seemingly rhetorical question: 'does it make sense to participate in political life if one does not trust the political system or decision makers?'. Yet this question conflates trust in political institutions at a systemic or regime level, with trust in political elites or political decision makers. In this conflation, political trust is treated as a uni-dimensional concept and encompasses the political system and occupants of decision-making roles alike. Similar properties across different political institutions, actors and levels of activity thus adhere to the notion of political trust. Not surprisingly, therefore, uni-dimensional conceptions of political trust have been criticised for their relational definition of political trust, reductionism, and lack of explanatory power (Fisher *et al.* 2011: 276–81). Hooghe (2011: 274), for example, in identifying a single independent variable – political culture – as the basis of political trust judgements, has encountered difficulties in explaining differences in citizens' assessments of trust across types of political actors and across institutional forms.

In contrast, multi-dimensional views of political trust make a distinction between specific trust (at the level of political actors or public policies) and diffuse trust (as a form of 'institutional confidence' that reflects more enduring and general orientations than trust in particular actors or policy programmes (Norris 2011: 61–6)). In these views, there is a recognition that, even at the level of institutional confidence, different trust judgements may conceivably apply from one institution to another and, indeed, are empirically observable. In this sense, there is a close proximity between Easton's (1965) broader conception of political support, with its specific and diffuse dimensions, and conceptions of political trust (see Fisher *et al.* 2010: 182; Norris 2011: 70–82).

Indeed, surveys in the UK reveal that citizens are capable of making discriminatory trust-judgements amongst and between politicians and political institutions. However, the difficulty in interpreting these survey results is that, if trust is taken to be contingent, relational and multi-dimensional, then most empirical surveys of political trust do not help greatly in understanding political trust in the UK. In part this is because of the survey questions asked of citizens to establish their trustfulness. In cross-national surveys, such as the World Values series, 'confidence' in named institutions is treated as a proxy for political trust. While there is a theoretical argument that confidence in institutions is the equivalent in modern complex societies to interpersonal trust (see Newton 2001: 205), there is a pragmatic recognition that the determination of 'confidence' requires some evaluation of the performance of those institutions. In the absence of widespread public knowledge or interest in political institutions (see below), assessments of 'confidence' based on behavioural indicators of institutional performance may differ markedly from attitudinal indicators of 'trust'. Even those surveys that specifically ask about trust tend to use questions focused upon particular institutions or groups of political actors and particular meanings of trust (whether probity, truthfulness or responsiveness).

This point can be illustrated in relation to the UK parliament. When asked whether the UK parliament was essential to UK democracy, over two-thirds (68 per cent) of respondents in the 2013 *Audit of Political Engagement* agreed (with 30 per cent strongly agreeing). Only 7 per cent disagreed. In fact, the 2013 result marked an 8 per cent increase on the 2010 result of 60 per cent who found parliament 'worthwhile' or 'essential' (Hansard Society 2010a: 41). This might be taken as a high level of general or diffuse support or trust for the institution. However, when specific trust in parliament's actual capacities was probed, levels of support/trust were found to be far lower. In 2013, 47 per cent of respondents agreed, for instance, that parliament held government to account (with 18 per cent disagreeing). In fact, the approval rating on this measure (agree minus disagree) had increased considerably within a two-year period. It was 12 percentage points higher than in 2012 and 17 percentage points higher than in 2011 (Hansard Society 2013: 57; 2012b: 52).

When the public is asked specifically about their 'trust' in parliament the results are lower still. Indeed, respondents to successive Eurobarometer surveys have consistently recorded a marked propensity 'to tend not to trust' the UK parliament rather than 'to tend to trust'. In 2013, 25 per cent tended to trust in contrast to 68 per cent who tended not to trust (Eurobarometer 2013: 42). This marked a nearly 50 per cent decline in those trusting parliament within the space of a decade (down from 47 per cent in 2001) and a nearly 40 per cent increase in those tending not to trust parliament (up from 43 per cent) in the same period. This low trust score is also mirrored in 'confidence' assessments of the UK parliament, with only 23 per cent of respondents to the European Values Study of 2008 recording a great deal or quite a lot of confidence in the Westminster parliament. Though, as noted above, exactly what respondents were assessing in making their confidence judgement, or what their cognitive basis for trust was, is unclear in these surveys.

When a more delineated measure of trust is used to assess the trustworthiness of MPs – 'trust to tell the truth' – MPs generally do not fare much better than assessments of trust at an institutional level. The Committee on Standards in Public Life's (CSPL) Survey of 2010, for example, found that 26 per cent of their sample trusted MPs to tell the truth (which was a slight decline from the average of 28 per cent in the preceding three years). Notably, however, 40 per cent of respondents believed that their own local MP would tell the truth; but even so there had been a more marked decline in trust at this level – from an average of 47 per cent in the preceding three years. Nonetheless, there is something of a mismatch between these two findings as, of necessity, the aggregate of 'MPs in general' is composed of individual 'local MPs'.

The figures cited in the last paragraph treated trust as dichotomous: respondents either trusted or did not trust MPs. However, when a four-point scale is used – with respondents able to choose between trusting 'a lot', 'a fair amount', 'not very much' or 'not at all' – then positive assessments of trust increase markedly. In the 2008 CSPL survey 45 per cent of respondents trusted MPs in general a lot/a fair amount, 62 per cent trusted their own local MP at these levels, and 57 per cent similarly trusted local councillors (in contrast to 45 per cent when a two-point scale was used).

When people are asked 'how much they trust politicians generally', just over one in four have a 'fair amount' or 'a great deal of trust'. This figure has been constant across three waves of *Audit of Political Engagement* surveys (26 per cent in 2010, and 27 per cent in both 2007 and 2004). At the other end of the scale, exactly 25 per cent had no trust at all in politicians in 2010 – an increase on 23 per cent in 2007 and 19 per cent in 2004. The bulk of respondents had not very much trust: 48 per cent in 2010, 47 per cent in 2007, and 51 per cent in 2004. How these results should be read, however, is uncertain, as not having much trust is still having some trust. Moreover, politicians are treated as a homogeneous group in the Audit, with no distinction made between elected representatives or governments at multi-levels. As noted above, however, different trust assessments have been obtained in the CSPL surveys for MPs in general, individual constituency MPs, and local councillors. In this respect, simply differentiating amongst different groups of politicians appeared to be capable of prompting more positive evaluations of trust.

UK citizens also had little trust in the UK government. The 2013 Eurobarometer recorded a 22 per cent to 76 per cent split between those who tended to trust and those who tended not to trust the national government. Similarly, the 2008 European Values Survey recorded only 19 per cent of UK respondents who had a great deal or quite a lot of confidence in their national government. Government ministers also (perhaps not surprisingly given the common institutional location) fared almost exactly the same as 'MPs in general' in being trusted to tell the truth, with 26 per cent of respondents recording a positive assessment in 2010, 27 per cent in 2008, and 44 per cent recording 'a lot' or 'a fair amount' of trust (on the four-point scale used in the CSPL 2008 survey).

Age and trust

Cross-national studies have tended to find that young people are more likely to display lower levels of political trust of politicians and political institutions than older age cohorts (Dalton 2004: 91–4). In this regard, the UK would appear to be no exception, with Henn and Foard's (2012: 61) online survey of 18 year olds finding that 'large majorities of young people report that they lack trust in democratic institutions as well as those individuals and agencies that inhabit them'. Some 66 per cent of respondents believed that, on the whole, UK governments were neither honest nor trustworthy. Only 15 per cent of 18 year olds held a positive view about the trustworthiness of governments. Other data from the survey also revealed that young people had a deep distrust of political parties and professional politicians (2012: 60–2).

In contrast to Henn and Foard's findings, however, the CSPL's 2010 survey revealed 'a clear age gradient to distrusting MPs and government ministers ... with younger people having more positive views of politicians/standards than older people, and particularly those over 45' (Committee on Standards in Public Life 2011: 19). The 18–24 cohort was significantly less likely than the over-45 cohort to distrust MPs in general or to distrust government ministers. This raised 'the interesting question' for the Report's authors of whether a life-cycle or cohort effect had been uncovered in young people's trust attitudes: the former would suggest that people became less trusting of governments and MPs as they aged, while the latter would suggest that the effects of a more trusting generation of voters would be felt as that generation aged collectively. An answer to this question would only be revealed in the long term, however, by tracking longitudinal data (Committee on Standards in Public Life 2011: 19).

Political trust, social trust and social capital

As noted above, political trust has often been associated with Easton's notion of diffuse support, and has routinely been considered an essential component of the civic culture and 'an essential resource for governing a society effectively' (Marien and Hooghe 2011: 5). In this sense, trusting citizens are predicted to be more likely to grant legitimacy to representative institutions and their outputs than distrusting citizens, in which case an erosion of political trust would have significant implications for the legitimacy of these institutions and for electoral participation by citizens (Denemark and Niemi 2012: 2). There is often also an implicit assumption that political trust is intimately related to social trust and, in turn, that both are related to 'social capital' and to the health and stability of democracy (Newton and Zmerli 2011: 170). Indeed, the relationship between political trust, social (generalised) trust and social capital in sustaining systemic legitimacy has preoccupied theorists of political participation and empirical researchers alike in recent years. The focal point of this preoccupation, for many, has been Robert Putnam's linkage of the importance of interpersonal trust with political engagement, with an identified propensity of 'trusting' citizens to be more willing to interact socially and participate politically (see Putnam 2000). Putnam (1993: 183) hypothesised, on the basis of his studies of community activity in Italian regions and the USA, that social interaction honed the skills that are preconditions for participation. In this sense, social interaction could be seen as 'the school of democracy' (1993: 89–90; Stolle 2007: 666).

In essence, Putnam (2000: 249) deployed the notion of 'voluntary association' as a proxy for civic engagement (Alexander *et al.* 2012: 44). By this view, when social interactions are structured in social networks – either in organised associations or in informal daily life – they serve to develop social trust. Such interpersonal trust provides the conditions for further collaboration – social capital – that enhances the potential and the capacity to achieve more efficient and productive communities. In this manner interpersonal trust and voluntary activity are linked in a 'virtuous circle' (Whiteley 2009: 789; 2012: 78). Social capital is thus effectively a reservoir of civic goodwill based upon social interactions.

Importantly, Putnam maintains that participation in voluntary social associations has the propensity to spill over into political participation. In essence a simple causal process is posited, with democratic value patterns arising from interactions in various forms of voluntary associations (Quintelier and Hooghe 2012: 65). In this sense social capital drives political participation.

While there might be a certain intuitive logic to this conception of causality, it has been challenged at both a conceptual and an empirical level. At the level of conceptualisation, it can be contested whether associational involvement necessarily leads to political engagement, as there might be strong *dis*incentives for political participation arising from associational activities (see van Deth 2008: 200–3). Questions have also arisen about the directionality of causation: does social capital generate participation or is it the other way round? (see Whiteley 2012: 82). At an empirical level, an unambiguous linkage between social capital and political capital, social trust and political trust, and a subsequent transposition into political participation, has often been difficult to find. Newton and Zmerli (2011: 172), in their review of existing studies, concluded that until very recently 'empirical research failed to deliver clear support for the social capital theory that social and political trust are linked at the individual level. At best the evidence was weak and patchy, and at worst it showed no clear associations between social and political trust' (see Newton 2001: 211, Whiteley 2009: 793). Even though Newton and Zmerli's (2011: 193) own research found a significant and positive relationship between general social trust and political trust, they still concluded that 'in spite of all the literature on the importance of voluntary associations for social and political trust, the evidence here, as in some other studies, is not particularly convincing'. In the specific case of the UK, the relative absence of adequate data to measure trends over time has complicated analysis of this relationship still further. On the one hand, according to Stoker (2006: 54) 'little support for a general decline in social capital' has been found in research on associational membership in Britain (see also Christoforou 2011: 716). On the other hand, more detailed diachronic analysis led Whiteley (2012: 85–7) to conclude that there had been a decline in social capital since 1981, and that there was a discernible link between declining levels of voluntary activity and declining levels of trust in Britain. As a result, 'social capital is declining partly because people are less trusting but also because they are less willing to volunteer' (Whiteley 2012: 87).

In fact, successive comparative studies have found that, although relationships exist between social trust and social capital, and, in turn, between political trust and political capital, these relationships are to be found at system level rather than at individual level. But even at the systemic level these relationships are 'complicated and indirect in manner' (Newton 2001: 211). In other words, little can be predicted about an individual's political trust on the basis of his or her social trust, but, at a system level, a relationship can be observed generally between high levels of social trust and relatively high levels of political trust (but this relationship is not necessarily close or symmetrical).

Knowledgeable citizens

The connection between political trust and an informed citizenry is explicit in Fuks and Casalecchi's (2012: 74) observation that the possession of 'relevant information' by citizens is the 'normative reference standard' by which citizens are able to judge political institutions and so to calibrate their degree of political trust. More generally, Dahl (1998: 37–8) listed 'enlightened understanding' – the 'opportunities for [citizen] learning about the relevant alternative policies and their likely consequences' – as one of five requisite criteria by which democracy should be judged (see also Hochschild 2010: 111). Indeed, some political scientists have gone further and argued that 'factual knowledge about politics is a critical component of citizenship' (Delli Carpini and Keeter 1996: 3). Such knowledge encompasses an understanding of basic institutional structures, information about electoral platforms, and familiarity with the performance of decision makers. More pragmatically, Norris prefers the concept of 'enlightened democratic knowledge', based upon practical knowledge of the basic principles, institutions and processes associated with liberal democracy, as the touchstone for conceptualising and measuring political knowledge (Norris 2011: 151).

Despite the importance of basic political information and knowledge in forming attitudes towards political competence and political trust, successive surveys in western liberal democracies have found a relative absence of even basic levels of political knowledge amongst the citizenry (see McAllister 1998). Surveys have also found that political knowledge is distributed unevenly within liberal democracies, with greater knowledge associated generally with higher socio-economic status, more formal education, increased age, and being male (see Frazer and Macdonald 2003). Nor has there been a significant increase in political knowledge, despite rising levels of education across all western societies (Gibson and McAllister 2011). And, if anything, the 'digital divide' appears to be widening the 'political knowledge gap' still further, as the use of the internet transforms the manner in which political information is disseminated and received (Gibson and McAllister 2011: 20).

In the UK, successive *Audits of Political Engagement* have recorded, with only two exceptions (in 2010 and 2011), a majority of respondents claiming to know 'nothing at all' or 'not very much' about politics. On average, across the Audits from 2004 to 2013, 54 per cent of respondents fell into the 'know not very much or less' category. And in 2013 the highest proportion of those who knew nothing at all was recorded – at 16 per cent (Hansard Society 2013: 31). At the other end of the scale, on average only 5 per cent of respondents claimed to know a great deal about politics. Perhaps not surprisingly, the proportion of 18–24 year olds claiming no political knowledge at all was far higher than for other age cohorts – at 30 per cent in 2013.

When respondents to the Hansard Society surveys were asked how much they knew specifically about the UK Parliament, levels of ignorance rose to an average of 61 per cent who knew nothing or not very much about parliament (across the six surveys in which this question was asked). On average, 15 per cent of respondents claimed to know nothing at all about the UK parliament. As with other indicators of political understanding, knowledge of parliament increased with age (Hansard Society 2013: 87).

More generally, nationwide surveys of 18-year-olds in 2002 and 2011 found that 'a large number of young people continued to lack confidence that they had as much [political] knowledge or understanding as they would like'. In 2011 47 per cent of 18-year-olds considered that they did not know enough about politics in general. The corresponding figure in 2002 was 53 per cent. Only 24 per cent in both 2011 and 2002 samples believed that they did have enough knowledge (Henn and Foard 2012: 54). The introduction of statutory citizenship classes in England in 2002, and similar initiatives in other parts of the UK, appeared to have had only 'a relatively marginal positive impact' upon the knowledge and understanding of 18-year-olds in 2011 (Henn and Foard 2012: 54). This conclusion mirrored the National Foundation for Educational Research's assessment, reached upon completion of its longitudinal survey of citizen education in England between 2001 and 2010, that overall 'the impact of citizen education is still relatively small' (Keating *et al.* 2010: 65; for a comparative review of the limitations of civic education see Manning and Edwards 2013).

Knowledgeable citizens: Who needs them?

The starting point for most discussions of political knowledge is agreement with Dahl's contention that 'enlightened understanding' is an essential feature of democracy. This does not mean that 'people need to know everything, but they do need to know something. They need to have enough information to keep politicians honest' (Tilley and Wlezien 2008: 192). In the face of empirical evidence that many citizens acknowledge that they do not 'know enough' about politics, then their capacity to act as 'minimally competent citizens', as required in democratic theory, is brought into question. This has led some to restate Lippmann's (1922) earlier answer that, in the face of such widespread public ignorance, 'rule by the people had become effectively obsolete' (Tilley and Wlezien 2008: 192). In turn, such a view has prompted calls that if citizens cannot be changed then conceptions of democracy should be changed (see Schattsneider 1960: 135–6). In contrast, a case has also been made that neither ignorant citizens nor the conceptions of democracy need to be changed, as an ill-informed and apathetic citizenry has proved effective in 'holding the system together' (Berelson *et al.* 1954: 322). In this elitist view, an 'apathetic segment' – of disengaged and minimally informed citizens – is useful in 'cushioning the shock of disagreement, adjustment and change' in political systems (Berelson *et al.* 1954: 322).

Other, less cynical and more empirically grounded, studies have recently made an alternative case (see for example Soroka and Wlezien 2010). First, citizens might not know very much about political processes or policies, but they do not need much information, or may easily obtain information, to inform their preferences sufficiently to cast a vote. Second, it is not necessary for all citizens to be informed about the range of policy options – only that 'some nontrivial number' are capable of tracking and responding to what decision makers do. Third, it is not necessary for all citizens to possess knowledge about all areas, but there will be informed interest by some 'issue publics' in different policy areas (Soroka and Wlezien 2010: 19). Ultimately, such arguments lead to the conclusion that 'individuals are not [political] "encyclopedias" and evidently need not be' (Soroka and Wlezien 2010: 170). Citizen self-assessments of 'not having enough' political information or knowledge might, therefore, overestimate the levels of understanding required to make political trust judgements, or to signal policy preferences, or to make accountability judgements about decision-makers.

Conclusion

This chapter has examined a series of theoretical and empirical incongruities surrounding 'the people' and their engagement in the UK's representative process. Whereas democratic theory posits a vision of active, participatory and knowledgeable citizens who are willing and able to participate when called upon to do so, the empirical reality is that significant sections of the UK's citizens do not participate in the minimal act of voting, or engage in any other form of institutionalised political activity, or, for that matter, possess deep resources of political knowledge or information capable of informing reasoned political choice. In addition, not only is the UK citizenry largely disengaged from formal politics, it also displays significant levels of mistrust in its political representatives and representative institutions. While some comfort might be sought in the conjoined facts that many other western polities also display low and often declining levels of electoral turnout and high levels of political distrust, such comfort is soon dissipated by the observation that the UK is ahead of the curve in these respects in comparison to most other liberal democratic states.

But nested within the headline incongruities of low electoral participation and high distrust are a series of sub-headline incongruities. At the level of theory there is a basic incompatibility between 'standard' versions of representative democracy and revisionist perspectives, such as those proffered by Hibbing and Thiess Morse on 'stealth democracy', or Saunders on electoral turnout, or Berelson on uninformed citizens. At an empirical level basic incongruities are evident in the definition of political trust and its measurement, and specification of the relationship between social and political trust, as well as in the calibration of 'decline' in relation to social capital. Analysis of empirical data also throws up incongruities in relation to measurement of political trust, the distinction between diffuse and specific levels of trust, or fluctuations in observed levels of citizens' trust in political actors and political institutions.

Perhaps the greatest incongruity, however, is to be found in the elision between the terms *political participation* and *political engagement*, and in the associated assumption that the two are positively, rather than negatively, correlated. In this elision, distinctions between formal and informal, institutionalised or non-institutionalised, and electoral or non-electoral modes of participation become blurred. This blurring was noted above in Putnam's use of 'voluntary association' as a proxy for civic engagement, and in his belief that participation in voluntary social associations had the propensity to spill over into political participation. Indeed, this blurring might help to explain why an unambiguous linkage between social capital and political capital, social trust and political trust, and a subsequent transposition into political participation, has often eluded empirical verification. Moreover, this blurring is of some significance in conceptualising 'the problem of the people' in representative democracy. 'Civic engagement', as deployed by Putnam, encompassed informal socialising, friendship circles, associational membership, and formal political participation (Berger 2009: 338). A decline in the interpersonal, informal and associational dimensions of engagement was posited to lead to a direct decline in formal modes of political participation and the performance of political institutions (Putnam 1995: 67; Stolle and Hooghe 2005: 152).

This is not the place to subject Putnam's thesis to sustained critical scrutiny, other than to note that criticism has been advanced on five fronts: first, on empirical grounds that the available data did not support the decline thesis; second, on comparative grounds that there were no consistent trend-lines of declining social capital across other liberal democracies beyond the USA; third, on analytical grounds that the nature and forms of social and political mobilisation were under-conceptualised, and, fourth, on normative grounds that a decline in social capital did not necessarily result in negative effects for social stability and democracy overall (for a summary see Stolle and Hooghe 2005; Whiteley 2012: 79–83).

It is the place, however, to question the assumption that 'it does not really matter how people participate as long as they do it' (Marien and Hooghe 2011: 17), for this assumption highlights the incongruities arising from fusing notions of civic engagement and political participation. If there is no direct connection between formal/institutionalised/ electoral modes of participation and informal/non-institutionalised/ non-electoral modes, to the extent that the enhancement of the latter does not necessarily enhance the former, then 'the problem of the people' in representative democracy is not mitigated. There may be displacement activity whereby low levels of political trust may not be associated with a general decline in participation as the 'distrustful' participate in informal/non-institutionalised/non-electoral modes (such as 'buycotting', volunteering, or protesting) but still prove reluctant to engage in formal/institutionalised/electoral modes (see Marien and Hooghe 2011: 12). In this respect 'the problem of the people' and their disengagement from formal representative political processes remains, for although these variant forms of participation intersect they do not necessarily overlap or reinforce each other systematically.

3
The 'Problem' of Representational Transmission of Power

Introduction

The standard account of representative democracy, as noted in Chapter 1, identifies at the heart of the representative system a principal–agent, territorially based, relationship between individual voters and individual representatives. Over time, however, the standard account witnessed a pragmatic accommodation of collective principal–agent relationships between aggregates of electors and representatives organised around political associations – primarily political parties as electoral representative organisations, but also interest groups, civil society organisations, and social movements as non-electoral representative associations. In this accommodation, representation became mediated, with these political associations facilitating the 'representational transmission of power' between citizens and state decision-makers. And in this accommodation recognition was also made that 'partial or partisan aggregations such as political groups or parties ... are not optional or accidental in a representative democracy' (Urbinati 2006: 134).

Political parties have been ascribed a particularly crucial role in the process of democratic linkage, to the extent that 'the existence of political parties is fundamental to the process of representation' (Alonso et al. 2011: 7). Indeed, as institutions of deliberation and aggregation, political parties have been identified as 'the primary representative agents between citizens and the state' (Dalton et al. 2011: 6). Yet, as this chapter will reveal, parties acting as 'representative agents' manifest a series of conceptual and operational incongruities. Whereas standard accounts of party representation identify the positive capacities of political parties to articulate interests, aggregate demands, formulate collective preferences, and mobilise electoral support, the practice of party representation highlights the incongruities of discordant policy preferences between parties and their electors, hazy voter perceptions of parties' positions, and diminished mobilisation capacities resulting from declining membership and restricted funding. At the same time, the positive contribution of parties to standard accounts of representative democracy – in their combination of representing and governing roles – have come to be viewed more negatively as the latter role came to be asserted over the former role.

As the positive representative capacities and potentialities of political parties came to be subject to increased critical scrutiny, so reconceptualisations of the 'representational transmission of power' explored conceptions of non-electoral modes of linkage and self-authorised, particularised forms of representation beyond electoral modes of party representation. As noted in Chapter 2, the notion of 'social capital' connected associational engagement to political participation and, correspondingly, linked social trust to political trust more broadly. A key point was that there were complex interconnections between formal representative processes and political participation and the norms and institutional networks of informal civic engagement (Putnam 1995: 65). Recognition of these interconnections also came to feature in many contemporary reformulations of representation. A common basic contention was that political representation was systemic and occurred not only through electoral processes and institutions but also through non-electoral processes, and 'informal' or 'self-authorised representation' of interest groups, civic associations, social movements, or even individuals. In this sense, there was little new in conceptualisations of representation 'beyond' electoral representation. What was new, however, was the constructivist emphasis upon representation as claim-making and claim-reception both within and outside formal political structures (see Saward 2010: 161, Chapter 1). Yet making a representative claim does not necessarily mean that it will be received or accepted, and the incongruities of non-electoral claim-making and claim-reception will be analysed in the latter part of this chapter.

Political parties

While political theorists have been antagonistic, or at best agnostic, towards 'factions' and parties, political scientists tend to view parties as 'vital agencies in the proper functioning of democracies' (Dalton *et al.* 2011: 3; see also Wilks-Heeg 2011: 22, Whiteley 2012: 57). In the specific context of the UK, Driver (2011: 209) maintains that '[f]or more than a century, the established narrative of British liberal democracy has relied on political parties to connect voters to government, citizens to state'. Taking this established narrative as the starting point of analysis, what needs to be explained is why the certainties of the recent past have come to be counterposed with a series of incongruities pertaining to the present party system in the UK. Such an explanation requires an examination of the roles of parties in democratic systems and the nature of party systems.

In essence parties have performed two major roles in representative democracies. Mair (2009: 5) neatly summarised these roles as parties acting as representatives and parties acting as governmental institutions. As representatives they articulated interests, aggregated demands, and formulated collective preferences into patterned policy programmes. As governing institutions they translated their distinct policy programmes into public policies. In this manner they 'organized and gave coherence to the institutions of government' (Mair 2009: 5). While there are far more elaborate specifications of the roles and functions of parties than this (for summaries see Clark 2012: 18–38; Driver 2011: 32–57; Ware 1996), the beauty of Mair's parsimonious specification is that it focuses attention on the 'linkage' role of parties. In this role there were few (if any) principal–agent problems, for, as Mair (2009: 5) notes, the principal was the agent. Yet, as Mair proceeds to argue, in most contemporary liberal democracies the representative and governing functions became disentangled, and the governmental role came to be privileged over the representative role. 'In this way, political parties become more like governors than representatives, at least within the mainstream or core of the party system' (Mair 2009: 6). This had an impact upon how parties organised themselves internally, how they constructed their electoral programmes, how they competed for votes, and in turn how voters perceived parties and their performance.

Before subjecting these claims to scrutiny it is advisable to say something about the nature of the party system in the UK. As noted in Chapter 1, Lijphart's (1999: 13–14) conception of the 'Westminster model' assumed that British electoral politics was dominated by two parties, with party programmes and policies differentiated by 'just one dimension, that of socio-economic issues'. Indeed, the 'established narrative' of UK parties, right up until 2010, was that there was a two-party system inside Westminster, which, for long periods in the post-war period, had mirrored two-party competition at elections. Underpinning this electoral two-partism in these long periods was a social cleavage structure based largely on social class, and an electoral system (single-member plurality) that amplified this bifurcation. Even by 1970, however, the 'established narrative' was under challenge from new narratives of multi-party electoral contests and of increasing partisan and ideological dealignment. Certainly, by the UK general election of 2010 a single two-party system was pronounced long-since dead. Yet incongruously, two-party contests still characterised electoral competition in 2010: but instead of a single Britain-wide system there were now multiple two-party contests spread across the constituent parts of Britain.

Party systems in the UK

A party system, as defined by Webb (2000: 1), following Sartori's lead ([1976] 2005: 43–4), is 'a particular pattern of competitive and cooperative interactions displayed by a given set of political parties'. Sartori ([1976] 2005: 111–78) categorised party systems not simply by the number of competitive parties (as in earlier categorisations (see Blondel 1968; Daalder 1983; Duverger 1964)) but also by the ideological distance that separated parties, the nature of contests for executive office, and the alternation – or more accurately the potential for alternation – of executive office among parties. On this basis Sartori identified distinct types of party system: two-party, moderate pluralist, polarised pluralist, and predominant-party. In a predominant-party system a single party serially dominates electoral competition and so secures successive parliamentary majorities and extended executive leadership. Success in three successive elections was deemed by Sartori ([1976] 2005: 175) to be necessary to differentiate a two-party system from a predominant-party system. In either two-party or predominant-party systems, however, competition for executive office constituted the 'core' of the system, serving both to structure and to institutionalise the party system (Mair 2009: 288). In these respects, academic categorisations, defined either as 'sets of parties' or as 'party interactions', corresponded to an empirical reality at the UK level in the 1945–1970 period – of electoral competition and executive formation focused upon two parties. Equally, when the competitive interactions between the two leading UK parties were recalibrated in Westminster elections between 1979 and 2010, this change could be accommodated within Sartori's typology.

This period marked a transition from a two-party to a predominant-party system, with four successive electoral victories for the Conservative party followed by three successive Labour victories in Westminster elections. While recognising that this transition had been effected, both empirically and typologically, Mair (2009: 288, emphasis in the original) suggested a further refinement to Sartori's categorisation: 'this predominant position has transferred from one party to another, a shift which is unprecedented in any other system ... the British case could also be regarded as an exceptional example of *alternating predominance*'. In this refinement, alternating predominance resembles 'two-partism in slow motion' (Quinn 2013: 396). But where it differs from a classic two-party system is that, whereas in its classic form there is intense competition, in the UK's alternating predominant system there is weak competition between the two main parties brought about by a decline in the share of the vote of the runner-up party in relation to the vote of the winning party. What differentiates an alternating predominance system from a classic two-party system, therefore, is the limited degree of competition of the former when compared with the high degree of competition of the latter (see Quinn 2013: 391–3).

In conceiving of party systems in terms of patterned interactions of competition (and potential cooperation) the focus of analytical attention thus comes to be redirected away from a simple numerical calculation of parties competing in elections to a matrix calculation of the combinations of the nature and outcomes of party competitions in the electoral, parliamentary, and executive arenas at a number of different levels. In a multi-level polity such as the UK – with variegated patterns of electoral competition at local, sub-national/regional, UK, and EU levels, and with kaleidoscopic patterns of party cooperation across legislative and executive institutions at all levels – empirical reality manifestly fails to correspond to the notion of a single-party system. If there are multi-party systems in the UK there are also multi-party contests across these systems. At each level, the number of parties competing in elections and the number of parties successfully returning candidates to representative institutions is well in excess of two. In terms of the number of parties that had contested elections successfully in the UK – to the extent of securing representation in elected assemblies – eight UK parties were returned to the European Parliament (EP) after the 2009 election; ten parties were represented at Westminster after the 2010 general election (rising to 11 after the Bradford West by-election in 2012 with the return of a representative of the Respect party); and the 2011 elections for the devolved assemblies and parliaments returned four parties in Wales, five in Scotland, and seven in Northern Ireland.

The proliferation of levels of electoral competition and governance accompanying the linked processes of Europeanisation (supranational) and devolution (sub-national) have manifestly had an impact upon the number of parties capable of successfully competing in elections and cooperating in executive office. The question is whether each system is structured largely independently of each other. One possible answer provided by Bardi and Mair (2008: 156) is that the existence of several levels of electoral competition and government may 'have negligible effects on the party system if one level of government, usually the national one, is overwhelmingly more important than the others'. Where national significance is attributed to electoral competitions at all levels, and where elections at supranational or sub-national levels are seen as 'second-order' contests, then competition patterns are likely to be structured by the 'first-order', national, party system. The incongruity in the UK, however, is that although elections to the EP, devolved assemblies, and local authorities are deemed to be second-order, and although campaigns invariably incorporate UK 'salience' issues, distinct and variegated party systems are clearly observable at these levels (see Clark 2012: 141–50).

Undoubtedly, the existence of nationalist parties with a major regional presence in Scotland, Wales, and Northern Ireland serve to sculpt the contours of distinctively different party systems in those territorial areas (see Clark 2012: 142). Yet if the UK has a series of party systems stacked one upon another at multi-levels of governance, it is necessary to return to the UK level to determine the nature of the UK party system in the wake of the 2010 general election. What the 2010 election confirmed was that although the UK had three 'relevant' parties (in terms of their UK government/coalition potential), the two-party system categorisation was not wholly redundant at national level. In effect, instead of a single two-and-a-half/three-party system prevailing throughout mainland Britain, there were *three* two-party, Britain-wide systems (and three other two-party systems at the Scottish and Welsh levels). Indeed, Johnston and Pattie's (2011: 19) examination of the 2010 election found that regional and urban–rural differences in party competition resulted in a geographical map where the Conservative and Labour parties were the leading contenders in only 45 per cent of contests; in the other contests one or other of these parties were in competition primarily with either the Liberal Democrats or a nationalist party. This electoral map has profound implications beyond categorisations of party systems – implications that reach into the heart of party organisation and party campaigning:

> At any election each party is fighting not only a national campaign to gain as many votes as possible everywhere but also at least two

separate types of local campaign, depending on which party provides the main opponent in the marginal seats where the election is eventually won and lost. This calls for two different local strategies – what works against one party may not against another: and the problem may be exacerbated because the party that forms your major opponent in the parliamentary constituencies in an area is the one with which you are in coalition in the local governments covering the same area. (Johnston and Pattie 2011: 24)

Party identification and party linkage

Just as the UK polity became more differentiated along a territorial axis (propelled by the twin forces of Europeanisation and decentralisation), so too was it subject to changes along a social axis. At the height of the two-party system in the 1950s and 1960s UK general elections could be caricatured as 'little more than an organized class struggle' (Driver 2011: 25), with both main parties secure in their core votes, rooted in the social class structure, and supported respectively by the representative associations of organised labour and organised capital. Some 50 years later, however, leading psephologists concluded that 'class had come to play a very limited role in determining the voting preferences of the British electorate' (Clarke *et al.* 2004: 50) and reinforced their message after the 2005 election by declaring that social class and other demographic variables were 'decided non-starters' in explaining electoral choice in the UK (Clarke *et al.* 2009: 190). Yet if there was widespread agreement that social class was not as closely linked as it once was to voters' party choice, there was little agreement as to why this was the case.

Two main contrasting explanatory models have been used to explain the decline of the class basis of UK politics (for details see Evans and Tilley 2012). The dominant perspective, which Evans and Tilley label the 'class heterogeneity model' (2012: 138), identifies a fracturing of class distinctiveness and the emergence of a less structured society as major explanatory variables. These social changes have been attributed variously to: economic development leading to increased affluence and rising living standards; enhanced participation of women in the labour market; a rebalancing of public and private sector occupations and service provision; changed patterns of home ownership; the expansion of mass higher education; generic processes of individualisation; more variegated notions of social identity; and the rise of post-material or self-expressive values. Whatever the precise cause of the decline of class distinctiveness, the assumption of the class heterogeneity model is that social class has been cross-cut by multiple social and political orientations, which has led to an unravelling of the intricate connections between objective class position, class identities, party identification, and voting preferences that characterised UK politics half a century ago (Clarke *et al.* 2004: 2).

The second model, identified by Evans and Tilly (2012: 139) as the 'political choice' perspective, starts from the assumption that the agent of political change is political rather than social. In this model, political parties and their attempts at strategic positioning influence the extent of social divisions 'by differentiating themselves in ways that are relevant to the choices of voters on relevant axes of competition, or conversely, minimizing their differences on these axes so that they are less relevant to party preference' (2012: 139). While changes in party positions reflect wider social structural changes, the assumption of the 'political choice' model is that social divisions based upon class have not necessarily been blurred by these changes. The main change has simply been the decline in the size of the manual working class. Confronted by a decline in their core vote, parties of the left have sought to reposition themselves more towards the central pivot of party competition to compensate for the decline in the size of the working class. This has been a common phenomenon of European social democratic parties in the 21st century, but it has been especially pronounced in the UK given the initial strength of the correlation between class and party identification.

In the UK, the Labour party's repositioning of itself towards the ideological centre, its adoption of 'catch all' strategies, and adherence to the logic of median voter competition, have been ascribed as a reaction to the changes in the social class structure and a resultant decline in the size of the working class (see Evans and Tilley 2012: 139). An incongruity arises, however, in that in responding to class fragmentation the Labour party's adoption of 'catch all' and 'market oriented' (Lees-Marshment 2008: 181–203) strategies led it to distance itself, consciously, from its core support. This move to the centre was clearly perceived by the British electorate, to the extent that, in the seven years after the election of the Blair government in 1997, there was a full point shift along a 0–10 left–right scale. Thus by 2005 'Britons viewed the Labour party as very close to the center of the party spectrum' (Dalton *et al.* 2011: 113–14). A corollary was that the perception of the Labour party as a party that 'very closely' 'looks after the interests of working class people' fell from 46 per cent in 1987 to only 10 per cent in 2005 (Curtice 2007: 42). The significance of such findings is that 'when there is ideological convergence the strength of the signals from parties to voters is weakened and the motivation for choosing parties on interest/ ideological grounds derived from class position is reduced' (Evans and Tilly 2012: 144). In such a case, the actions of political parties and their strategic positioning significantly impact upon the salience of social class as a determinant of voting behaviour. Intriguingly, 'the future strength of class politics could depend more upon party strategy and electoral appeals than the social changes usually envisaged in discussions of post-industrial society' (Evans and Tilly 2012: 161).

Thus to conclude that class differences in political choices in the UK have weakened as parties have adopted centralist ideological platforms does not mean that class differences have evaporated completely. There are still statistically significant differences between classes in terms of a Labour/Conservative choice (Evans and Tilly 2012: 151). As Denver *et al.* note (2012: 80), the proportion of voters who identify themselves as belonging to a particular social class has changed little since the 1960s. What has changed, however, is how the parties position themselves in relation to social class and the distinctiveness of the ideological signals they transmit to the electorate. Over the period of New Labour in government there was a convergence of party positions as the Labour party moved to the centre under Blair, with the Conservative party remaining relatively static in its post-Thatcher location on a left–right spectrum.

Moreover, as parties reoriented their representative function away from 'traditional large collective constituencies' (Mair 2009: 7), voters have been induced to adopt an alternative logic of choosing which party best represents their interests. If voters perceive little ideological distance between the parties then 'valence politics' and 'voting decision heuristics' become of increased importance. 'Valence politics' focuses primarily upon voters' perceptions of the 'ability of governments to perform in those policy areas that people care most about' (Clarke *et al.* 2004: 315). This entails judgements about the competence of parties to deliver the most favourable outcomes on important issues (such as economic management, public services, and security). In parallel, voters use 'heuristics' or 'cognitive shortcuts' to make voting decisions by assessing the overall competence, trust, and likeability of party leaders. Indeed, the comparative judgements made by electors of the respective party leaders in 2005 and 2010 were found to be of some significance in explaining the outcomes of those general elections (see Clark 2012: 204–5; Clarke *et al.* 2009: 101).

One further, and relatively unexplored, consequence of the positional convergence of the major UK parties has been the cost in terms of citizen satisfaction with electoral democracy. In an analysis of the representativeness of the British party system, Brandenburg and Johns (2013: 17), in deploying a conception of collective representation as 'many-to-many', argue that 'voters are not only interested in competence and delivery, even if the structure of party competition offers them little other basis for choice'. Their findings, based upon data from the British Election Study, suggest that voters might not simply want 'solutions' and 'valence competition' but might prefer instead 'a certain type of solution that is consistent with their values and preferences' (2013: 18). Linked to this argument is the finding that at recent UK general elections, while there has only been modest ideological convergence among voters, the two major parties have converged 'almost to the point of superimposition' (2013: 9). This has left many voters 'a long way from the representational "action"' in the sense that they are faced with choosing between parties that are both difficult to distinguish ideologically and also distant from voters' own ideological positions and policy preferences. In this sense 'the party system as a whole [is] less representative of the ideological diversity within the electorate as a whole' (2013: 16). In turn, this unrepresentativeness erodes political satisfaction as it leaves voters, on average, some distance from their nearest significant party (2013: 2). In turn again, this leads Brandenburg and Johns (2013: 17) to believe that 'we can reasonably infer that the vote-seeking strategies of British parties contributed to dissatisfaction with democracy'. This finding reveals the incongruity that if electoral representation is conceived as a process then achieving congruence between government policies and the preferences of the wider public over time might well be achieved through alternation of differentiated parties in office rather than 'the alternative in which governing parties continuously take centrist positions' (2013: 8).

Party organisation

As cleavage structures became more intricate in UK politics, with an increased emphasis upon other identities other than class (national, ethnic, gender), so parties found it 'more and more difficult ... to read interests, let alone aggregate them within coherent electoral programs' (Mair 2009: 6). At the same time as the representative function became increasingly complex, the rise of valence politics paradoxically served to simplify the nature of electoral competition between the two major parties at UK level. Along with other European parties, '[t]he ambitions of the party in public office were transformed into the ambitions of the party as a whole. For many party leaders, parties were governors or they were nothing' (Mair 2009: 6). Party organisations designed for one purpose – representation – were confronted with pressures to modulate their activities to changed party ambitions and objectives focused upon the related purpose – governing. This is not to argue that this tension is new, only that it has become more pronounced in an era of partisan/ideological dealignment. Nor is it to argue that parties are homogeneous organisations with unambiguous objectives and ambitions. There have always been intra-party tensions between mass membership and party elites, between activists and professionals, and between organisational structures designed to enhance participation and those designed to promote leadership. The organisational configuration of parties at any particular time reflects the intricate balance of electoral priorities, the profile of the competitive environment, and agency relationships within parties.

It is not surprising to find, therefore, that changes in this intricate balance find reflection in changed organisational structures. It is a mix of endogenous and exogenous change. In themselves, neither environmental change (social, political, constitutional) nor internal change (membership, factional, leadership), determine causality. Moreover, there is a further connection between changed broader conceptions of democracy and the nature and purposes of party competition within a polity and changed party organisational structures.

This connection was made most explicitly in Katz and Mair's (1995) examination of transitions from a 'mass party' model, to a 'catch-all' model, to a 'cartel' model. In these transitions the representative/democratic role of parties in the wider polity is reformulated alongside a specific restructuring of representative/democratic relationships within parties. A mass party in Duverger's (1964) conception is both a representative strategy and an organisational form. The problem with applying this conception to the UK, however, is that from the outset 'none of the main British parties has ever equated fully to a mass party' (Webb 2000: 213). In this respect, arguments that start from the premise that British parties have 'metamorphosed from ... large membership-based "mass bureaucratic" parties to today's "catch-all" "electoral professional" parties' (Heffernan 2009: 448) start from shaky foundations. Similarly, judgements as to whether the major UK parties are currently 'catch all' parties, 'electoral professional' parties, or 'cartel' parties also need to bear in mind the fact that such typologies are essentially 'ideal types'. And as such any particular categorisation 'may be heuristically useful, [but] it will inevitably be incomplete' (Katz and Mair 2012: 108).

Labour party

With Katz and Mair's cautionary dictum in mind, it should be noted from the outset when analysing the Labour party that 'of all the mass membership parties, ... [it] is perhaps the one where membership recruitment has been taken least seriously' (Ware 1987: 146). For most of the Labour party's history, its affiliated membership (predominantly drawn from trade unions but also from other socialist societies such as the Fabians) provided the party 'with the consoling myth of a mass membership' (Quinn 2004: 155). Its affiliated membership also provided a nominal headcount – and financial resources – sufficient, until the 1980s at least, to obviate the need to 'foster an army of voluntary individual activists' (Webb 2000: 200). Moreover, 'the mass' (of affiliated members) held the added advantage, for the party's leadership, of being largely inactive in the party's internal decision-making processes. In this 'hollowed out' organisational space the symbiotic, asymmetric, and tensile relationships between trade union leaders, constituency activists, and the party leadership were acted out. Yet, at key junctures, the organisational equilibrium was punctuated by changed intra-party power constellations between these groups (see Driver 2011: 89–104; Judge 1993: 77–100; Webb 2000: 190–217). The primary driving force for major organisational reforms, particularly after 1983, was electoral: change was needed to provide an internal structure capable of generating electorally attractive policy programmes, and to convince voters that in government these policies 'would not be put at risk from leftwing activists and union barons' (Quinn 2004: 175–6). In effect this meant that: 'if both the unions and the party's activists were to be weakened, this required a third group to be strengthened. Neither side would readily consent to handing control directly to the leadership, so the "ordinary member" became the target of empowerment' (Russell 2005: 28).

Essentially, after 1983, reforms sought to relocate the locus of authority within the party away from the trade unions and 'the organized party on the ground' towards individual members. Successive organisational reforms effected: One Member One Vote for candidate selection; a reduced weighting of the unions' block vote at conference; payment of Trade Union (TU) funds directly to the central party; and, with the adoption of *Partnership in Power* in 1997, the further restriction of conference's role, the extension of plebiscitary processes, and the identification of a Joint Policy Committee and the National Policy Forum as the key institutions of policy development within the party. Following the party's electoral defeat in 2010 and the election of a new leader, Ed Miliband, the party embarked on a self-proclaimed 'radical project of party reform' (Hain 2012). The *Refounding Labour* review established a new Labour Supporters Scheme to recruit 'potentially many tens of thousands of Party supporters registered on a data base'. At the 2011 Conference it was confirmed that supporters would be given between 3 per cent and 10 per cent of the votes in the party's next leadership election provided that 50,000 supporters were recruited. In parallel, the *Partnership into Power* process was to be updated 'to reform and simplify the cycle of policy development and strengthen the National Policy Forum' (see Labour party 2012). The stated intention was to transform Labour into 'a grassroots campaigning movement' in order to achieve 'street-level range' and secure electoral success (Hain 2012; see Labour party 2011).

While *Refounding Labour* was billed as 'the most significant shake-up in Labour's 111-year history' (Hain quoted in *The Independent*, 23 September 2011), suspicions remained that these reforms continued a strategy of what Webb (1994: 120) described as 'democratization as emasculation'. *Refounding Labour* did little to reverse the cumulative effect of earlier organisational reforms that had led to accusations of the party's policy-making process becoming 'hollowed out' (Marsh 2013: 228–9). Proclamations of the need 'to open up our process of making policy, both to give party members much greater say and to enable supporters and voters to feed in their ideas' (Labour party 2011: 18) held the potential, simultaneously, to dilute the intra-party policy contributions of formal members while still maintaining the leadership's centralised strategic control (see Gauja 2013: 116). The increased emphasis upon the involvement of volunteers and supporters, beyond traditional activists and members, has significant potential organisational ramifications. Indeed, as Fisher *et al.* (2013a: 18) observed, this development 'suggests that models of party organisation may require a degree of refinement. Existing models focus on members as *the* source of volunteer activity. ... Thus, a growth in the use of supporters coupled with a decline in members may indicate the development of an enhanced form of cadre party or at the very least, greater leadership domination'.

Conservative party

The Conservative party, as in the case of the Labour party, did not move towards an 'electoral professional' party from the starting position of a being a 'mass party'. In fact, Webb (2000: 192) makes it quite clear that 'the Conservative party's organizational model never closely approximated that of an authentic mass party'. Before the *Fresh Future* review, instigated as a response to the general election defeat of 1997, the party made little pretence of subscribing to internal democratic norms and structures: it had no corporate legal identity and was constituted in three separate organisations. In this manner the Conservative parliamentary party was formally insulated from the party's professional and voluntary arms, other than through the integration of all three organisational hierarchies in the position of the party leader. Indeed, between 1965 and 1998 the Conservative parliamentary party had sole responsibility for the election of the party leader. However, since 1998 the party's organisational structures have continued to privilege leadership and centralisation, but there has been a simultaneous, novel promotion of democratisation and decentralisation.

Fresh Future brought about a single unified party, with a Party Board at its centre acting as the 'supreme decision-making body' on all matters concerning party organisation and management. In pursuing the commitment to make the reformed party 'open and democratic', *Fresh Future* proposed that, for the first time, every member would have a direct vote in the election of the party leader and introduced a Policy Forum to encourage political discussion throughout the party. It also created Regional Policy Congresses to discuss policy proposals. It was envisaged that the Conservative Policy Forum would have 'major input into the annual party conference agenda', yet the party's Committee on Conferences was to determine the final agenda. The annual conference itself was afforded no decision-making capacity and was identified simply as 'the main party gathering of the year'. At the time Conservative commentators noted: 'Despite the rhetoric of democracy ... the thrust of the [modernising] proposals is towards centralisation' (Peele 1998: 146). In retrospect, the problem with the *Fresh Future* reforms was seen to be not only that they were 'justified in the somewhat contradictory language of both intra-party democracy and [electoral] efficiency' but also that they 'failed to help the party progress electorally' (Clark 2012: 177).

In fact it took three consecutive election defeats before the relative autonomy of local Conservative associations over the choice of election candidates was more forcefully constrained by central party direction. The introduction of a 'priority list', known as the 'A-list', of approved central party candidates was announced by David Cameron within a week of becoming party leader in 2005. The 'A-list' was seen by many constituency party activists as an erosion of their autonomy (Bale 2011: 301–2). Yet although the resulting process constituted a substantial centralisation of power, the subsequent abandoning of the priority list in 2007 and its replacement with an extended list of centrally approved candidates, and a commitment that at least 50 per cent of the final shortlist should be women, pointed to the uneven trajectory of centralisation within the Conservative party. Surprisingly perhaps, the introduction of primary elections for candidate selection, which undermined the control of local activists directly over the final choice of candidate, was met with less intra-party resistance. Before the 2010 election, primary elections were held in 116 constituencies, and in two cases 'open primaries' were used to allow all registered electors in a constituency to vote for candidates shortlisted by local Conservative associations.

Members, mobilisation, and money

Members and mobilisation

There is no doubt that formal party membership in the UK has declined: in 2012 it was estimated that the Conservative party had approximately 175,000 members, the Labour party had around 156,000 and the Liberal Democrats had 65,000. This meant that collectively the members of the main parties constituted less than 1 per cent of the electorate, and this marked a significant decline from an estimated 3.3 million party members in 1964 (11 per cent of the electorate) (Wilks-Heeg *et al.* 2012: 187). Yet, despite this decline, the major political parties still have the capacity to mobilise supporters and to use them as a key electoral resource – even if campaigns have become more centralised and professionalised (see Clark 2012: 214–19; Denver *et al.* 2012: 180–2). Certainly the two main UK political parties now have fewer formal members, and this is one contributory factor towards the increased use of more centrally managed techniques of communication with voters in constituencies. Partially offsetting this decline of 'paid-up' local activists, as noted above, has been an increase in the use of registered volunteers and supporters in constituency campaigning. At the 2010 general election, for instance, 78 per cent of local Conservative, Labour, and Liberal Democrat parties involved supporters (that is non-members) in campaigning (Fisher *et al.* 2013a: 7). Importantly, the 2010 election also provided evidence that 'free campaigning' by volunteers could have had significant campaign effects (see Fisher *et al.* 2013b: 14).

Money

The fact that political parties are vital to the functioning of representative democracies was reiterated by the Committee of Standards in Public Life (CSPL) in its report into political party financing in the

UK (Cm 8208 2011: 21). The starting premise of the CSPL was that in order for parties to continue to perform their vital democratic roles they needed to be adequately funded. At its simplest: democracy is costly. The expenditure patterns of the major UK parties confirm this simple truism: in the period 2001–2010 the Conservative party spent on average £29.5 million a year, the Labour Party £30.9 million a year and the Liberal Democrats £7.5 million a year (Cm 8208 2011: 39). On average, 80 per cent of expenditure was on routine operational costs and staffing, with only 20 per cent of the three parties' spending devoted to campaigning. At the 2010 election a total of £31.5 million was spent by all political parties across the UK; over half of this total was spent by the Conservative Party alone (£16.7 million), a further quarter by the Labour party (£8.0 million) and 15 per cent by the Liberal Democrats (£4.8 million) (Electoral Commission 2011: 7–11).

Yet, as the Committee of Standards in Public Life (Cm 8208 2011: 21) noted, '[a]ll parties have found raising the funds necessary to undertake their democratic functions extremely difficult'. Clearly, however, some parties have found it more difficult than others. In the relative absence of state funding for political parties in the UK – other than direct grants to opposition parties in both Houses of Parliament to assist them in performing their parliamentary duties, and limited grants (amounting in total to £2 million a year) to assist parties develop policies for inclusion in election manifestos – parties are dependent upon generating income through a mixture of donations, membership fees, affiliation fees, commercial income, and loans. In this respect the UK 'remains something of an outlier compared with other European countries, and for good or for bad ... British exceptionalism [continues]' (Fisher 2009: 315). Unlike many other states, such as Australia, Canada, Germany, France, Norway, and Sweden, the UK provides little public funding for parties. In Germany, for example, public subsidies amount to 30–40 per cent of party income, and in Norway the state provides between 67 and 88 per cent of party revenues (Cm 8208 2011: 44).

In the absence of significant public subsidies, the alternative sources of revenue for UK parties all come with their own problems. As a corollary of the decline in party membership noted above, membership fees have declined significantly. Over the period 2001–2010 these fees accounted for 3 per cent of the Conservative party's total income, 10 per cent of the Liberal Democrats' income and 13 per cent of the revenue of the Labour party. The Labour party received £74.8 million in affiliation fees, which was 25 per cent of its total income between 2001 and 2010. The overwhelming proportion of these fees came from the trade unions.

No other party received such affiliation fees. This income stream appeared to become more uncertain, however, in the wake of the Labour party leader's decision to call a special party conference (scheduled for 2014) to examine the financial relationship between the party and trade unions. The collective fees system, whereby affiliated trade unions paid a political levy remotely for their members unless individuals opted out of the scheme, came under review and an alternative 'opt-in' payment scheme for individual trade unionists came into consideration.

A further 30 per cent of Labour's income came from donations (Wilks-Heeg and Crone 2010: 8). The corresponding proportion of donation income for the Conservative party was 59 per cent in the period 2005–2009. Research by Wilks-Heeg *et al.* (2012: 197) revealed the extent of the concentration of the sourcing of donations. They found that between 2001 and 2010 single donations in excess of £50,001 accounted for 54 per cent of the Conservative party's and 76 per cent of Labour's declared donation income. In the same period approximately 30 per cent (£45.5 million) of the Conservative party's donation income came from just 15 'donor groups'. Moreover Wilks-Heeg *et al.* (2012: 197) reported that some 50 per cent (£11.4 million) of Conservative party donation income in the general election year of 2010 came from individuals or companies associated with the financial services sector. The Labour party similarly benefited from large donations from individual donors or from the trade unions. Indeed, in the period 2001 to 2010, 62 per cent of Labour's total donation income (£98.6 million) came from the trade unions, and in the election year of 2010 71 per cent (£17.9 million) of the party's donation income came from this source. In the case of both the Labour and Conservative parties 'the reliance on "big money" is very striking' (Wilks-Heeg *et al.* 2012: 197).

While the Committee on Standards in Public Life (Cm 8208 2011: 63) adjudged the UK's system of party financing not to be actually corrupt, it also concluded that: '[a]n arrangement which makes the main parties dependent for their continued functioning on a small number of individuals, trade unions or other organizations is fundamentally flawed'. The same point had been made earlier in the review of the funding of political parties undertaken by Sir Hayden Phillips (Phillips 2007: 2). Both the Phillips Report and the Committee of Standards in Public Life's Report recommended increased public funding which would be conditional upon restrictions upon donations, further limitation of regulated campaign expenditure, and linked to measures of popular support – such as 'a pence-per-vote scheme' (Cm 8208 2011: 70), and/or matched funding under 'a registered subscriber scheme' (Phillips 2007: 18).

The costs of increased state funding proposed by these two reviews was estimated respectively at between £20 and £25 million a year and around £23 million a year (Cm 8208 2011: 10; Phillips 2007: 8).

Not surprisingly, historically, state support for political parties has been a matter of deep contention between the main parties in the UK, particularly when linked to the regulation of donations and affiliation fees (which would impact upon the two major parties asymmetrically). Although there is a fundamental cross-party agreement that something needs to be done to reform party financing, there is also a fundamental disagreement as to the constituent elements of any particular package of reform. Cross-party talks initiated in the wake of the Phillips Report and Committee of Standards in Public Life's Report were, on both occasions, suspended without agreement within a matter of months. In part, this was a reflection of a return to what Phillips (2012: 322) calls the 'default position of party introspection'. In part also, it was a reflection of the difficulty of convincing the public of the need for increased financial assistance to political parties at a time of deepening restrictions on public expenditure generally (see Clegg HC Debates, 15 November 2011: col 683).

Yet state funding of political parties is no panacea. One of the defining characteristics of a modern cartel party in Katz and Mair's (1995: 18; 2009: 755–7) conceptualisation is the use of state subventions to fund party organisation. In their opinion, this has an impact not only upon internal party organisation, through the enhancement of professionalisation, capital-intensive campaigning, and bureaucratisation, often at the expense of membership participation and decisional decentralisation (Katz and Mair 2009: 759), but also at a systemic-level with the 'movement of parties towards the state' (Katz and Mair 2009: 755). In the interpenetration of party and state, brought about by the regulation and subvention of the former by the latter, a pattern of inter-party collusion develops. First, parties collude in shaping the form and distribution of state subventions (and regulation); and second, they collude in the containment and management of electoral competition within the bounds of 'valence politics' and competing capability claims to effective and efficient policy management (Katz and Mair 1995: 19). In turn, cartel collusion has significant implications for competitive party models of democracy, not least in constraining the policy space between parties (Blyth and Katz 2005). As Katz and Mair (1995: 22) observe: 'As party programmes become more similar, and as campaigns are in any case oriented more towards agreed goals rather than contentious means, there is a shrinkage in the degree to which electoral outcomes can determine government actions'.

Katz and Mair's cartel party model has attracted close attention both as to its empirical validity and to its theoretical rigour (see for example Detterbeck 2005; Fisher 2009; Koole 1996; Loomes 2011; Pierre *et al.* 2000). While found wanting in both respects, nonetheless, this model has served the important purpose of highlighting the organisational and legitimation costs associated with increased state funding of political parties. Parties in the UK, however, are caught by conceptual immobilism, where the respective costs of models of voluntarism and state assistance for party funding are known and sufficient to militate against collusion over funding, while at the same time being insufficient to mitigate collusion of party leaders as 'apologists for and defenders of policies that have become more generically policies of the state' (Katz and Mair 2009: 759). In this manner they are caught, incongruously, between being parties as governors and parties as representatives.

Representational transmission beyond parties

> [As] parties have moved from representing interests of the citizens to the state to representing interests of the state to the citizens ... [m]eanwhile, the representation of the citizens, to the extent that it still occurs at all, is given over to other, nongoverning organizations and practices – to interest groups, social movements, advocacy coalitions, lobbies, the media, self-representation, etc. – that are disconnected from the party system. (Mair 2009: 6)

While Mair's assessment overstates the extent to which the representative role of parties has altered and the extent to which other representative institutions and actors are disconnected from parties, nonetheless, it does convey a widely held view that parties are 'damaged goods' as institutions of representation and that they have effectively become 'a broken link in the chain which connects voters and their representatives' (Wilks-Heeg and Crone 2010: 17). But the demise of parties as representative institutions should not be exaggerated (see Kitscheldt 2012: 146; Urbinati and Warren 2008: 400). In particular, the bi-directionality of party representation, should not be underestimated, for not only does it echo Mair's view, but it also means, as Saward (2010: 131) notes:

> It may be the case ... that parties are no longer rooted deeply in, or deriving strong and consistent partisan support from, relatively

settled societal groups. But that does not mean that they are no longer representing. The representative claims that they tend to make, or which are best enabled, are simply different from those that are characteristic of a different mode of claiming. In their claims – their presentation of themselves and the portrayals of constituents and nation that they offer – they may simply have 'moved up a level' [from civil society to state]. Parties, in this mode, are 'state actors' more a vehicle of state to society than vice versa.

In this regard, Saward's notion of representative claim is of value in identifying the reciprocal and 'contraflow' directionality of political party representation – with parties representing, in one direction, the opinions and interests of their members and voters to the state; yet, in the other direction, representing constructions of the state/national interest to the electorate. Saward's notion of representative claim is of even greater significance, however, in revealing the extent to which political representation occurs beyond political parties and the electoral transmission of power.

Non-electoral representation: Beyond parties and elections

One of the 'most critical key assumptions' about representative democracy over the past 40 years, in Saward's opinion (2010: 140), is that it 'is all about elections, and only elected officials can be classed as democratic representatives'. In this sense 'representative democracy as a political system in which elected officials make collective decisions for constituents is too familiar'; and what is needed, therefore, is to 'make democracy strange again' (Saward 2010: 167). The strangeness is to be found in non-electoral forms of representation. Yet in making this case Saward forgets his initial premise that 'political ideas and practices are more closely intertwined than we often think' (2010: 1). In fact, in the period specified by Saward, the practice of political representation in the UK accommodated non-electoral forms of representation to the extent that pluralist, corporatist, network, and governance models – as variants of non-electoral 'interest' representation – challenged the view that 'representative democracy is all about elections' to the extent that they came to be seen as 'new orthodoxies' (see Judge 1999: 121–48; Chapter 5). In the same period contemporary political theorists, such as Rosanvallon (2008) and Urbinati (2006), openly acknowledged that 'insofar as electoral representation works, it does so in conjunction with a rich fabric of representative claimants and advocacy within society' (Urbinati and Warren 2008: 402). In this sense, non-electoral, self-authorised representation is not new: 'history is replete with unelected leaders and groups making representative claims ... on behalf of interests and values they believe should have an impact' (Urbinati and Warren 2008: 403).

While non-electoral representation may not be new, what is new is the increased attention paid by political theorists and political scientists to the scope and diversity of such forms of representation. As Alonso *et al.* (2011: 18) note: 'The ecology of representation is rapidly changing ... plausible claims by leaders and groups that they are representative despite the fact that they are unelected are surfacing'. Non-electoral representation may be targeted and specific (as with interest groups); or be more generally concerned with the 'negative power of the people' – as manifest when electoral representation fails to reflect adequately the collective identities and interests of, for instance, women, ethnic groups, the marginalised, and the dispossessed, or the collective goods of the environment, peace, human rights, non-human life, or future social and economic sustainability (as with social movements). The nature of the representative claims made by non-electoral representatives, their organisational (and often 'non'-organisational) forms, and their relative territorial 'unboundedness' all warrant close attention.

In many ways the attention now paid to non-electoral representation constitutes part of an intellectual and academic rebranding of earlier normative and empirical enquiries focused upon organised groups, associations, and collective action. Established interest group scholars point out, with some irony, that the neologisms of 'social movements', 'non-governmental organisations' (NGOs), and 'civil society organisations', along with 'newly fashionable' usage of the term 'civil society' itself, has led to a 'positive bestowal of legitimacy', and a 'more (normatively) wholesome and attractive' perspective of 'what were once seen as interest groups' (Jordan and Maloney 2007: 193).

Interest groups

When examining the representational dimensions of organised groups, the starting point is often an observation that somehow groups have filled a 'linkage void' left by political parties (Jordan and Maloney 2007: 6). Indeed parties and interest groups have occasionally been conceived as having a zero-sum, rather than a positive-sum, relationship with each other, with the 'strength of parties tend[ing] to be inversely related to the strength of interest groups' (see Allern and Bale 2012: 8; Jordan and Maloney 2007: 6). Whereas parties are concerned with aggregative and collective representation, interest groups are defined by their 'particularised' representational focus. The exact degree of the 'particularity' of interest does, however, vary with the type of group, with a broad distinction commonly made between two types of groups. The first type is 'sectional', 'interest', 'functional', or 'associational' (SIFA) (designated respectively by Stewart 1958; Baggot 1995: 13–14; Moran 2011: 128; Heffernan 2011: 177). Such groups are formally organised and represent the interests of specific social or economic collectivities. In this sense, they have a restricted membership base, normally confined to those sharing a particular functional relationship, for example trade unions, professional associations, or sectoral trade organisations. The second type of group is designated variously as 'cause', 'attitude', 'preference', or 'promotional' (CAPP). The representational focus of such groups extends beyond their immediate membership to include representative claims raised by and through members, but made on behalf of a wider constituency of non-members – for example, and often most visibly, in the fields of civil liberties and human rights (Liberty, Amnesty International), or the environment (Greenpeace, Friends of the Earth), or child poverty and protection (Child Poverty Action Group, Barnardo's, Save the Children).

'Sectional', 'interest', 'functional', or 'associational' (SIFA) groups

For Saward (2010: 49) all representatives are 'claim-makers', and all 'claim-makers offer a construction of constituency to an audience'. A constituency may be actual or intended. 'Actual' constituencies 'consist of those who recognize a given claim as being made about and for them, or those who see their interest as being implicated in the claim' (2010: 49). In this sense they 'judge that the claim is indeed for and about them' (2010: 148). In making such judgements constituents are ultimately assessing the legitimacy of claims made on their behalf (2010: 149). An 'intended' constituency is 'the group that a maker claims to speak *for*; ... all claims to speak for also speak about: all claims that speak about can also be understood, however indirectly, as claims to speak for' (2010: 49; emphasis in the original).

In advancing a claim to represent a constituency, leaders of SIFA groups have ready-made, 'actual' constituencies for which they claim to speak. In the case of functional or professional constituencies these are coherent, self-delimited and legitimated through their restricted membership. Leaders can claim, authoritatively, that they speak for and on behalf of their members precisely because of the limited focus of representation – a specific industry (for example farming, or chemicals), or profession/occupation (for example doctors, or teachers, or miners) – and the specialist knowledge or expertise derived from that representational focus. Indeed, although professionalised and bureaucratised in their organisational structures, such organisations often strive to display their representative credentials through internal democratic processes (including leadership elections, membership consultations, conferences, surveys, and, in the case of trade unions seeking to embark upon industrial action, state-sanctioned membership ballots). Such legitimation exercises, when combined with high membership density, serve to authenticate the voice of group constituencies and to encourage acceptance of group representative claims by 'the audience' to which those claims are directed.

An audience, in Saward's model (2010: 49), is the recipient of representative claims. As part of an 'ongoing, dynamic process' a claim has to be evaluated by audiences (as well as constituencies) through 'acceptance acts' (Saward 2010: 151–3). These acts entail some assessment of the legitimacy of the claims made, and are also capable of prompting negative as well as positive evaluations. Claim-makers are subject to vagaries in how their claims are communicated, who receives them and how receptive an audience is to these claims. As in the case of constituencies there are actual and intended audiences. An 'actual' audience is one where members are conscious of receiving a representative claim. In this case, acceptance (or rejection or contestation) of the claim is dependent upon the recipient. An 'intended' audience, on the other hand, is the group to which the claim is addressed. In this case the audience is 'maker-driven' (Saward 2010: 50).

For SIFA groups the primary audience for 'claim-makers', in seeking to perform their routine functional duties, is often to be found within the particular sectoral world they inhabit. However, given the significance of many of these groups in key economic and societal sectors, claims addressed to sectoral audiences spill over, whether with deliberate intent or consequential effect, into audiences of state (at multi-levels) decision-makers, media (formal and informal, new and old) and 'the public'. State decision-makers are invariably the actual audience that receives and decodes claims directed to other delimited sectoral audiences, as well as the intended audience to which SIFA groups address their claims directly when seeking to influence state policies. The extent and degree to which state decision-makers, as 'audience', accept, reject, or contest representative claims moves the discussion towards the 'policy influencing' dimensions of the representational transmission of power (see Chapter 5). For the time being, however, the representative claims of 'cause', 'attitude', 'preference', or 'promotional' groups will be examined.

'Cause', 'attitude', 'preference', or 'promotional' (CAPP) groups

CAPP groups are often self-authorised representatives in that they make 'representative claims on behalf of interests and values that they believe should have an impact' (Urbinati and Warren 2008: 403). What has attracted attention is the recent proliferation of such groups and that they 'have proved extremely skilful in identifying and organizing "constituencies"' (Stoker 2006: 109). In fact, many of these groups take it upon themselves to speak for those who have no organised voice (Näsström 2011: 505) – be they the poor, those whose human rights have been infringed, those of future generations, or even non-human species in the natural world. Groups such as Child Poverty Action, Save the Children, Liberty, Friends of the Earth, and the World Wildlife Fund make claims to represent, or to speak for, intended constituencies of their own making. In Saward's terms they construct a constituency. Their success in doing so is then assessed by an audience's acceptance of this construction and the representative claims that flow from that construction. Indeed, the intended audiences for most CAPP activities are state decision-makers and agencies (at multi-levels), the media, and the public. In some formulations of 'representative claims' (see Montanaro 2010: 159; Saward 2010: 150), the claim to act as a representative, in the absence of an actual constituency, is substantiated simply if the intended audience accepts those claims. Such acceptance is likely to be facilitated if the claim-maker is able to identify that the representative claim is based upon some form of authorisation by and responsiveness to the constructed constituency. Direct authorisation is problematic where the constituency literally has no voice (in the case of animals or yet unborn future generations), or has a limited capacity to express a voice (those incarcerated, dispossessed, or impoverished). In these instances, the focus of attention is upon an intended constituency where surrogate measures of 'constituency construction' (primarily through mass membership) serve both to authorise and hold representatives accountable through group organisation (in so far as membership retention or exit indicates satisfaction or otherwise with the status of being a surrogate constituent). In practice, however, mass membership may measure little more than 'chequebook participation' (Jordan and Maloney 2007: 12). Nonetheless, CAPP organisations 'see "big numbers" (of members/supporters) as an important part of the policy-influencing armoury' (Jordan and Maloney 2007: 157). Equally, 'big numbers' may contribute to the legitimation of non-electoral representative claims made by CAPP organisations.

Social movements

Beyond CAPP groups, as formal organisations, are a range of social movements (both 'new' and 'old'). Whether a meaningful distinction can be made between 'interest groups' and 'social movements' – in terms of organisational structures, the construction of representational constituencies, or their mobilisation strategies in pursuit of collective goods – still divides academic opinion (for an overview see Diani 2012: 27–8). Some analysts have proposed instead that both terms should be subsumed within a more generic category of 'interest organization' (Burstein 1998: 45). The problem with such an approach is that viewing social movements as simply rebranded interest groups reduces their distinctiveness as informal networks of sustained interactions amongst collective action organisations. In other words, social movements are not simply aggregations of individual organisations or specific acts of pressure politics performed by coalitions of interest groups. Instead, as Diani (2012: 28) argues, the collective action dynamics of social movements can best be characterised as: 'sustained interactions between organizations and individuals taking part in movement campaigns and coalitions [that] generate regular patterns of resource coordination between several groups and organizations that maintain their independence, yet are involved in a sustained joint collective effort'. The concept of 'social movement families' (see Amenta *et al.* 2010: 288) has similarly been deployed to capture the sustained interactions and collective endeavours of social movement actors. The most active movements in the UK in recent decades have included those focused upon women (though doubts exist as to the continued vibrancy of the women's movement in the UK (see Mackay 2008a)), gay and lesbian rights, peace/anti-war (especially since military deployment in Iraq and Afghanistan), anti-nuclear, anti-globalisation/global justice, and the environment.

A distinction between CAPP groups and social movements has also been sought by pointing to the latter's adoption of unconventional styles of political engagement, most particularly a proclaimed emphasis upon protest strategies and disruptive forms of action (for an overview see della Porta and Diani 2006: 165–81). But, as della Porta and Diani (2006: 233) point out, protest is only a small part overall of the political repertoires of social movements, and one that is likely to prove ineffective unless accompanied by more traditional lobbying strategies.

When viewed through the analytical lens of representative claims, social movements can be conceived as claim-makers. Indeed, Saward uses the example of anti-globalisation demonstrators to show how they 'set up themselves and their movements (subjects) as representatives of the oppressed and marginalized (object) to Western governments (audience)' (Saward 2010: 37). As with other claim-makers, social movements have to construct constituencies. As with many CAPP groups, social movements have to do so in the absence of actual constituents with 'a voice'. In other words, in claiming to speak for a constituency they also 'portray and offer some conception of the group's interests' (2010: 49). Moreover, the dynamic interaction between claim-making and claim-receiving (between constituency and audience) may play a key role in shaping a conscious sense of identity on the part of intended constituents (2010: 51). This is of particular significance where constituencies are not territorially anchored (global justice/environment) or temporally defined (peace/future generations).

In parallel, social movements identify audiences that are not necessarily territorially delimited (or more accurately not defined by the boundaries of 'the state') and so make their claims –'speak to' – decision-makers in international organisations (such as the G8/ G20 (Group of 20), United Nations, European Union, International Monetary Fund, World Bank, or World Trade Organization) and multinational corporations, as well as to global media and to like-minded publics across state boundaries (increasingly through social media). Thus, as governance has come to be conceived, and to operate, at multi-levels, so social movements have developed multi-level strategies. In this sense social movements are active in a political arena that offers 'no discrete domain of institutional processes' (Urbinati and Warren 2008: 404). In fact, social movements may not necessarily prioritise action in formal political arenas, preferring instead to engage in cultural strategies aimed at changing values systems (della Porta and Diani 2006: 170–1). Where political action is prioritised, however, social movements are predisposed to pitch their representative claims to wider audiences than elected decision-makers, not least because 'social movement actors usually occupy a peripheral position in decision-making processes' and so need 'to mobilize public opinion to maintain their pressure capacity' (della Porta and Diani 2006: 28). In this respect, protest and disruptive forms of action remain integral to processes of claim making by social movements: 'social movement politics is still to a large extent "politics in the streets"' (della Porta and Diani 2006: 29). Indeed, the notion of the 'word from the street' is used by Saward (2010: 99) to capture the idea that the interests that are claimed to be represented 'emerge from specific grassroots techniques or events'.

Demonstrations and protests

In making the case that a representative claim can be based on a 'massive and tangible demonstration of popular support', Saward (2010: 99) cites the example of the anti-war demonstration in London of 15 February 2003. Not only was this demonstration unprecedented in size in recent UK history (organisers estimated 2,000,000 marchers on the streets of London, although the police estimated 750,000), it was also part of an international day of protest. The BBC (2003) estimated that between six and ten million people took part in protests in 60 major cities across the world on that day. Certainly social movements are acutely aware of the 'logic of numbers' (DeNardo 1985: 35) as, amongst other things, 'demonstrations by their size ... give the regime an indication of how much support the dissidents enjoy' (DeNardo 1985: 35–6). Indeed, della Porta and Diani (2006: 172) suggest that 'the logic of numbers is coherent with the principles of representative democracy: an attempt is made to influence public opinion [who are also voters]'.

Alongside the anti-war marches, any number of large public demonstrations in the UK could also be cited as examples of 'tangible public support' for some cause or other. Certainly, popular protests 'from the street' have been a recurring feature of representative politics in the UK. They have included: social movement protests (anti-war demonstrations noted above, as well as global justice protests against the G20 in London; Occupy London Stock Exchange (Occupy LSX) demonstrations; interest group protests (TUC anti-cuts rallies, NUS/UCU organised protests against student fees); or of public sector workers to 'save our pensions' (TUC Day of Action)). Similarly, the 'performance protests' coordinated by, for example, UK Uncut in campaigns against, variously, corporate tax avoidance (with sit-ins at shops owned by Vodafone, Topshop, and Fortnum & Mason) and NHS cuts (the blocking of Westminster Bridge), or by Plane Stupid (with protests on the roof of the Palace of Westminster) against the expansion of Heathrow airport, constituted clear, non-electoral, representative claims.

A dramatic, headline-catching representative claim was deployed by Occupy LSX in the slogan 'we are the 99 per cent'. Occupy LSX claimed to 'imagine itself from the beginning as the broadest possible community of resistance – the 99 per cent, as against the 1 per cent' (Davis 2011). Yet, in terms of numbers, the Occupy LSX participants camped outside St Paul's Cathedral in the autumn of 2011, or demonstrating outside the Bank of England in May 2012, were counted in hundreds rather than thousands (but with a more numerous electronic 'presence' through Facebook, Twitter, and other social media). But numbers, even in Saward's logic, are not of paramount significance in making and sustaining a representative claim. In making their respective claims, both anti-war and anti-capitalist protestors, in Saward's (2010: 48–50) terminology, 'constructed a constituency' – in the sense of when 'speaking about' the negatives of war and capitalism they also, indirectly, claimed to be 'speaking for' those in opposition to existing policies/systems. The intended constituency is thus far broader than the actual constituency of those who recognise a claim through their presence in the act of protest (whether physically or virtually through electronic media). Correspondingly, the actual audience which receives the claim (through direct or indirect communication: speech, news media, social media, etc.) and 'respond in some way' (Saward 2010: 49) is but one segment of a wider intended audience to whom the claim is addressed – of other social movements, civil society organisations, opinion formers (media), and decision makers, both 'public' (members of formal political institutions) and 'private' (corporate/financial capitalist organisations). In both of the main examples used here – anti-war and anti-capitalist claims – the intended constituency and audience transcend the state boundaries of the UK, as in both cases there are parallel movements in other liberal representative democracies making similar claims.

But, as noted above, making a claim does not guarantee that it will be accepted. It has to be evaluated by constituencies and audiences through 'acceptance acts', and can generate negative as well as positive assessments. In the case of Occupy LSX, significant sections of the intended audience – 'the 99 per cent' – proved resistant to the representative claims, with only 39 per cent of a YouGov (2011a) sample supporting the aims of the protestors outside St Paul's, 26 per cent opposing and 35 per cent not sure. Within a few weeks, however, support for the protest was down to 20 per cent, with 46 per cent opposing and 33 per cent neither/don't know (YouGov 2011b). In the 'percentage game' much was made of the fact that Occupy LSX did not, and could not, speak for 'the 99 per cent'. In the case of anti-war claims in 2002–2003, at the time of the mass demonstrations, a large proportion of the UK public, 45 per cent of respondents to an ICM poll (fieldwork conducted 11–13 February 2003), agreed with the claim that Britain should not go to war. Yet, within less than a month of the 15 February demonstration, a subsequent ICM poll (28 March 2003; see also Lewis 2004) reported that 52 per cent approved of military intervention in Iraq, with 34 per cent opposed to such action.

While anti-war and anti-capitalist demonstrators, along with others articulating 'the word from the streets', sought to construct, through their representative claims, wider constituencies within the public, and to appeal to wider audiences through social networking and formal and informal media, their ultimate claim was to affect the policies of concern to these constituencies. Their ultimate target was an intended audience of governmental decision makers that was situated within the electoral representative process (no matter how indirectly that audience was approached).

Conclusion

In making the move from individual to collective representation the principal–agent relationship between citizens and government came to be mediated through collective representational associations of political parties, organised political groups, and social movements. Of these associations, political parties – as electoral institutions engaged in interest articulation, demand aggregation, collective preference formation, and popular mobilisation – are deemed to be fundamental in the representational transmission of power. Yet, equally, they have come increasingly to serve as governing institutions and, through their electoral programmes, to compete in representing conceptions of 'the state' and its interests to citizens. In so doing, the directionality of 'representational transmission', initially prescribed in the standard model of representative democracy, is reversed, and parties are placed in an incongruous 'contra-flow' position of representing, in one direction, the opinions and interests of their members and voters to the state, and, in the other direction, representing the state to the electorate. In turn, this incongruity generates further incongruities as to the political terrain upon which political parties compete at elections, and how they organise themselves internally to secure relative competitive advantage on this terrain. In Britain the positional convergence of the major parties on the national electoral terrain has impacted upon voter choice and, in Brandenburg and Johns' (2013: 9) words, left many voters 'a long way from the "representational action"'. As competing for office has become 'the core of what British parties now do' (Clark 2012: 227), voters have adopted cognitive shortcuts to assess governing competence and 'valence politics' has become a powerful variable in explaining the outcomes of recent UK general elections. Correspondingly, as the major parties have come to privilege 'governing' over 'representing', so attempts have been made to reverse organisational polarity and to redirect the flows of intra-party authorisation, with the requirements of leadership and governing competence asserted over participatory processes and membership direction of policy programmes. But attempts to reverse this polarity have generated fluctuations in the flows of authorisation. Hence, while leadership has been prioritised in both major parties, there have been parallel organisational initiatives designed to 'open up' internal policy processes to supporters and volunteers. The incongruity remains, however, that these initiatives, launched in the name of decentralisation and democratisation (while simultaneously circumventing formal members), were designed not to subvert the leadership's centralised strategic control of party programmes.

In circumstances in which, for political parties, 'representational transmission' is more bidirectional than the unidirectional flow outlined in a standard model of representative democracy, the standard model has been challenged still further in the ideas and practices of 'non-electoral' and 'self-authorised' representation. Indeed, as noted above, for some analysts these developments are linked, as the representational terrain vacated by parties in their transmutation into 'governing institutions' has been occupied by a plethora of political associations and movements. Self-authorised representation is not new, but has now achieved a significance such that the mismatch between the *self*-authorisation and *disaggregated* claims of non-electoral associations and institutions and the *other*-authorisation and *aggregative* claims of political parties and electoral institutions has led to increased questioning of how, let alone if, the former can successfully conjoin representative and democratic claims. This basic incongruity will be examined further in Chapters 5 and 6. In the meantime, Chapter 4 examines in more detail the linkage effects of political parties in the processes of electoral representation, and locates that examination in a broader analysis of other nodes of electoral linkage and their associated democratic incongruities.

4
The 'Problem' of Elected Representatives

Introduction

Whereas Chapter 3 was concerned with the representational transmission of power – of the institutions and processes linking citizens to their representatives – this chapter is concerned with the end point of that linkage and with the representatives themselves. Conceived as a one-to-one, person-to-person, principal–agent relationship, representation is relatively unproblematic. It becomes more problematic, however, when both 'the represented' and the 'representatives' are collectivities. One solution, historically, has been to subsume individual differences amongst the represented within sets of segmented collective interest – of a territorial constituency, or a political party, or a political association – constituted respectively around a community of local interest, or an ideological programme, or a specific functional interest or political cause which can then be represented. Such conceptions have attracted criticism, however, for assuming that such collective interests are relatively static and exist 'out there' ready to be represented (Celis *et al.* 2008: 101); and for conceiving of representation as doing/acting rather than being/standing for (Pitkin 1967: 61). Notions of representative claims (see Chapters 1 and 3) and of descriptive representation (see below) have been developed in response to such criticisms and have attracted increased attention and importance in the contemporary theorisation and practice of representation.

The fundamental question underpinning these responses remains, however, the same question initially posed by Pitkin (1967: 8–9 original emphasis): what is entailed when representatives claim to 're-present' by 'mak[ing] present again ... *in some sense* something which is nevertheless *not* present literally or in fact'? An answer to this question requires consideration of three further questions: 'what' is being made present again; 'how' (whatever it might be) is being represented; and 'who' is doing the representing? But these questions have tended to be rephrased, and simplified, by making a basic dichotomous distinction between the 'focus' of representation (how are the represented constituted?) and the 'style' of representation (how does the representative act on behalf of the represented?) (Wahlke *et al.* 1962). In this rephrasing, attention came to be focused largely upon the 'what' and the 'how' questions. Only recently has the 'who' question come to the forefront of attention. Proponents of descriptive representation, particularly spokespersons of disadvantaged groups, have placed the emphasis upon the importance of the 'who' of representation: of 'representatives [who] are in their own persons and lives in some sense typical of the larger class of persons whom they represent' (Mansbridge 1999a: 629).

This chapter examines each of the 'what', 'who' and 'how' questions in sequence. Starting with the 'what' question, the historical and contemporary importance of territorial constituencies and notions of locality as a focus of representation are examined, before the 'who' question is addressed in an analysis of descriptive representation (and its relationship to ideas of substantive representation). Finally, the 'how' question is addressed in examining the complex interactions between delegate theories of party representation and trustee notions of the exercise of representatives' independent judgement.

The 'what' of representation

Territorial constituency

> The practice of using territory to define constituencies is widespread: almost every modern democratic government uses territory in some form to construct constituencies for their national legislature. (Rehfeld 2005: xii)

Historically, the core principles of representation in Britain – of consent, legitimation and the authorisation of decision-making – were built upon territorial foundations (see Judge 1993: 8). The origins of territorial representation can be traced back to Medieval English parliaments where, at that time, constituencies effectively constituted geographically defined 'communities of interest' and representatives were drawn from local communities simply 'because that is where and how people defined themselves' (Rehfeld 2005: 71). Even as the composition and function of the English/British parliament changed in the face of significant economic and social change and a restructuring of the state after 1689, representation remained rooted in territory; or, more particularly in Edmund Burke's classic formulation, in locality and specific, objective local interests (see Burke ([1780] 1801 vol 4: 73)). At the end of the 18th century this might have been a defensible position for a Whig such as Burke to adopt, but in 21st century Britain how is the continuing significance of territorially based representation to be explained?

One explanation might simply be that territory remains 'a seemingly "natural" part of representation' (Rehfeld 2005: 72); or, at least, basing representation on geographical constituencies is still used 'without giving much thought to its alternatives' (Rehfeld 2005: 9).

Another, less unthinking, explanation is that geographical constituencies provide for a residency-based franchise, which apportions representatives to the represented in territorial segments within territorially defined states (states that often are conflated with nations in terms of identities). If the national legislature is deemed to represent the collectivity of the 'political nation' (conceived in terms of *demos* in a representative democracy), then one, admittedly arbitrary, mode of constituting (yet simultaneously segmenting) that collectivity is through a residency-based territorial franchise (Urbinati and Warren 2008: 387). This gives rise to two principles of territorial segmentation: one based on 'community of interest' and the other based upon numerically equal populated geographical districts.

The contemporary relevance of these (often contrasting) principles was apparent in the debate surrounding the redistribution of parliamentary constituencies in the UK following the decision of the post-2010 coalition government to reduce the number of MPs from 650 to 600 with effect from 2015 (but later postponed until 2018). This reduction was deemed necessary by the coalition partners, first to reduce the cost of politics and also to help to rebuild trust in the representative process in the wake of the MPs' expenses scandal in 2009; and, second, and of particular interest to one coalition partner, to remove an anti-Conservative bias in the way in which votes were translated into seats under the existing distribution of electors across constituencies. Under the provisions of the *Parliamentary Voting System and Constituencies Act 2011* the four Boundary Commissions within the UK were required to ensure that every constituency (with four named exceptions) had an electorate within 5 per cent (higher or lower) of a UK national electoral quota of 76,641 voters. Although the perceived partisan advantage to be gained by the Conservative party was a major stimulus for redistribution, the reform was framed in the more principled language of equality and fairness (see HC 437 2010: 24; Clegg HC Debates 6 September 2010: col.35).

The proposed redrawing of constituency boundaries thus constituted a 'major shift in the relative importance of two separate criteria for defining constituencies – the "organic", in which constituencies are created so that their MPs represent distinct communities, and the "arithmetic", in which equality of constituency populations/electorates predominates' (Johnston *et al.* 2012: 4). The inherit danger of such a shift was that an increasing number of constituencies would have 'little internal homogeneity' or 'organic' sense of community. In emphasising arithmetical equality and privileging electoral wards in defining constituency boundaries in England post-2011, the 'organic' principle was in danger of being eroded. And with it a challenge was posed to historic notions of territorial representation:

> The implicit theory of representation that underpins the UK's model of democracy has each Member of Parliament (MP) representing not only a certain proportion of the national electorate but also an area of the national territory which is more than an aggregation of those individuals' homes. Part of the MP's role, it is argued, is to represent a place, a spatially bounded territorial unit whose residents have common interests; the place is thus more than a sum of its component parts – and is often equated with the elusive concept of a community. (Rossiter *et al.* 2013: 856–7)

The continuing importance of this 'implicit theory' finds practical manifestation in a convention whereby MPs address each other in the Chamber of the House of Commons by the name of the constituencies that they represent. Attempts to remove this arcane form of address, as part of procedural modernisation projects, have met with principled opposition on the grounds that: 'Members do not sit in the House as individual citizens, they are there as representatives of their constituencies: and it is in that capacity that they should be addressed' (HC 600 1998: paras 38–9). The danger inherent within the proposed boundary changes after 2011 (even though their implementation was delayed until 2018) was that many new constituencies would have different and often longer names (to reflect the incorporation of two or more separate geographical areas). As a result, as Rossiter *et al.* (2013: 884) concluded, 'increasingly such names will have less relevance' for parliamentary representation in the UK.

Locality

Coincidentally, at the very same time that the redrawing of constituency boundaries in the UK was threatening the territorial basis of the representation of 'communities of interest', UK political scientists showed an increased interest in the 'case for local representation'. At the forefront of making such a 'case', Childs and Cowley (2011: 8 original emphasis) started from a basic assumption that a local representative would be 'a *better* representative than someone from outside'. 'Better' in the sense of having a better understanding of the needs of local people in a constituency, and/or because a locally resident representative was more likely to have individual social capital invested in the area, and to have a greater incentive to promote the 'success' of that area, than a representative from outside. In making this case Childs and Cowley sought to draw parallels between the representation of locality and other forms of descriptive representation (see below; see also Cowley 2013: 159). Their case ultimately distilled into the argument that 'the representative must be "of" that constituency' (Childs and Cowley 2011: 8).

Yet the basic problem confronting Childs and Cowley is in determining what constitutes being 'of' a constituency. It is one thing to note that voters prioritise for their MP 'representing the views of local people in the House of Commons', or that most candidates' election materials spotlight local issues, or that most MPs spend some two-thirds of their working time dealing with constituency matters (see below). It is entirely another to say that there is a cohesiveness of 'community interest', or a 'local identity', sufficient to underpin the 'descriptive representation of the local [DRL]' (Childs and Cowley 2011: 3). Indeed, the very calibration of the scale of 'locality' presents a conceptual problem for Childs and Cowley, and they are forced to acknowledge openly that 'a definitive definition of what "local" means' (2011: 6) is beyond their reach.

Taking locality seriously

Childs and Cowley (2011: 5) point to 'a widespread acknowledgement within the political parties themselves that a "local candidate" can be an electoral asset', but then lament that there has been 'almost no recent academic writing on the subject'. Survey evidence has consistently pointed to the fact that voters state a preference for local candidates (Cowley 2013: 22; Childs and Cowley 2011: 5; Johnson and Rosenblatt 2007); and survey experiments have revealed the impact of local residency upon voters' perceptions of parliamentary candidates (Campbell and Cowley 2013: 10–13). Yet empirical verification of the likelihood of the residential location of candidates affecting voter choice has only recently been undertaken. Arzheimer and Evans (2012) provided the first statistical test of the 'distance hypothesis' through their intricate statistical modelling and scenario simulations of party competition and distance interactions between voters and candidates. In essence they found that the residential distance between a voter and candidates (from the three main UK parties in English constituencies) was of statistical significance. Admittedly the electoral advantage accruing from a candidate who lived closer to voters was substantively small. Nonetheless, Arzheimer and Evans (2012: 309) believed their findings to be robust and to confirm the proposition that: 'Candidate distance does matter, with voters finding distant candidates less appealing than local ones, even when pre-campaign party feeling and personal incumbency effects are controlled for ... local is better'. But equally they recognised that spatial distance and residential location by themselves do not necessarily define 'local', and that other dimensions of 'localness' need to be explored (2012: 309).

Local representation

The most important criterion deployed by many constituents in determining the effectiveness of MPs as representatives is 'being local' (see Hansard Society 2011: 33–5). For most of the participants in the Hansard Society's survey, residency in the constituency for a number of years was the measure of 'being local'. As a local resident it was assumed that 'the MP would know and care about [the local community] and its people, that they would understand any issues and problems and know what would be in the best interest of the community' (2011: 34). Indeed, 'being local was closely connected ... with the idea that the MP was good at their job' (Hansard Society 2011: 34). This perception was not simply the preserve of voters, but also found reflection in the Report of the *Speaker's Conference on Parliamentary Representation* (see HC 239 2010: 38).

Being good at their job: Constituency representation

Territorial representation, as noted above, has been at the core of parliamentary government since medieval times. What changed dramatically in recent years, however, was the increased scope and volume of constituency demands, and a concomitant increase in the expected involvement of MPs in 'constituency work'. Indeed, this seemingly exponential increase in constituency workload has been likened by one MP to 'a tidal wave ... that overwhelms you' (Martin Slater HC 337 2007: Q160;

see Rush and Giddings 2011: 24). Not surprisingly, therefore, successive surveys of the working patterns of MPs have revealed that most MPs spend significantly more time dealing with constituency matters than any other activity (HC 337 2007: Ev 32; HC 330 2012: Ev. w97–120; Korris 2011: 6–7; Rush and Giddings 2011: 112–3).

The work patterns of MPs closely reflect their individual prioritisation of roles, to the extent that representing constituency interests and dealing with individual constituents were identified respectively as the single highest priority by 29 per cent and 19 per cent of MPs in the 2012 Procedure Committee's sample ('holding government to account' was the highest ranked role by 36 per cent of MPs). This prioritisation was also broadly in line with the expectations of constituents. Constituency activities, such as representing the views of local people, dealing with the problems of local people, participating in local meetings and events, and communicating with constituents, were identified as key elements of how MPs should spend their time by constituents (Hansard Society 2010a: 93; 2011: 47). While the precise components of constituency work – policy advocacy, policy congruence, and service responsiveness, including the dimensions of 'welfare officer tasks', 'individual case-work', 'local promotion', and 'territorial advocacy' (for an overview see Gay 2005; Judge 1999: 151–7) – are not of prime concern here, what is of more immediate interest are the representational incongruities that are exposed by the magnitude of 'the tidal wave of constituency work'.

Incongruities of the constituency role

What constituents believe MPs should be doing is what MPs are in fact doing

Survey evidence reveals that the work patterns and role prioritisation of MPs correspond fairly closely to the stated preferences of electors. Nonetheless, despite the significant attention and effort devoted by MPs to their constituency activities – to the extent that one leading parliamentary analyst, Philip Cowley, raised the spectre that '[t]here must now be a real concern that MPs are so focussed on the parochial they have no time for the national, let alone the international, picture' (HC 337 2007: Ev. 14) – voters, generally, appear largely oblivious to work done on their behalf by their MPs. Indeed, surveys have found a significant and continuing 'perceptions gap' – what has been characterised more dramatically as a 'huge gulf' (Hansard Society 2010a: 90) – between what constituents thought MPs should do and what they actually did (Hansard Society 2007: 56; 2010a: 39). Despite the importance placed upon constituency service by electors, many of them remained uninformed about who their MP was and how MPs engaged with constituents. The basic incongruity arising from this 'perceptions gap' is that MPs appear be performing in ways that electors want, but constituents are largely unaware of such activity.

Basic knowledge about the name of their local MP was beyond the grasp of most constituents, with the first seven Hansard Society *Audits* routinely recording that only two in five voters knew the name of their local MP (2012a: 63). By the 2013 *Audit* (2013: 51) this figure was down to one in five (22 per cent). A corollary of these findings is that many of the participants in the Hansard Society's focus groups who did not know their MP's name proceeded to extrapolate that their MP 'must not be doing a good job of representing them because, if they did not even know who he or she was, how could they be doing so?' (Hansard Society 2011: 32). Moreover, while many believed that MPs should hold regular events where MPs should meet with their constituents to find out and discuss the interests and concerns of the represented, most participants were unaware that most MPs already held advice surgeries and local meetings to do precisely that (Hansard Society 2011: 32).

What MPs are doing in relation to their constituencies is not necessarily what MPs should be doing

Alongside the incongruity that MPs are spending much of their time on constituency service, which is what most voters say they want but yet most voters do not know that this is indeed the case, is the further, contradictory incongruity that many commentators and analysts believe that MPs are spending too much of their time on constituency service. As Riddell (2011: 20) opined: 'one worry is that [MPs] have become too constituency-oriented'. This view is shared by many former MPs and serving MPs alike (see HC 330 2012: Ev w113–7; Wright 2010: 301–2; 2012: 211). Yet the increased emphasis on 'constituency casework' is entirely understandable and predictable in periods of public expenditure cuts and economic 'austerity' and of rapid change in the nature and jurisdictional boundaries of state service. In these circumstances MPs receive a substantial number of requests from individual constituents to intervene on their behalf to resolve some administrative problem or other. Typical problems relate to social security provision, housing, schooling, the NHS, immigration services, and policing matters, and reflect the mix of institutions that MPs are expected to mediate with – local authorities, central government departments and agencies, and private utilities and private welfare service providers. There is, however, a fundamental ambiguity about the status of MPs in dealing with these matters, as the responsibility for service delivery is often in the hands of local officials who are responsible to locally elected councillors, or of devolved executives responsible to sub-national assemblies and parliaments, or of NHS Trusts with responsibility to Strategic Health Authorities, or (after 2012) police authorities responsible to directly elected Police and Crime Commissioners in England and Wales, or to private companies which are responsible to their shareholders or state regulators. In these circumstances MPs act as intermediaries, literally 're-presenting' the grievances of individual constituents to service providers. Whether MPs should be performing such roles in the first place, or even if, in the second place, it is decided that they should, whether they should be devoting so much attention to constituency service, has been open to question.

Indeed there has long been an argument that: 'MPs should take a decision no longer to deal with matters which are properly the responsibility of those elected at local level, or to a [devolved] parliament' (Riddell, *The Times* 25 August 1997; HC 330 2012: Ev w6). Yet the response by MPs to this suggestion is essentially fatalistic: 'Whatever the reasons [for increased constituency workload] it is clear that these pressures, once raised, are very unlikely to diminish' (HC 330 2012: 9; for the reasons why see HC 330 2012: Ev. 3–4; Wright 2012: 17–8).

Are MPs representing territorial constituencies when they represent their constituents?

If the case is made that constituency representation revolves around the identification of essentially economically defined 'community interests' then, beyond specifically geographically contingent industries such as agriculture and those associated with 'heavy industries' (which have also been in steep decline in the UK in recent decades), most constituencies have a diversity and plurality of economic interests which makes the identification of 'a community economic interest' difficult to discern. Alternatively, if the spatial location of concentrations of people from the same ethnic, religious, or racial groups, or for that matter social class, is used as a basis for 'communities of interest' then territory might be taken to serve as a 'reasonably good proxy for communities of interest that happen to be territorially segregated' (Rehfeld 2005: 158). The difficulty with such an argument is, however, that:

> When territory becomes a proxy for some other community of interest, the 'communities of interest' justification no longer justifies the use

of territory per se. Rather, territory is justified as a means to represent the other interests for which it serves as a proxy ... [but] were we to take this road of justifying territory as a proxy for other communities of interest, we then run into [the] problem: Territory can serve as a proxy only for interests that are territorially contiguous, and there is no reason to think that only territorially contiguous interests are the most relevant to national politics. (Rehfeld 2005: 158)

Indeed, in Rehfeld's (2005: 158) estimation, 'given the multifaceted functions of national representation, territory ranks low as a strongly relevant interest, and seems hardly justifiable as a weak one'.

The 'Who' of representation

Descriptive representation: Women

Descriptive representation denotes a correspondence of social characteristics between representatives and the represented. The characteristics deemed to be of importance vary both over time and in relation to socially constructed priorities. At the heart of a definition of descriptive representation is the notion of 'shared experiences' between represented and representative, which allow the latter to be 'in some sense typical of the larger class of persons whom they represent' (Mansbridge 1999a: 629). Historically, as noted above, the 'shared experience' of most significance in most representative democracies was 'geographic location' (Dovi 2002: 739). And, as Mansbridge (1999a: 644; see also Pitkin 1967: 85–6) points out, 'the original geographic representation of voters ... was undoubtedly intended in part to capture this form of descriptive representation'.

Beyond the immediate relationship between the represented and their representative, Mansbridge's (1999a: 648) conception of descriptive representation is of broader significance in outlining the crucial role of 'the representative assembly in constructing social meaning and de facto legitimacy'. This role is particularly apparent when 'major status differences connected with citizenship' occur, for at those points 'a low percentage [or even the absence] of a given descriptive group in the representational body creates social meanings attached to those characteristics that affect all holders of the characteristics' (Mansbridge 1999a: 649). The created social meaning is that the un-represented, or under-represented, group 'cannot rule or are not suitable for rule' and carries with it 'a legacy of second-class citizenship' (Mansbridge 1999a: 649–50).

Yet identifying quantitative under-representation of a particular social group 'does not in itself add up to a normative case for their equal or proportionate presence' in representative institutions (Phillips 1995: 39). Some groups, most commonly identified as the stupid, the mad, or the maleficent (see Pennock 1979: 314; Phillips Griffiths 1960: 190), are treated as exemplars of groups deemed to be at the furthest limits of the normative case for descriptive representation. Other groups – most notably those framed by 'shared experiences' of being female, or of ethnicity, or of race, or of sexual orientation – have articulated more convincing cases for descriptive representation. In this manner, feminist movements (alongside black, ethnic, and other social movements) have interjected into the discussion of representation the issue of 'who represents' alongside the 'what' and 'how' questions (see Dahlerup 2009: 5; Galligan 2007: 557).

In posing the question 'who represents women?' feminists already know the empirical answer: mostly men. In the UK, after the 2010 general election, 22 per cent of MPs, 143 of 650, were women. This was the highest number of women ever elected to Westminster and represented a doubling of the proportion of female MPs returned at the 1992 election (9.2 per cent) and a quintupling since 1966 (4.1 per cent). Yet, despite this increase, women remain significantly under-represented in Westminster. But, as noted above, the empirical fact of exclusion does not automatically translate into a normative case for the greater inclusion of women. Nonetheless, it does provide a basis from which to construct such a case. The first step in constructing such a case is often to couch the argument in terms of 'principles of justice' (Lovenduski 2005: 22) or, more specifically, 'democratic justice' (Norderval 1985: 84). By this argument, increased female representation is conceived as an end in itself, as it is 'patently and grotesquely unfair for men to monopolise representation' (Phillips 1995: 63). Indeed, Lovenduski (2005: 177) is willing to contend that, 'considerations of justice are enough to support the increased representation of women'.

Similarly, a stand-alone case for descriptive representation can be made in relation to 'symbolic equity' (Norris and Lovenduski 1989: 107). Here the focus is changed to consider the legitimacy of representative institutions (Krook 2010: 236), or of the wider political system, and the claim is made that if representation is designed to secure legitimation then 'political decisions made by all-male or predominantly male governmental processes can no longer serve this legitimizing function' (Darcy *et al.* 1994: 18). The exclusion of women may undermine 'the democratic legitimacy and public confidence in institutions'

(Norris 1996: 89; Norris and Lovenduski 1995: 209), whereas their inclusion can bolster 'democratic participation and the legitimacy of democratic institutions' (Dovi 2002: 742).

But these claims for more proportionate representation logically stand independently of the actual impact of increased female representation upon policy outputs. The 'justice' and 'symbolic equity' cases are not concerned primarily with whether or not women have any practical impact on decisions, but rest, instead, on the claim that it is only 'fair', it is only 'equitable', that they should be represented more proportionately.

Substantive representation: Women

Rarely, however, are cases for descriptive representation pressed by themselves and without reference to claims for the substantive impact of increased female representation upon policy outcomes. Although analytically distinct, descriptive representation ('standing for') is often conceived by feminists as an enabling condition for substantive representation ('acting for' women) (Celis and Childs 2008: 419). Substantive representation is often linked, therefore, with 'policy responsiveness' where '[w]omen are thought to be represented when deliberations about public policy consider the potential impact on different groups of women' (Campbell *et al.* 2010: 172). Yet, as Childs and Lovenduski (2013: 496) recognise: 'While the requirements of descriptive representation are at least superficially straightforward in that only women can descriptively represent women, those of substantive representation are more complicated'.

A major complication is how the 'shared experiences' of women, identified by Mansbridge as the essence of descriptive representation, are translated into policy outputs as the essence of substantive representation. This complication is revealed starkly in the elision of the notion of 'shared experiences' into 'shared interests'. In turn, the identification of 'women's interests' has been used by feminist theorists to underscore the case for increasing the numbers of elected female representatives, but without a consensus upon what these interests are, or the extent to which women share these interests. The complexity of conceptualising women's interests and deploying this notion in empirical studies has been thoroughly examined by feminist scholars and lies beyond the immediate focus of the present discussion. What only needs to be noted here, however, is that, in seeking to avoid the essentialism and determinism associated with stipulations of women's interests in relation to female biology or in terms of innate women's psychologies (Campbell *et al.* 2010: 174), feminist researchers have reached the position that 'women's concerns are *a priori* undefined, context related, and subject to evolution' (Celis *et al.* 2008: 105–6; Childs and Lovenduski 2013: 499). This position switches attention from problematising women's interests in terms of 'sex', and the biological differences between men and women, to 'gender', and the construction of social meanings about these distinctions. In seeking to avoid a binary division between the sexes and to emphasise the social construction of gender (Campbell *et al.* 2010: 174), some feminists have gone further and conflated such an undertaking with feminist understandings of gender constructions. As a result, the substantive representation of women has often been subsumed within a narrower notion of feminist substantive representation.

To move beyond constricted feminist notions of substantive representation, and to acknowledge the essential contestability of 'women's interests', researchers have canvassed a 'new approach' to identifying the existence and nature of 'women' as a group to be represented. The new approach entails a conceptualisation of representation as 'claims making' and returns the discussion to that started in Chapter 1 in relation to Saward's work. Indeed, Saward (2010: 120) claims that 'seeing representation as claim-making provides further resources to criticize any persistent essentialism in characterizing women's identities or interests'. Acknowledgement of the value of this approach has been widespread (see for example Celis and Childs 2012: 219–20; Celis *et al.* 2008: 106; Childs and Krook 2009: 133; Childs *et al.* 2010: 203; Evans 2012: 184; Krook 2010: 236; MacKay 2008b:135; Squires 2008: 191–2). Critical reflection upon this approach, however, has been far less widespread (see Childs and Lovensduski 2013: 492; Severs 2012: 179).

Squires (2008: 191), in adopting a claims-based perspective, argues that representation is a constitutive process in so far as it entails the construction of a constituency in whose interest the representative claims to speak. It is a creative process in which 'when claiming to speak for women, representatives are actively engaged in making claims about women, participating in the construction of feminine subject-positions' (Squires 2008: 192). This has been interpreted to mean that representatives 'are regarded as making claims to know what constitutes the interests of those they seek to represent' (Childs and Lovenduski 2013: 492). This allows for interests not to be predetermined, and hence to be non-essentialist, and also for representatives, of any gender, to claim to 'speak for' those interests (Severs 2012: 169–70). As a result, contradictory constructions and competing discourses as to who 'women' are and what women want may arise. The logic of this position is that feminist conceptions of women's interests or issues are simply one construction of, often 'uncrystallized or not fully articulated', interests (Campbell *et al.* 2010: 173–4; Celis *et al.* 2008: 106). Indeed, somewhat belatedly, feminist researchers have come to recognise that representative claims to speak and act for women can just as legitimately be made by those located in a centre-right/conservative position of the ideological spectrum as by those in the left/feminist position (Celis and Childs 2012: 214). Equally, researchers have come to acknowledge the role that men may play in the substantive representation of women (see Evans 2012: 184).

This 'analytical turn' towards men has been facilitated by a conceptual move from 'critical mass' to 'critical actors' in explaining the promotion of women's interests and issues through public policy outputs. 'Critical mass' studies have tended to emphasise the importance of numbers – of the proportion of female representatives in decision-making bodies – on the assumption that the greater the presence of women representatives the greater the potential for outcomes favourable to women, despite inconclusive empirical evidence in support of such an assumption. The focus of 'critical actor' studies, however, is upon 'legislators who initiate policy proposals on their own and/or embolden others to take steps to promote policies for women, regardless of the numbers of female representatives' (Childs and Krook 2009: 138). Significantly, critical actors do not need to be women: men may also advance the substantive representation of women (Childs and Krook 2009: 138; Childs and Lovenduski 2013: 497; Evans 2012: 184; Saward 2010: 124).

One incongruity arising from this rethinking of traditional approaches to women's substantive representation is, as Evans recognises (2012: 185), the contention that 'non-descriptive representatives (in this case men) may even in some circumstances have a greater ability and propensity to represent the substantive interests of a group (women) risks undermining the argument for the increased descriptive representation of women'. A further incongruity arising from this 'rethinking' is that the emphasis placed upon representative claims as constitutive claims tends to lose sight of Saward's (2010: 54) initial stipulation that such claims 'construct in some measure the groups that they purport to address (audience), along with the groups that they purport to speak for or about (constituency)'. Claims only exist or work if audiences or constituencies receive, recognise, and respond to such claims. Judgement of claims rests 'in how they are received rather than by whom they are made' (Saward 2010: 124). In making the case that substantive representation involves competition to act 'for women' – as it presupposes diverging views about women's gendered interests, and stipulates that there are no *a priori* women's interests – the constitution of claims becomes effectively a top down process (see Squires 2008: 188). In this process, multiple women's constituencies and audiences, both actual and intended, are conceived and addressed – with increased potential for communicative distortions and multiple, differentiated and unreceptive responses by those audiences and constituencies to representative claims made on their behalf. In other words, 'any simple understanding of congruency between the interest of the represented and subsequent action by representatives [in initial formulations of substantive representation] appears incompatible with more creative [claims based] or anticipatory understandings of representation' (Childs and Lovenduski 2013: 507). Indeed, such is the magnitude of the potential incongruities associated with claims-making that 'we might wish to withhold our judgement that women are being represented' (Childs and Lovenduski 2013: 507; see also Severs 2010: 420).

A return to descriptive representation

While 'claims making' and 'critical actor' approaches to substantive representation have successfully dismantled essentialist, homogeneous conceptions of 'women's interests' and unambiguous notions of women representatives alone being capable of 'acting for' women; they have been less successful in sustaining the conceptual linkage between substantive and descriptive representation. In many ways feminist arguments in favour of descriptive representation have regressed into assertions that 'the strength of the justice argument for women's descriptive representation should be sufficient in and of itself; women's presence matters, above and beyond whether or not it can be "proved" that they are more likely to act for women' (Evans 2012: 185). Similarly, the Speaker's Conference on Representation (HC 239 2010: 17) identified justice as the 'primary case for widening Parliamentary representation' (ahead of arguments relating to effectiveness and enhanced legitimacy).

No matter what the theoretical grounds for supporting enhanced descriptive representation, the adoption of practical measures to bring about closer gender correspondence between represented and representatives in the UK parliament has proved to be contentious, protracted, and tortuous. Overwhelmingly feminists in the UK have sought to secure greater descriptive representation through mobilisation within political parties (see Lovenduski 2005: 106–30). Three broad strategies to promote greater representational equality have been pursued, asymmetrically, within the major UK parties: equality rhetoric, equality promotion and equality guarantees (HC 239 2010; Lovenduski 2005: 90–2). While all three major UK parties have willingly adopted discourses recognising the centrality of fairness and justice for women (and other under-represented groups) in the representational process, and have sought to promote women's candidacies through training and financial support (as well as through diversity awareness programmes for party selectorates), they have been more hesitant in advancing 'equality guarantees' or other forms of positive discrimination. Historically, such hesitancy has been occasioned, variously, by: legal obstacles and challenges; accusations of 'tokenism'; principled defence of intra-party organisational decentralisation; and universalistic contentions about 'meritocracy' and 'competence'. As a result, only the Labour party – in its adoption of all-women shortlists for targeted Westminster seats – implemented a modified quota, or equality guarantee, system (for details see Ashe *et al.* 2010: 470–2). The Conservative party, under Cameron's leadership, chose instead an enhanced equality promotion strategy, the so-called 'A-list' (noted in Chapter 3), but failed to introduce all-women shortlists or other forms of equality guarantees (Krook 2009: 154). The party imbalance in the number of women representatives in the House of Commons suggests that equality guarantees are to date 'the only mechanism to have produced a significant step-change in representation in the House of Commons' (HC 239 2010: 57). In turn, this imbalance underscores the simple fact that adoption of such guarantees and other equality promotion measures are party-dependent, as embedded histories and cultures within parties impact differently on intra-party attitudes to equality strategies (see Webb and Childs 2012: 47–8). What is beyond doubt is that women in Britain depend largely on political parties for their political representation. Before examining the centrality of 'party representation' in UK politics, however, it is instructive to analyse arguments relating respectively to the descriptive representation of black, Asian and other minority ethnic (BAME) groups and the 'working class'.

Descriptive representation of black, Asian and other minority ethnic groups

The arguments in favour of greater descriptive representation of minority ethnic groups in the UK parliament closely replicate those advanced on behalf of women (see Judge 1999: 42–3). The case for BAME descriptive representation is built upon the same justice and equity arguments as for the proportionate representation of women (Durose *et al.* 2011: 2–3; HC 239 2010: 17). Similarly, the case for descriptive representation often spills over into a case for substantive representation. Yet, equally, the difficulty of identifying shared interests and experiences for BAME citizens offers a conceptual and empirical challenge for their substantive representation. Conceptually, as James (2011: 901) notes: 'Looking at race, we might ask if the "black experience" is universally shared among all members of this group, or whether some individuals possess different experiences not typical of the group'. James' answer is that 'there is no purely philosophical solution to this puzzle: it must be answered empirically' (2011: 901).

Early empirical studies suggested that there appeared to be no distinctive set of policy priorities that divided BAME and white British voters (Studlar 1986) and that 'race specific issues do not play an important role in the political priorities of black voters' (Saggar 1992: 43). More recently, Heath *et al.* (2013: 74) concluded that: 'In many ways Donley Studlar's argument from twenty five years ago still holds true'. BAME voters still tended to share the same political concerns as white British voters about the state of the economy, the financial crisis, and unemployment, but diverged from majority opinion on issues connected to the detention of terrorist suspects and to asylum. Where there was a 'distinct and dramatic majority/minority difference', however, was on the issue of equal opportunities for ethnic minorities. This was an issue that united different minorities and on which 'issues of representation may well arise', as within-group differences were minute when compared with the overall difference between BAME and white British groups (Heath *et al.* 2013: 75).

The shared experiences of BAME citizens of discrimination and perceptions of differential discrimination, alongside greater exposure to distinctive minority cultural values and practices, thus appear to provide cognitive prompts for them to think and act differently from white British voters. But there is a complex and variegated picture of the intensity of perceived discrimination, and participation in mainstream British cultural practices and competence in the usage of English language, across BAME groups sufficient to question any essentialist understanding of BAME 'shared experiences'. Indeed, the sheer heterogeneity of BAME communities in the UK – incorporating major groups of Black African, Black Caribbean, Southern Asian (Pakistani, Bangladeshi, Indian), and Eastern Asian (Chinese) alongside less numerous and more recently arrived groups from East Africa and Western Asia – reflected in diverse cultural, social, and religious heritages further compounds the difficulties of articulating 'shared experience' beyond perceptions of discrimination. At best a 'plural ethnic assertiveness' may be identified rather than an all-inclusive conception of interest and identity as 'non-whiteness' (Modood 2010: 486).

The absence of 'essentialist' definitions of BAME interests and experiences may make substantive representation complex and contested but does not fatally undermine the case for more proportionate representation of BAME members in the House of Commons. If anything, following Mansbridge's (1999a: 636) argument, 'a variety of representatives is usually needed to represent the heterogeneous, varied inflections and internal oppositions that together constitute the complex and internally contested perspectives, opinions and interests characteristic of any group. This range of views is not easily represented by only a few individuals'.

Attempting to facilitate greater descriptive representation of BAME groups in the Westminster parliament, however, has proved to be a protracted process. In 1987 four BAME MPs were elected, and these were the first BAME representatives in the House of Commons since 1945. By 2010 the number of BAME MPs had risen to 27 (4 per cent of all MPs), 11 of whom were Conservatives and 16 Labour. This marked an increase from 15 BAME MPs in the previous parliament, but was still a proportionate underrepresentation of the estimated 11 per cent of BAME UK citizens in the UK in 2010 (see Cracknell 2012). In the absence of formal equality guarantee strategies before the Equality Act 2010, the major parties, along with non-party advocacy groups such as Operation Black Vote, adopted equality promotion strategies (including mentoring and shadowing programmes for BAME prospective parliamentary candidates). After the recommendation of the Speaker's Conference, that the enabling provisions of the Sex Discrimination (Election Candidates) Act 2002 should be extended to allow political parties to use all-BAME shortlists, the Equality Act 2010 enabled political parties, for the first time, 'to reserve places on electoral shortlists for those with a protected characteristic, such as race, that is under-represented in politics' (Cm 7824 2010: 15). However, this provision stopped short of allowing all-BAME shortlists, not least because of problems of definition, and in determining eligibility to stand on an all-BAME shortlist (HC 239 2010: 58). Yet Keith Vaz, in introducing a ten-minute rule bill to permit the creation of shortlists on the grounds of ethnicity, had earlier challenged the practical significance of such 'problems':

> Some may argue that a problem exists regarding which boundaries and terms can be used to define an 'ethnic minority'. I can assure the House that ethnic minorities know exactly who they are, and

so do the political parties; they will be well able to identify them. (HC Debates 6 February 2008: col 974)

Representing the poor: Working or otherwise

One of the undoubted achievements of the reconceptualisation of representation in recent decades has been to identify representation as a mediated relationship in which constituencies and audiences are constituted in relation to group histories and shared experiences (Urbinati and Warren 2008: 394). In so doing, the fundamental inclusion–exclusion paradox of representation has been brought to the forefront of debate. Of particular relevance, Phillips (1995), in seeking to develop a 'different understanding of representation', managed to insert the issues of group difference directly into the normative and practical debates about representation, and to identify which groups had been systematically excluded from decision-making and so to consider the conditions for their political inclusion. This circumvented the problem of calling for equal representation of all disadvantaged groups and concentrated attention instead upon 'those particularly urgent instances of political exclusion which a "fairer" system of representation seeks to resolve' (Phillips 1995: 47). In this respect, and as noted above, women and ethnic minorities stood out as 'particularly urgent instances of political exclusion'. And once difference is conceived in terms of 'identity-based politics' and in relation to 'those experiences and identities that may constitute different kinds of groups' then it 'becomes far harder to meet demands for political inclusion without also including the members of such groups' (Phillips 1995: 6).

Such was the impact of Phillips' argument that after the publication of *The Politics of Presence* 'no one regarded descriptive representation [of women and ethnic minorities] as unimportant' (Childs and Lovenduski 2013: 490). The downside to this seemingly universal acceptance, however, was the residualisation and re-categorisation of interests based upon differences of social class. Phillips (1995: 171) was well aware of the 'remarkable absence' of class from her discussion, but claimed that a basic distinction could be made between social class on the one hand and gender, ethnicity or race on the other. Her argument in defence of this distinction distilled essentially into a series of six linked assertions (1995: 173–6), but ultimately her argument regressed into the contention that: 'When it comes down to it, the real reason for my silence on class is simply that it does not lend itself to the same kind of solutions' (1995: 178).

Recent reconceptualisations of representation, however, allow for this silence to be broken. Depending on which strand of reconceptualisation is pursued, at least two contrasting arguments for representation of the 'working class' (broadly defined to include unskilled workers and the non-working poor) can be advanced: one for greater descriptive representation and one for closer substantive representation. The first argument notes that: 'since one of Phillips' arguments against the need for the descriptive representation of class was that it was already represented within the political battle, then as the dividing lines between the parties become less class based, so the need for descriptive representation of class would increase rather than decrease' (Childs and Cowley 2011: 12; see also Wauters 2010: 186–7). The second argument, rooted in a claims-based approach to representation, would allow for the substantive representation of working class/poor interests as a constitutive process of constituency building by elected representatives who do not necessarily have to be drawn from the same class background as their intended class constituency. In this process, the representative offers some conception of a group's interest, which the intended constituency has to acknowledge in some way (Saward 2010: 48–9). As noted earlier in this chapter, this allows for interests not to be predetermined, and hence to be non-essentialist, and also in this instance for representatives, of any class, to claim to 'speak for' working class interests.

Social class is notoriously difficult to define, with notable differences between objective classifications based primarily upon occupation and subjective class self-assignment. In 2009 36 per cent of Chief Income Earners in the UK were classified as manual workers, with a further 8 per cent assigned to the Social Grade of 'causal, lowest grade workers, or the unemployed with state benefits or state pensioners' (Ipsos MediaCT 2009). After the 2010 UK election, 25 (4 per cent) of 621 MPs from the three main UK parties had been manual workers in their former occupations. All but two were Labour MPs (McGuiness 2012: 20–1). Some 30 years earlier, in 1978, 62 per cent of Chief Income Earners in the UK had been manual workers, unemployed, or state pensioners, while the 1979 election returned 86 former manual workers to the House of Commons (14 per cent of MPs in the three major parties), 83 of whom were Labour MPs.

In view of this continuing proportionate under-representation, the Labour party announced, initially in 2011, a Future Candidates Programme to align Labour representatives to 'reflect what Britain looks like and the jobs which people do' (Chuka Umunna, *Guardian* 17 July 2012; see also Jon Trickett, *Times* 16 July 2012). One strand of this programme was to enhance the political prospects of those in lower paid jobs. Indeed, Denis MacShane (then Labour MP for Rotherham) raised the prospect of 'all-working class shortlists' as an equality guarantee measure to work in parallel with all-women shortlists and reserved places shortlists for BAME potential candidates (BBC 2012). To avoid definitional problems associated with 'working class', MacShane suggested that all parties should set aside 10 per cent of seats for candidates earning the minimum wage. In September 2012, the Labour party's conference accepted the less ambitious change, proposed by the party's National Executive Committee, that 'social class' would now be taken into account in its selection procedures along with sexuality, ethnicity, and disability.

Underpinning these calls for greater descriptive representation was an implicit acceptance that social class, and the social and economic contexts associated with class position, shapes attitudes and beliefs. Indeed, comparative empirical studies have confirmed differences in policy preferences between income groups that are 'quite substantial and ... cover a wide range of issues' (Giger *et al.* 2012: 49; Soroka and Wlezien 2010: 166–7). In turn, such policy preference differences are of importance in making the link between descriptive representation and a substantive argument that 'differential representation is always in disfavor of the poor' (Giger *et al.* 2012: 57).

Professional politicians: Not representing 'people like us'?

In pointing to the 'under-representation' of lower-paid socio-economic groups, Labour politicians also drew attention to the 'over-representation' of so-called 'professional politicians'. Estimates of the number of MPs whose primary occupation before entering the House of Commons in 2010 had been 'politics' ranged from 14 per cent who had been a 'politician or political organiser' (McGuiness 2012: 20) to 24 per cent who had worked previously in 'politics' (Hackett and Hunter 2010: 7). Jon Trickett (Labour shadow minister) pointed to the descriptive imbalance of the occupational profile of MPs in contrasting the proportion of low-paid workers to those previously engaged in 'politics': 'Roughly one in four MPs, before they became MPs, were effectively full time politicos already ... Nobody wants to say you should be excluded because you were a speechwriter. But it is disproportionate' (*Times* 16 July 2012).

Here, the term 'professional politician' is used to denote those who have worked primarily as ministerial aides, special advisers, parliamentary researchers, party staffers, or representatives in other elected institutions; or, more broadly still, those who have worked in NGOs, INGOs, advocacy groups, or think tanks before becoming an MP (for categorisations of professional politicians see Allen 2013; Cairney 2007; Rush and

Giddings 2011). Such pre-parliamentary experience is often dismissed, in terms of MPs not having done a 'proper job', or providing 'absolutely no experience of working in the real world' (Groves 2012), or for having 'barely touch[ed] the sides of real life' (Wright 2012: 221). Yet there is another more positive dimension to the rise of the 'professional politician'. As Riddell (2011: 167–8) appreciates, while on the one side they might unfavourably skew the descriptive representation of parliament, on the other, substantive representation might benefit through the process-expertise and advocacy skills possessed by professional politicians (see also HC 239 2010: 43). In this instance the enhancement of substantive representation may be linked to claims-based arguments that representatives 'act for' constituted constituencies in portraying or framing their interests (Saward 2010: 47). In so doing, their 'professional' skills might endow them with capacities to 'speak for', and 'act for', constituted groups more efficiently and efficaciously than members of the disadvantaged groups themselves. What is at issue is securing congruence between the policy preferences of 'descriptive groups' and the policy responsiveness of their 'non-descriptive' representatives as reflected in substantive policy outputs. As noted above, and elsewhere, male representatives may speak and act for women, whites may speak and act for BAME, and middle class MPs may speak for the working class and act for the poor and the dispossessed. Substantive representation is not inextricably and incontrovertibly bound to descriptive representation: for reasons of justice, equality and legitimacy it might very well be the case that it should be, and, certainly, in instances where the policy preferences of the represented diverge significantly and consistently from those of their representatives, equally a normative case can be made in favour of such linkage.

Party representation

The preceding discussion of the descriptive representation of various under-represented groups – women, BAME, and working class – identified political parties as institutions capable both of constraining (through 'selectorate' biases) and of enhancing more proportionate representation (through equality rhetoric, equality promotion, and equality guarantee programmes). Equally, parties have proved to be of significance in the substantive representation of under-represented groups, with 'presence effects' mediated through party affiliation, cohesion, and ideology (Childs and Lovenduski 2013: 506; Evans 2012: 184; Wängnerud 2009: 62). In the particular case of women, for example, it is still the case that

British women remain dependent on political parties for their political representation.

In essence, as noted in Chapter 3, parties have acted traditionally both as representative and as governmental institutions. As representative institutions they articulated interests, aggregated demands, and structured collective preferences into patterned policy programmes. As governing institutions they translated their distinct policy programmes into public policies. This dyadic role in the UK has been the foundation of conceptions of party representation and party government, in which the translation of voters' aggregated policy preferences into specific government outputs has usually been modelled in terms of an electoral or a party mandate.

In the UK permissive and prescriptive mandate models have been identified (Norton 2013: 204). The permissive model is a grant of legitimacy for a party (or, as in the case of the coalition government after 2010, a combination of parties) with a majority in the House of Commons to govern. This model found official confirmation in the *Cabinet Manual* (Cabinet Office 2011a: 39): 'the Government derives its democratic mandate from its command of the confidence of the Commons'. The prescriptive mandate is 'one in which a party is elected to fulfil particular promises laid before the electorate in a general election' (Norton 2013: 204). This model had earlier found official endorsement in the then Labour government's statement: 'the Party which secures a majority [at a General Election] has the right to form a Government and, subject to sustaining its Parliamentary majority, to carry through the programme set out in its election Manifesto' (Cm 5291 2001, paras 13–17). What is a relatively simple principal–agent model of delegation in theory (see Judge 2005: 37–41) is, however, far more complicated in practice. Exactly what constitutes 'carrying through' a manifesto programme is subject to both qualitative and quantitative contestation. Qualitative assessment of a programme as a list of specific policy pledges or as more a general statement of issue priorities leads to different quantitative measures of the congruence between electoral programme and policy outputs and outcomes. A 'pledge approach' evaluates the degree of congruence by determining the extent to which specific policy commitments are fulfilled. A 'saliency approach', based upon a saliency theory of party competition (see Chapter 3), examines the congruence between programme and policy by 'examining the association between parties' emphases on various policy themes in their platforms and subsequent governments' spending priorities in related policy areas' (Thomson *et al.* 2012: 3). A further approach, the 'spatial approach', has been developed by Louwerse (2011: 433–5) to capture the positions of parties on issue dimensions in political space and to compare the congruence of 'issue dimensions' in electoral competition and in parliamentary party competition.

In each of these approaches programme-to-policy linkage is not exact but is stronger than is popularly conceived (Louwerse 2011: 443; see also Rallings 1987; Thomson *et al.* 2012: 18; Webb 2009: 273). This led Louwerse (2011: 443) to identify a 'paradox of party mandate research' wherein 'studies show fair levels of fulfilment, while many people are convinced mandate fulfilment is low'. While the complexities of gauging congruence between party manifesto commitments and the policy outputs of parties in government should not be underestimated, none-theless, incongruence between manifesto pledges and policy outputs is viewed unfavourably by voters, as Liberal Democrats MPs found to their cost in the 2010 parliament. The reversal, when in office, of the manifesto pledge to 'scrap unfair university tuition fees' in the long term (Liberal Democrats 2010: 33), and the more immediate pledge to the National Union of Students in support of its campaign against increased tuition fees, led Nick Clegg, as leader of the party, to offer a public apology: 'We made a pledge, we did not stick to it, and for that I am sorry' (*Guardian* 20 September 2012). The apology, though ambiguous in intent, reflected acknowledgment of the continuing importance of sustaining the linkage between electoral pledges and parliamentary action held by the electorate. Indeed, in making the apology, Clegg was at pains to emphasise the broader point that the Liberal Democrats had secured significant advances towards achieving the four 'core priorities' emphasised in the party's manifesto.

What is of most relevance for the discussion of representative roles of MPs, however, is that 'the party in government can, and does, utilize the claim to have a mandate as the basis for requiring the loyal support of its MPs' (Norton 2013: 204; see also Norton 2012: 68). This claim is supported empirically in the findings that some 60 per cent of sur-vey respondents believe that governments 'are elected on a mandate' (Hansard Society 2005: 6) and that 63 per cent believe that MPs pay most attention to the policy of their party leadership in parliament when voting on legislation (Kellner 2012: 24). In addition, 72 per cent of YouGov respondents in 2012 believed that MPs, when voting in the Commons, should pay a great deal of attention to 'the promises they made at the most recent election'. A survey of public attitudes con-ducted on behalf of the Committee on Standards in Public Life in 2010 also found that 84 per cent of respondents agreed that it was reasonable for MPs to take into account election manifesto promises when voting in the Commons (the average across four surveys between 2005 and 2010 was also 84 per cent). Perhaps not surprisingly, in view of the discussion in Chapter 2, only 15 per cent of respondents to the same survey believed that MPs actually paid attention to party election promises; and even more strikingly only 2 per cent of YouGov respondents believed that MPs paid attention to their election promises in practice.

Equally, surveys of MPs reveal that the party manifesto and notions of 'electoral mandate' feature prominently in influencing their voting decisions. Some 98 per cent of new entrants to the Commons in 2010 believed, after the experience of their first year, that their votes in Parliament should be 'most often determined by their election pledges and party manifesto promises' (Korris 2011: 9). This reflected the extant findings of broader surveys of MPs that 'party looms large' in influencing MPs' voting decisions (Rush and Giddings 2011: 113–5). Indeed, Rush and Giddings (HC 330 2012: Ev. w26, emphasis in original), on the basis of a longitudinal survey (in the period 1992–2005) concluded that MPs 'say that party, not constituency is the most important influence on their *parliamentary* behaviour'. Rush and Giddings were keen to point out that: '"Party" here means not the narrow context of the party whips, but the wider context of MPs being members of parties with which more often than not they agree' (HC 330 2012: Ev. w26). Tony Wright (2012: 214), writing then as a Labour MP, reinforced Rush and Giddings' findings in his observation that MPs 'might (and do) say that their constituency function is more important than anything else, but in practice it is the partisan function'. This led him to conclude: 'Party is what matters, but this is not because of slavish submission to the whips. Politicians are party animals by both instinct and interest. Party cohesion is not an imposition from without' (Wright 2012: 173; see also Riddell 2011: 91).

Indeed, party cohesion continues to be pronounced in the Commons, despite increased and increasing levels of dissension in successive parliaments (see below). MPs primarily support their party leadership in parliament not out of fear, or out of inducement, but because, variously, they: share common overarching political perspectives and norms (which are sufficiently different from those of other parties); are subject to intra-party socialisation processes; secure psychological reinforcement from collaborative activity; and recognise for the most part, but not absolutely, the potential individual career dividends and collective electoral advantage to be derived from intra-party unity (see Cowley 2002: 176–9; Cowley 2005: 22–7; Judge 2005: 40–1; Kam 2009: 21–31;

Rush and Giddings 2011: 165; Russell 2012: 3–4). Despite these positive incentives, however, 'unity is not preordained … MPs can and do dissent from the party line' (Kam 2009: 21).

Party unity has never been absolute in Westminster, although it came close, at levels of party voting above 95 per cent, in the majority of parliamentary sessions between 1945 and 1959. In fact, between 1945 and 1970 no government suffered any defeat caused by MPs defying their party whips (Cowley 2005: 2–3). By the 2001–2005 and 2005–2010 parliaments, however, Labour governments encountered rebellions by their own backbenchers in 21 per cent and 28 per cent of divisions (Cowley and Stuart 2012: 47). In the 2001–2005 parliament 229 Labour MPs voted against their own party in 259 divisions but the government remained undefeated throughout that period. Even the 139 Labour MPs who voted against military intervention in Iraq in March 2003, and hence against their whip, did not bring about defeat for the government. This was despite the fact that this had been 'the largest rebellion by MPs of any governing party … on any type of policy since modern British party politics began' (Cowley and Stuart 2005: 23). In the 2005–2010 parliament 174 Labour MPs voted against the government in 365 divisions (totalling 3,318 votes against the whips) (Cowley 2010). In that parliament the Labour government (headed by Blair and Brown respectively) also suffered its first defeats since 1997 (four defeats in 2009 and three in 2010).

In the first session of the 2010 parliament 116 coalition MPs (86 Conservatives and 30 Liberal Democrats) voted against the government in 45 per cent of all whipped votes. This meant that just over 25 per cent of Conservative MPs and over half of Liberal Democrats MPs had rebelled by the end of the first session (Cowley and Stuart 2012: 46). This led Cowley and Stuart to conclude that the level of rebellion was 'extremely atypical', as most first parliamentary sessions recorded relatively low levels of dissent (2012: 44–5). By the second session the overall rate of rebellion within the coalition had dropped to 27 per cent, but this was still relatively high in comparison with most post-war parliaments, and culminated in three defeats for elements of the coalition's programme (Cowley and Stuart 2013: 2). Indeed, what was notable, given the two-party composition of the coalition government, was that the rebels in the two parties rarely coalesced on the same issues. This undoubtedly reflected the coalition's broader ideological spectrum in comparison to that of single-party governments.

Moreover, the dissonance between party theory – with its emphasis on electoral mandates and party discipline – and parliamentary behaviour is revealed in the perceptions of both the electorate and MPs themselves. On the one hand, voters believed that MPs paid most attention to their party leadership when voting in parliament (63 per cent of YouGov respondents), and that it was acceptable for MPs to vote in accordance with the party leadership's wishes (41 per cent of CSPL respondents in 2010). On the other hand, only 29 per cent of the YouGov sample thought that MPs *should* pay a 'great deal' or 'most' attention to their party leaders. Correspondingly, the proportion of CSPL respondents who believed that it was acceptable for MPs to vote in accordance with the party leadership's wishes was less than half of those (84 per cent) who thought that it was reasonable for MPs to base their parliamentary decisions upon the promises made in their party's manifesto (Committee on Standards in Public Life 2011: 30). These perceptual differences reflect in part the pragmatics of parliamentary government, where the policy pledges made at elections are mediated by policy inheritance (extant programmes and expenditure commitments), policy perturbations (domestic and foreign policy crises, with overseas military interventions providing classic examples), or simply changed circumstances.

MPs, to a lesser extent than voters, also recognise the potential dissonance between what their party promised and what party leaders and party whips might require in voting divisions. Whereas 98 per cent of new MPs in 2010 expected their parliamentary votes to be influenced by election promises and pledges, a smaller proportion, 91 per cent, acknowledged the influence that party whips were expected to play (Korris 2011: 9). What is far clearer, however, is that MPs have a propensity to prioritise party manifestos and party leadership ahead of constituency opinion when voting (Korris 2011: 9; Rush and Giddings 2011: 113–16). Notions of party representation help to legitimise this prioritisation, as the core element of all interpretations of party representation is the justification of party discipline within Parliament (Judge 1999: 71). What party theory has to justify, in essence, is a 'system in which the elected representative may be forced by his party managers to vote for a policy which is contrary to the apparent interests of his constituents, contrary to the prevailing opinion in his constituency, and contrary to his own personal judgement about what is best for the country' (Birch 1971: 97). While MPs might be less willing to succumb to such 'management' than at the time Birch made his stipulation, nonetheless, their representative practice in Westminster still largely conforms to the prescriptions of 'party theory' as outlined by Birch.

The 'How' of representation

> [A]t the core of political representation there is a *relational*
> element between the entity that represents and the entity
> that is represented. Although this observation is obvi-
> ous, its implications are not always fully appreciated.
> (Castiglione and Warren 2006: 6 emphasis in original)

This relational element was captured in Pitkin's notion of representation
as 'acting for'. As she states: 'The activity of representing as acting for
others must be defined in terms of what the representative does and
how he does it' (Pitkin 1967: 143). It is in the action of representation that the represented is made present (Pitkin 1967: 145). How a
representative should act has typically been conceived as a continuum
defined by the two polar positions of 'trustee' and 'delegate'. Despite
recognising that a variety of intermediate forms of action can be,
and have been, identified between these polar positions the classic
normative position of Pitkin (1967) and the classic empirical studies
of Wahlke *et al.* (1962) have attracted the 'dissatisfaction' of contemporary theorists for supposedly focusing their attention upon a simple dichotomous trustee–delegate relationship rather than a complex
multidimensional relationship (see Andeweg and Thomassen 2005:
524–6; Mansbridge 2011: 621; Rehfeld 2011: 635–8). This multidimen-
sionality and 'relational complexity', identified at the core of the current
'rethinking of representation', leads Mansbridge (2003: 515) to identify
four relational categories and Rehfeld (2011: 632) to produce eight ideal
relational types to replace the simple delegate/trustee dyad.   While
this is not the place to examine the intricacies of such 'rethinking',
it is worth isolating for further consideration Rehfeld's (2009: 229) contention that: 'the trustee/delegate debate ... does not arise as a feature
of representation per se, but on account of the role that a representative
takes on as a decision maker'.

As noted above, representatives and represented alike recognise the
primacy of party when MPs make their voting decisions in Westminster.
Yet MPs also rank highly their own 'personal opinion' as an influence
upon their parliamentary actions and voting (Korris 2011: 9; Rush and
Giddings 2011: 113–16). In most circumstances 'personal opinion', conceived as ideological and normative positioning, is in congruence with
'party opinion' in determining voting choices. In this respect, as Rush and
Giddings (2011: 113) observe, the prominence given by MPs to their own
opinions 'is generally within the context of party, not separate from it'.

Members of the public have a somewhat more ambiguous view than MPs themselves of the extent to which it is reasonable for MPs to take into account their own personal beliefs when voting in parliament. On one side, in the 2010 CSPL survey, 68 per cent of respondents believed that it was indeed reasonable (with an average of 69 per cent sharing the same view across four surveys between 2004 and 2010). Yet, on the other side, in the 2012 YouGov survey, when asked whether MPs should vote according to their own judgement on free votes (not subject to the party whip) rather than the majority view of their constituents, only 29 per cent thought that MPs' independent judgement should prevail (Kellner 2012: 14).

Free votes are most commonly used on 'conscience issues' (see House of Commons Library 2011). Such issues have traditionally encompassed abortion, embryology, and capital punishment, as well as some aspects of family law reform and certain issues relating to homosexuality. In part this is a reflection of the fact that 'morality issues live on the periphery of British [party] politics' (Thorup Larsen *et al.* 2012: 114). Indeed, according to Cowley and Stuart (2010: 173), '[w]ith "conscience issues" ... the parties do not take a stance, the executive remains neutral, and parliamentarians are given a "free vote", left to decide on their own consciences'. An incongruity arises, however, in that when left to decide in this manner MPs still tend to vote in accordance with their party colleagues (see Cowley 2005: 23–4; Cowley and Stuart 2010: 173–4; Pattie *et al.* 1998). The Human Fertilisation and Embryology Bill 2008, provided a clear example of cohesive party voting on what was essentially a 'cross party' measure. In fact, the extent of cohesion was such that every vote on the bill witnessed the majority of Conservative MPs voting in opposition to the majority of Labour MPs. On this bill, therefore, party still remained fundamental to the outcome (Cowley and Stuart 2010: 175). This illustrates the broader point, however, that, even in the absence of formal voting cues from party managers, informal party norms and party ideational frames often serve to sustain party voting cohesion.

Conclusion

The realities of modern representative politics in the UK parliament are that MPs are primarily representatives of their party, increasingly attentive to their territorial constituencies, marginally more descriptive of the population at large than two decades ago, yet still retain a propensity to assert the value of their own independent judgement.

Disparate and contending theories, about 'what' and 'who' is to be represented and 'how' they are to be represented, are thus deployed simultaneously to legitimate representative practice. Pre-democratic notions, which answer the 'what' and 'how' questions by reference to territorial 'communities of interest' and Burkean notions of 'trusteeship', co-exist alongside more contemporary collectivist theories that answer the same questions by reference to socio-economic interests (long encapsulated in the rhetoric of 'class') and mandate notions of 'party representation', and operate alongside descriptive theories which, in turn, raise the 'who' question and provide an answer by using the idea of 'shared experiences' to connect the represented and their representatives. In this answer, descriptive theories seek to mitigate the exclusionary consequences of representation for marginalised social groups. They do so by positing an inclusionary dynamic – in the 'politics of presence' – and by justifying the 'making present' of those groups that, historically, had been largely absent from state decision-making processes. Incongruously, however, further analytical refinement (in the separation of descriptive from substantive representation, and in the exploration of constitutive notions of 'representative claims') has resulted in the proposition that 'non-descriptive' representatives may legitimately claim to speak and act for 'descriptive' constituencies framed in terms of difference, identity, and class. Perhaps not surprisingly, therefore, the mismatches of theory, and the coexistence of admixtures of different theories, have found reflection in mismatched ideas amongst the represented as to what the bases of representation are, and which communities, interests, and experiences should be reflected if their representatives are to 'be like' and 'act like' them.

5

The 'Problem' of Representative Government

Introduction

The official description of contemporary representative government in the UK, as outlined in Chapter 1, is clearly premised on representative democracy. Implicit within that description is the conception of representative democracy as a political system. At the heart of that system is a deceptively simple process: people vote in UK elections for MPs who will represent them and act in their interests in Parliament; an executive is drawn from and is accountable to Parliament, which has supreme legislative authority; and, in turn, representatives are responsible to the electorate for their legislative and policy performance. Thus the basic claim to be 'democratic' is a systemic claim. This is captured by Pitkin (1967: 221) when she notes: 'Perhaps when we call a governmental body or system "representative" we are saying something broader and more general about the way in which it operates as an institutionalized arrangement ... as embodied in a whole political system'.

In the UK the shorthand term 'the Westminster model' has commonly been used to capture a distinctive 'institutionalised arrangement' of representative government. In Lijphart's (1984, 1999, 2012) formulation, the Westminster model is used as a synonym for a majoritarian model of democracy and as an antonym for a consensus model. The difference between these models is both empirical and normative. Empirically, the former identifies government by the majority and in accordance with the majority's wishes, whereas the latter accepts majority rule simply as a minimum requirement while specifying broader agreement and consensus in decision-making. The concentrated decision-making power of the Westminster model is thus differentiated from the dispersed and bargaining mode of the consensus model (Lijphart 2012: 2).

Normatively, Lijphart (2012: 295) advances the case that consensus democracies, in comparison to majoritarian democracies, display a 'kindness and gentleness' in their public policy orientations, and have more effective policy-making processes. The difficulty in accepting Lijphart's version of the 'Westminster model', however, is that its portrayal of UK government is purposely caricatured in order to distinguish it from a 'consensus model'. Yet, in outlining the UK model, 'deviations' from the model, noted by Lijphart himself (2012: 10–20), weaken both its categorical distinctiveness while simultaneously highlighting its 'misleading interpretation of British policymaking' (Jordan and Cairney 2013: 255; see also Rhodes *et al.* 2009: 228).

Beyond Lijphart's caricature of the Westminster model, however, lies the 'problem' of finding agreement on the common elements of that model, or even finding consensus on whether or not it constitutes a 'model' in the first place. Yet, as already noted in Chapter 1, core ideas have been embedded within the Westminster model, and these ideas derive primarily from a longer-standing model of 'representative and responsible government' (Birch 1964). In its UK variant, this traditional liberal model presented an idealised view of a serial flow of authorisation and democratic control approximating to a 'standard model' of representative democracy. Yet, when set within the context of a simple plurality electoral system and, for long periods, duopolistic party competition, the idealised view – of popular legitimation, policy congruence, accountability, and transparency – of representative government mutated into the legitimation of a centralised, executive-dominated, and opaque system of government in which pre-democratic legalistic notions of parliamentary sovereignty overrode democratic conceptions of popular sovereignty. In essence, this mutation produced what Flinders calls a 'basic meta-constitutional orientation of power hoarding' (Flinders 2010: 75).

In this mutated 'power concentrating' form, the Westminster model poses a series of related 'problems' for representative democracy: first, the inversion of the basic principles of the representative and responsible model from which it derived; second, an acceptance by the model's critics that the mutated version was the authentic version; and, third, that the mutated version bore little relation to the practice of 21st century UK government. In setting out these problems serially two major incongruities become apparent: first, the core principles still prescribe an idealised form of representative and responsible government, even though the practice has rarely corresponded to those prescriptions. Second, in focusing upon the mutated version – and in emphasising the institutional concentration of power within the core executive – contemporary critics, as with earlier critics of the 'mythology the constitution', have 'fallen into the trap' of assuming that other modes of representation 'are outside of the political process [as conceived in the Westminster model] rather than part of it' (Birch 1964: 238). This trap was set in a failure to recognise a plurality of coexisting modes of representation – of the interconnections of electoral and non-electoral representation – in a broader political 'process' and political 'system'. Translated into the language of governance: the trap was set in defining the Westminster model exclusively in relation to government rather than allow for 'something broader than government'. In arguing that 'governance' presents a more disaggregated view of state decision-making than 'government', critics of the Westminster model have often chosen to ignore the 'processual' elements of that model. Yet, even Lijphart's (2012: 3) formulation of the Westminster model has, as one of its dimensions, a particular pluralist 'interest group system'. And lest it be maintained that pluralism is distinct from governance it should be noted that Bevir (2012: 2, 19), as an influential theorist of governance, willingly accepts that governance is an example of pluralism. However, before proceeding further with this argument, some clarification of what the Westminster model 'is' (and 'is not') is required.

Westminster model

For a model that has attracted sustained criticism from political scientists for most of the past 25 years or so, and one that provides the counterpoint for a self-proclaimed new 'conventional wisdom' (see Jordan 1990: 471) or a 'new orthodoxy' (Marsh 2011: 32) in the conceptualisation of British politics, the Westminster model has proved remarkably resilient. In part this resilience stems from the simple fact that there is no agreed definition of the Westminster model, and no real agreement on whether it is an 'organising perspective' (Gamble 1990: 404–6), part of a 'political tradition' (see most recently Hall 2011: 92–120), or simply an empirical descriptive perspective. Similarly, the fact that some 14 key beliefs and core institutions can be, and have been, identified as constituent elements of the Westminster model at various times (Rhodes *et al.* 2009: 7) makes it relatively easy to identify some continuities of 'key beliefs' or institutional configurations over time. Conversely of course it also makes it relatively easy to identify discontinuities or disjunctions of some other elements over time, as indeed critics of the model have demonstrated persistently. So it is perhaps worth examining

Gamble's original depiction of the Westminster model as an authoritative point of departure for the following discussion.

In Gamble's formulation the key components of the Westminster model were: a sovereign parliament which exercised supreme legislative authority; a parliament which was representative of the political community; parliamentary representatives who were accountable to the people; parliamentary procedures that institutionalised political opposition; a political executive drawn from parliament; 'an executive which was subject to parliamentary scrutiny and approval but retained its capacity for independent action, leadership and decision'; and central state institutions that were at 'the disposal of the parliamentary majority'. Overall Gamble (1990: 407) concluded that, 'at its best', the Westminster model provided for both responsible and representative government; and that 'understanding British politics meant understanding the workings of British parliamentary government'.

It is instructive that one of the most recent, and most detailed, examinations of the Westminster model identified at its core a set of four interrelated components that not only echoed those identified by Gamble but which, more significantly, reflected the central ideas of the Westminster model 'as understood by its constitutive actors' (Rhodes *et al.* 2009: 10). The four components were: responsible government with political executives drawn from parliament and ultimately dependent upon sustaining the legislature's confidence; an executive whose members are individually and collectively accountable to parliament; a professional, non-partisan, and 'permanent' public service; and, in the UK at least, a legally sovereign parliament (Rhodes *et al.* 2009: 10). These are deemed to be core ideas in that they have the deepest historical roots and 'typically gravitate' (Rhodes *et al.* 2009: 9) around the constitutional fusion of the executive and legislature (see also Richards 2008: 15–16; Richards and Smith 2002).

Over time other ideas have been 'grafted on' to this core: some for categorical/taxonomic reasons, in the sense of being used to categorise and differentiate majoritarian from consensual systems (Lijphart 2012: 1–8); some for normative/rhetorical reasons, to highlight the elitist nature of the UK's political tradition (Hall 2011: 28–35; Tant 1993: 71); and some for descriptive accuracy in the sense of reflecting changed practices in relation to electoral processes, party systems, and inter-institutional interactions. Yet the emphasis upon inserting more elements into the model skewed the debate towards empirical positivist analysis and towards measuring the degree of separation between model and political practice. In this respect critics started from the premise that the Westminster model constituted an accurate representation of political reality. Not surprisingly they discovered that it was not. What the Westminster model sketched, in the pivotal period of its inception in the second half of the 19th century, was an idealised 'liberal view of the constitution' that constituted 'a theory of legitimate power' (Birch 1964: 65). As such from the outset it was an artificial contrivance that arose out of the conflation of liberal theories of representation with a Diceyean view of liberal government (see Judge 1993: 138–40). The brief and exceptional convergence between the prescriptions of the liberal view of the constitution and the practice of liberal government, approximately between the two Reform Acts of 1832 and 1867, became petrified in seminal academic writings, most notably those of Dicey (see below), despite the manifest erosion of the precepts of the liberal view after 1867. Indeed, for much of the period thereafter 'adherents to the Liberal theory of the state [encapsulated in the Westminster model] have been regretfully aware that political practice has departed from [these] principles' (Birch 1964: 80).

Just such awareness has, since the late-1970s, been an analytical stem cell in the genetic development, mutation, and transmutation of models of policy communities, networks, governance, multi-level governance, differentiated polity, and asymmetric power (see, for example, Bache and Flinders 2004; Bevir and Rhodes 2003; Marsh *et al.* 2003; Rhodes 1997; Rhodes and Marsh 1992a; Richardson and Jordan 1979): all of which started from the premise that they provided 'alternatives' or posed a 'direct challenge' to the Westminster model (Marsh 2012: 46–8). The 'challenge' was empirical in so far as these alternatives sketched a more realistic representation of the British polity (see, for example, Bevir and Rhodes 2003: 198–9).

While governance is a fiercely contested concept, all definitions 'refer to something broader than government' (Kjaer 2004: 3). In particular in the UK it has been taken to mean 'a shift from a hierarchic state to governance in and by networks' (Bevir 2010: 81). As such, 'governance has become the most widely accepted term for describing the patterns of rule that arise from the interactions of multiple organizations in networks' (Bevir 2010: 85). The idea of policy networks reflects the fact that relationships between groups and government are institutionalised, but that these interactions are segmented (Richards and Smith 2002: 175). The fragmentation and differentiation of policy-making – the characteristic of networks – has been accompanied by the development of territorially and spatially differentiated policy processes – the characteristic of multi-level governance (see Bache and Flinders 2004: 97–106; Flinders 2008: 40–5).

In the UK, devolution upwards to the European Union and other international organisations and devolution downwards to Scotland, Northern Ireland, and Wales has transformed a unitary (or at least a union) state into a multi-level polity. The cumulative result, in the view of Bevir and Rhodes (2003: 59), was that the UK was now 'best viewed as a differentiated polity – an Unruly disUnited Kingdom'.

The differentiated polity is characterised by non-standardised administrative structures, a complex institutional nexus and variegated patterns of decentralised policy processes. It emphasises 'political devolution, fragmentation and interdependence, and decentralisation' (Bevir and Rhodes 2003: 60). In this view, the UK central government is just one (admittedly privileged) actor amongst many in multi-level, multidimensional, multi-sectoral (public and private) policy-making matrices. Within the encompassing frame of these matrices the UK state was seen, in some versions of the differentiated polity, to have been 'hollowed out' (Bevir and Rhodes 2003: 58–9; Rhodes 1994: 151). For Rhodes the notion of 'hollowing out' was deemed to be a 'core idea'; as it identified that governance required negotiations within and between networks, rather than a unilateral assertion of authority by government (Marsh 2008: 256; Rhodes 2008: 1249).

As a 'core idea', however, hollowing out was deemed, by many of Rhodes' critics, to be deficient on conceptual, historical, and empirical grounds (see Bellamy 2011: 84; Holliday 2000: 175; Lowe and Rollings 2000: 117). In the face of such criticism, Rhodes (2008: 1248) conceded that there was nothing new in the task confronting British governments in 'managing packages' (packages of services, organisations, and governments) or in the skills required to do so. Nonetheless, he still maintained that while the state intervened more it had less control over the outcomes of such interventions (2008: 1248). In this sense, the state remained hollowed out as it continued to be 'less reliant on a command operating code and more reliant on diplomacy'. In contrast, his frequent co-author, Bevir (2010: 89), was more willing to acknowledge that:

> The transformation associated with the new governance is ... less a hollowing out of the state than a complex and variegated shift in the pattern of rule. ... this change is one we might characterize less as a hollowing out and more as a shift in its activity from something like governance to something more like metagovernance.

The concept of metagovernance developed, in part, out of recognition that there has been no simple unidirectional shift from government to governance, or a hollowing out of the state; instead government and governance coexist. For Fawcett and Daugbjerg (2012: 202) effective 'meta-governance is about generating governance arrangements that deliver adequate levels of input and output legitimacy'. Without examining the complexities of the theorisation of metagovernance, and the arcane debates about strategic relational, critical realist, or form-analytical approaches to the state, the important point for present purposes is that the strategic relational approach conceives of the state as a complex social relation that 'strategically selects' or privileges some outcomes over others (Jessop 2004: 70). In this sense it has an affinity with the asymmetric power model – while being critical of that model's conceptualisation of the state.

The asymmetric power model starts from the premise that the unequal distribution of resources within the UK economy and society privileges some groups and disadvantages others, and this is reflected in access to policy processes (see Marsh 2008: 257; Marsh 2011; Marsh 2012; Marsh *et al.* 2003). The main features of the asymmetric power model, as summarised by Marsh (2008: 257; Marsh 2011: 41), are:

> [it] accepts that there has been a move from government to governance, but suggests that there has been much more path-dependency than Bevir and Rhodes acknowledge. More specifically, it contends that hierarchy, rather than networks, remains the dominant mode of governance and government remains strong, although increasingly challenged; the power-dependencies and the associated exchange relationships are clearly asymmetric; there is a dominant, if contested, political tradition; and the structured inequalities in society are reflected in asymmetries of power.

In this view the relationship between institutions and ideas is seen to be dialectical. In essence this relationship is anchored in a 'particular view of democracy', which is a 'top down' conception associated closely with 'a limited liberal notion of representation and a conservative notion of responsibility', and which is encapsulated within the 'British political tradition' (Marsh 2008: 263). The British political tradition is deemed to be of importance in understanding how the British political system works in three different ways: first, it constitutes the view of democracy underpinning the institutions and processes of government; second, debates about institutional and constitutional reform are permeated with, and delimited by, this tradition; and, third, it is a view to which most politicians in government and 'almost all' civil servants subscribe (Marsh 2008: 265–6).

While Marsh and acolytes have been insistent that the relationship between ideas and institutions was dialectical, the nature of this interactive and iterative relationship was largely left unexplored. In particular, the ideational linkage between the British political tradition and the Westminster model was asserted rather than analysed. As a result, as Hall (2011: 42) points out, the tradition and the model tend to be conflated. The extent to which the Westminster model was the institutional embodiment of the ideas incorporated within the political tradition was assumed, and in so doing the oppositional discourses at the heart of dialectical processes were left largely unexamined. While the Westminster model is unambiguously dismissed empirically, the ideational realm from which this model draws its institutional meaning still continues to display 'the historical and contingent patterns of belief that inform current governmental practices in Britain' (Bevir and Rhodes 2003: 195). If institutional configurations and practices are informed by 'broad patterns of belief' (Bevir and Rhodes 2003: 195), and if that practice is seen to be deficient, then the explanatory capacity of the dialectic between institutions and ideas would also appear to be deficient. Before examining these deficiencies it is appropriate, here, to reiterate the extent to which the 'institutional reality' of the Westminster model has been found wanting in the respective models of differentiated polity, asymmetrical power, and decentred governance (see Bevir 2010: 82; Bevir and Rhodes 2003: 198; Rhodes 1997).

Initially such 'corrective' accounts were especially critical of the privileging of electoral representation and institutions at the centre of the Westminster model's notion of representative and responsible government. In particular they were initially largely dismissive of parliament's contribution to such new narratives, with parliament variously being seen to be insulated from networks, or residualised in the policy process, or in fact superseded in a 'post-parliamentary' polity (see for example Jordan and Richardson 1987: 288; Rhodes 1997: 38; Rhodes and Marsh 1992a: 13; Richardson 1993: 90; 2000: 1006; see also see Chapter 7). There was also acknowledgement that, if these alternative models better encapsulated the processes of UK governance, then there were 'normative grounds for concern' (Grant 2000: 51). Indeed, Rhodes and Marsh (1992b: 265) raised just such a normative concern, bordering on pessimism, at the extent to which the 'output legitimacy' claimed by networks served to insulate their activities from the 'constraint of political, especially electoral, legitimacy'.

Legitimating frame of the Westminster model

The degree to which new modes of governance were insulated from electoral representative processes was questioned, however, in the argument that these modes were in fact nested in a process of parliamentary representation and in the legitimation of government and government outputs derived from that process (see Judge 1990, 1993). Indeed, the 'legitimating frame' provided by the Westminster model is now widely recognised even by those intent on demonstrating that political practice does not correspond to the political prescriptions of the Westminster model. More precisely, Rhodes *et al.* identify the Westminster model as a 'legitimizing interpretation' which allows 'various actors' to provide legitimacy and context for their actions (2009: 228). Similarly, other contemporary analyses of UK governance are replete with reference to the Westminster model as a 'legitimising mythology' (Diamond and Richards 2012: 192; Hall 2011: 12; Richards 2008: 199), or as a 'legitimating tool' or a 'legitimating framework' (Flinders 2010: 25). This framework is strikingly evident too in official descriptions of UK governance. Official views – enunciated for example in the *Cabinet Manual* (Cabinet Office 2011a: 2–4) – still proclaim the four key elements of the Westminster model. These are not false statements, as the term *myth* might suggest (Keating 2008: 111), but reflect instead the ideas of legitimate government as refracted in the vision of the executive. What is important about these official statements is that they combine statements about 'what is' with 'what should be'; and these ideas extend beyond formal official pronouncements. Of particular relevance, Richards (2008: 199) noted, from his interviews with ministers and civil servants, that 'it is important to appreciate the extent to which actors from the core executive have continued to draw from the Westminster model in defining, shaping and legitimising their behaviour'. Diamond and Richards (2012: 182) also reaffirmed the 'continuing salience of narratives that have emerged from within that [Westminster] model which still condition the mindset of ministers and civil servants' (see also Bevir 2010: 125; Richards and Mathers 2010: 516–18). In case it is suspected that the salience of the Westminster model for members of the executive pertains mainly to the centralisation/hierarchical dimensions of the model, it is worthy of note that the responsibility/accountability dimensions continue to feature predominantly in the mindset of ministers and civil servants as well (see for example Rhodes 2011: 38, 229; Stark 2011: 1151). In parallel to this internal executive recognition of the continuing significance of parliament, academics, many of who started as parliamentary sceptics, were willing to concede – even if grudgingly – the importance of electoral representation and institutions to the processes of policy legitimation (see Daugbjerg and Marsh 1998: 62–3; Marsh *et al.* 2001: 244–7; Marsh *et al.* 2003: 314; Richardson 1993: 90).

Double incongruity: Image and 'truth'

Yet even if there is now greater recognition of the centrality of electoral representation and institutions to the Westminster model, and of the extent to which members of the core executive in the UK seek to legitimise their institutional position and their policy preferences in terms of this model, there is equally a consensus that the UK polity does not necessarily adhere closely to those ideas in practice. Smith (2008: 150) makes this point neatly in his observation that: 'as a myth the Westminster model may represent how officials and ministers present the political system, but however strong their beliefs ... it does not represent the truth about either the power of ministers or of officials [or how the system works]'. A double incongruity arises, therefore: on the one hand, the practice of UK governance differs markedly from the precepts of the Westminster model; yet on the other hand the model still survives 'as an image to which politicians and public officials orient themselves' (Bevir 2010: 125).

The 'truth' of how the UK's political system operates, to borrow Smith's phrase, rests in the inversion of the core principles of the Westminster model – of responsibility, openness, and representativeness. Without going into the details here, the key components of the Westminster model as outlined at the start of this chapter have been systematically transmogrified. First, parliament, as noted in Chapter 4, falls short of being 'representative of the political community'. Second, while the official view continues to reflect the critical morality of the constitution in so far as 'Ministers have a duty to Parliament to account, and to be held account, for the policies, decisions and actions of their departments and agencies' (Cabinet Office 2011a: 40) and that members of the core executive have a responsibility 'to provide accurate, truthful and full information' (Cabinet Office 2010a: 1), the positive morality continues to reflect systematic transgression (on constitutional morality see Flinders 2010: 289–90; Judge 1993: 138–40). As a result, the normative logic of the doctrine has effectively been inverted, with parliament having to seek, through successive reform initiatives, to 're-invert', or more idealistically still to 'revert', to a more favourable balance between executive and legislature in order to lever greater executive accountability and responsibility (see Judge 2005: 52–64; Kelso 2009: 75–135; Wright

2012: 165–90). Yet parliament seeks to effect these changes in the context of an 'executive mentality' that still demands a 'safe space' in which policy may be formulated and which is insulated from the requirements and culture of transparency (see HC 96 2012: 54–77). Third, the features of a public service embedded in the Westminster model (although some refer to this dimension in terms of a subcategory 'Whitehall model' or an amalgamated 'Westminster–Whitehall model' (for an overview see Page 2010)) – professionalism, non-partisanship, and permanence of the UK civil service – have been subject to a potentially corrosive mix of neo-liberal initiatives, new public management reforms, agencification, politicisation, broader 'governance' tendencies, and specific legislative change (most dramatically in the 2010 Constitutional Reform and Governance Act). The cumulative impact of this has been sufficient to question the continued salience of these public service features to the Westminster model. Even so, definitive empirical confirmation that the 'Westminster–Whitehall model' has been fundamentally recalibrated has yet to be provided (see Page 2010; Pyper and Burnham 2011; van Dorpe and Horton 2011). Fourth, parliamentary sovereignty, described by Bogdanor (2009: 12) as 'perhaps the only principle at the basis of [the UK's] system of government', has now been 'severely qualified' to the extent that he believes 'it is no longer the governing principle of the British constitution' (2009: 283). It is to this fourth key component of UK representative government that the analysis of this chapter now turns.

Parliamentary sovereignty

> [T]he fundamental, perhaps only principle at the heart
> of our system of government, has been the sovereignty
> of parliament, the idea that Parliament can legislate as
> it chooses and that there can be no superior authority
> to Parliament. (Bogdanor 2009: 12–13)

As a 'fundamental constitutional principle' (Bogdanor 2009: 14) parliamentary sovereignty is a central component of the Westminster model. Yet it is a profoundly contested component. Conceptually, it has been deemed to be 'incoherent' (McLean 2010: 11), 'entirely redundant' (Lakin 2008: 730), 'hazardous' (Barber 2011: 144), and 'obscures more than it illuminates' (Bogdanor 2012: 195). Empirically, valedictory assessments have been offered of the 'quiet death of parliamentary sovereignty' (Barber 2011: 149) in the face of the challenges posed by EU membership, devolution to Scotland, Wales, and Northern Ireland, and the incorporation of the European Convention on Human Rights into UK law. Despite the depth and breadth of these negative assessments, parliamentary sovereignty remains, as will be seen below, the cornerstone of the official view of the UK's political system.

Dicey and parliamentary sovereignty

'Parliamentary sovereignty' is a shorthand phrase, most commonly associated with the 19th century constitutional lawyer A. V. Dicey. Writing in 1885, in *An Introduction to the Law of the Constitution*, Dicey proclaimed that 'the sovereignty of Parliament is (from a legal point of view) the dominant characteristic of our political institutions' ([1885] 1959: 39). The essence of his argument was stated succinctly:

> The principle of Parliamentary sovereignty means neither more nor less than this, namely, that Parliament thus defined [as the monarch, House of Lords and House of Commons] has, under the English constitution, the right to make or unmake any law whatsoever; and further that no person or body is recognised by the law of England as having a right to override or set aside the legislation of Parliament' ([1885] 1959: 39–40)

Dicey also added that 'Parliament cannot so bind its successors by the terms of any statute, as to limit the discretion of a future Parliament' ([1885] 1959: 67). This became the third element locked into the Diceyan 'orthodoxy'.

Dicey made it clear that his identification of the defining elements of parliamentary sovereignty were not derived from 'deduction from abstract theories of jurisprudence' but from the 'the peculiar history of English constitutional law'. The reason why a legal conception of 'the power of law-making unrestricted by legal limit' ([1885] 1959: 72) was symbiotically linked with parliament, in Dicey's opinion, was the 'peculiar development of the English constitution' ([1885] 1959: 69). Hence, in the case of England/Britain/UK, there was an inextricable historical linkage between the legal concept of sovereignty and parliament ([1885] 1959: 73). This linkage had been reconstituted at crucial periods with the transference of legislative supremacy from the monarch alone, to the monarch and both houses of parliament acting jointly, and, thereafter, effectively to the elected House within a triadic constitutional formulation of 'the monarch in parliament'. In particular, the Constitutional Settlement of 1689 had secured a 'system of real representative government' ([1885] 1959: 83) wherein there was a 'coincidence between the wishes of the sovereign and the wishes of the subjects'. This coincidence was deemed by Dicey to be the 'essential property of representative government' in the UK ([1885] 1959: 84). At this stage in the discussion it is important to note that Dicey's focus was upon representative government rather than representative democracy. The significance of the extension of the franchise and the 'democratisation' of UK politics for Dicey's analysis will be examined later in this chapter.

Dicey derived his legal theory of parliamentary sovereignty primarily therefore from the experience of the English/British/UK state. After 1689 the boundaries of legitimate power were marked out, with legal supremacy residing in parliament rather than in any other state institution – whether monarch or courts. From the 18th century onwards 'the Crown-in-Parliament was recognized as wielding an authority that both legally and constitutionally was absolute' (Loughlin 2010: 270). Moreover, Loughlin (2010: 270) proceeds to argue that the doctrine of parliamentary sovereignty has been accepted by jurists and judges ever since – a view shared by Loveland (2012: 26) in his observation that the 1688 revolution was 'generally regarded as having settled the question of the relationship between Parliament and the courts'. So that when Dicey wrote *The Law of the Constitution* he took it as a matter of legal fact that: 'Any Act of Parliament ... will be obeyed by the courts' ([1885] 1959: 40).

By this interpretation, Dicey was describing a political process resulting from fundamental political change wrought by the 1688 revolution. The significance of this interpretation is that understanding the relationship between parliament and the courts 'is not an exercise in logic, or in the recovery of "true" historical fact, or in the elaboration of fundamental principles of morality ... but is rooted in an appreciation of the nature of the contemporary political condition' (Loughlin 2010: 272). If this is the case then, as that 'condition' changes, so too does the relationship between parliament and the courts, and so too do their respective understandings of parliamentary sovereignty. The advantage of this interpretation is that it helps to explain how changes in Dicey's own understanding of parliamentary sovereignty came about. Equally it helps to foreclose, for present purposes at least, detailed consideration of the extensive and vibrant philosophical and theoretical debates about the meaning and limits of parliamentary sovereignty (see for instance Dyzenhaus 2013; Eleftheriadis 2009; Goldsworthy 1999, 2010, 2012; Hart 1994; Lakin 2008, 2012; Young 2009). Instead, attention will be focused upon the political and constitutional changes that have prompted leading legal theorists and political scientists alike 'to debunk' the very idea of parliamentary sovereignty.

Parliamentary sovereignty in 'the real world'

Perspectives on parliamentary sovereignty, whether self-consciously empirical or theoretical, are rooted in the real world in as much as they seek to understand, explain or justify the changing inter-institutional practice of parliament and the courts (and their interactions with 'the people'). Perspectives on parliamentary sovereignty develop in a proximate relationship to 'the nature of the contemporary political condition'. They are themselves as much political claims (in that they refract that contemporary condition through differing political interpretative lenses) as they are constitutional claims, in that they simply explain the nature of constitutional rules and conventions. When confronted by constitutional change – whether in the forms of extension of the franchise, the Parliament Acts 1911 and 1949, EU membership, incorporation of human rights, territorial devolution, or referendums – legal theorists, politicians and judges seek to interpret those changes by reference to claims about the nature and trajectory of inter-institutional interactions. These claims seek to understand change in terms of established precepts or to question the utility of those precepts in the light of changed circumstances.

At this point it is worth returning to Dicey to see how his conception of parliamentary sovereignty coped with profound political changes, and their associated constitutional ramifications, in the late 19th century. It should be noted, however, that Iain McLean (2010) would strongly counsel against adopting such an approach, as for him Dicey was merely a 'deeply prejudiced law professor' who, at the time of writing *The Law of the Constitution*, deployed an already 'outdated framework' that was historically inaccurate and Anglocentric (in misconceiving the creation of the UK through two political unions between England and Scotland in 1705–07 and Ireland in 1800–01). McLean (2010: 8) claims that Dicey's doctrine was wrong descriptively, even in 1885, in failing to recognise the constraints that had been imposed upon the UK parliament by these treaties/acts of union (see also Keating 2009: 39; 2012: 109–10; MacCormick 1999, 2000). While Dicey recognised that the terms of union might be conceived as fundamental or constitutional law, with which 'it would be political madness to tamper gratuitously' ([1885] 1959: 145), nonetheless, he resolutely maintained that the Act of Union had the same status as any other statute and could therefore 'be legally altered or repealed' ([1885] 1959: 145).

Not only does McLean contest Dicey's conclusion that the Act of Union had the same status as any other statute and could therefore 'be legally altered or repealed' ([1885] 1959: 145); but he also proceeds to argue that Dicey's opposition to Home Rule in the late 19th and early 20th century led him to move away from a conception of continuing sovereignty to one of self-embracing sovereignty. Indeed, at various stages after the publication of *The Law of the Constitution*, Dicey is claimed to have supported self-embracing sovereignty and, through advocacy of the referendum, popular sovereignty and the notion that ultimate legal sovereignty did not rest in parliament but 'in the people' (see McLean 2010: 130–4; Weill 2003: 488). Thus, within two decades of the publication of *The Law of the Constitution*, Dicey is adjudged to have 'abandoned parliamentary sovereignty altogether' (McLean 2010: 130).

That Dicey did change his perspective on the weighting of legal and political sovereignty is beyond question. That he did so in response to political change is worthy of emphasis. Significantly, Dicey's conceptual reformulations came in reaction to the challenges to the settled constitutional order (between 1689 and 1832) that had led him to nest his constitutional notion of parliamentary sovereignty within the broader political frame of representative government. In the face of seismic changes at the very time, and immediately thereafter, that Dicey was drafting *The Law of the Constitution* – most notably the interconnected events of the extension of the franchise, the development of party government, and executive dominance within parliament – the nature of representative government altered dramatically. Thus, whereas in 1885 Dicey maintained that, 'the special truth of the English House of Commons' had been ensuring the 'coincidence between the wishes of the sovereign' and the 'will of the nation expressed through the House of Commons' ([1885] 1959: 84/[1885] 1959: 82), by 1894 the 'truth' of representative government had become that 'Party becomes everything, the Nation sinks to nothing' (Dicey 1894: 68). In a personal letter written to the editor of the *Spectator* in 1894, Dicey made clear that his 'preference' remained for 'real Parliamentary government as it existed up to 1868', but that he did 'not have the remotest doubt that under the present condition of things sham Parliamentary government means a very vicious form of government by party' (cited in Cosgrove 1980: 107).

The exemplar of this process for Dicey was the attempt to force though Home Rule in 1886, 1893, and later in the Third Home Rule Bill of 1913 (see McLean 2010: 129–35; Weill 2003: 484). In circumstances that Dicey took to reveal dissonance between the expressed will of the nation and parliamentary actions, he advocated the use of the referendum. Despite objecting to the introduction of the referendum in 1884, by the turn of the century he favoured the referendum as 'the only check on the predominance of party'. The referendum allowed 'democracy itself' to serve as 'a check on party tyranny', and to do so without undermining the system of representative government (Dicey quoted in Cosgrove 1980: 107). Dicey's advocacy of the referendum thus came at a constitutional moment when the inbuilt capacity of representative government to 'produce coincidence between the wishes of the sovereign and the wishes of the subjects' had, in his judgement, been negated by the rise of party government, executive dominance of the Commons, and the legislative ascendency of the Commons over the Lords as confirmed in the Parliament Act 1911 (see Dicey [1915] 1982: cxvii; Qvortrup 1999: 539; Weill 2003: 484–6). Indeed, in 1915, in the introduction to the 8th edition of *The Law of the Constitution*, Dicey identified the 1911 Act as the 'last and greatest triumph of party government' ([1915] 1982: cxviii). To mitigate this triumph he identified the referendum as 'an institution which, if introduced into England, would be strong enough to curb the absolutism of a party possessed of a parliamentary majority' ([1915] 1982: cxiv). In which case: 'The obvious corrective is to confer upon the people a veto which may restrict the unbounded power of a parliamentary majority' ([1915] 1982: cxvi). Significantly, in making this case Dicey did not renounce parliamentary sovereignty 'from a legal point of view'. He still maintained that its 'truth has never been denied' ([1915] 1982: xxxvii), and that in practice 'the correct legal statement of the actual condition of things is that sovereignty still resides in Parliament' ([1915] 1982: xlii), but he acknowledged that within parliament 'the share of sovereignty' possessed by the House of Commons had greatly increased.

Whether the political constraint of the referendum, as a manifestation of the political sovereignty of the people, effectively served to curb the legal sovereignty of parliament has been a preoccupation of constitutional lawyers ever since. Without entering into that debate it is important for present purposes simply to note that Dicey was concerned with the recalibration of power within the triadic institutional formulation of the 'monarch in parliament' in favour of the elected House and ultimately therein in favour of party government. His concern was with the potentially malign effects of this recalibration, and whether, in the face of such political change, it remained accurate to describe parliamentary sovereignty as 'the dominant characteristic of our political institutions' ([1915] 1982: xxxvi–xxxvii).

In this sense Dicey was preoccupied with many of the same concerns that led successive generations of critics to dismiss his notion of parliamentary sovereignty. As with his critics, he sought to address the impact that political change had had upon the relationship between parliament, the people, and the courts.

Political change and parliamentary sovereignty

> We are at present in a period of transition when a traditional interpretation of parliamentary sovereignty, that Parliament cannot bind itself, is falling into desuetude ... power and effective authority has been ceded in large areas of policy to the European Union; and, insofar as ... domestic policies are concerned, to the devolved bodies of Scotland, Wales and Northern Ireland; and also, in matters of human rights to the judges. ... The powers of Parliament have been severely and probably permanently circumscribed. (Bogdanor 2009: 282–3)

Bogdanor's view has not been shared, however, by successive UK governments. The official position is that the sovereignty of parliament has not been constrained by any of these political developments.

Parliamentary sovereignty: The unwavering official position

UK accession to the EEC was by the Treaty of Brussels 1972, which was effected by the European Communities Act 1972. The 1972 Act was a simple statute, with no 'special' status, and, as with any other statute, could thus be repealed at any later date by parliament. During the passage of the 1972 Bill MPs were reassured 'that nothing in the Bill undermined the "ultimate" sovereignty of Parliament' (Loveland 2012: 367), a point that was emphasised in 1975 when the Labour government sought popular approval for continued EEC membership (see *Britain's New Deal in Europe* (HM Government 1975: 12)). This point was repeated again in 2010 when the coalition government announced its intention to introduce a European Union Bill to address concerns that 'the doctrine of Parliamentary sovereignty may in future be eroded by decisions of the courts' (Explanatory notes para 106 in HC 633 2010: 15). At the time of the Bill's introduction, however, the Minister for Europe insisted that 'the doctrine of Parliamentary sovereignty has not been affected by membership of the EU' (HC 633 2010: 15). What the government claimed to be doing in the EU Act, therefore, was to respond to 'legal and political speculation' about the continued absolutism of parliamentary sovereignty in order to 'reinforce the rebuttal of contrary arguments in the future' (Liddington in HC 633 2010: 15).

Similarly, official pronouncements on the creation of sub-national legislatures in Scotland, Wales, and Northern Ireland displayed no ambiguity about the continued resilience of parliamentary sovereignty. In granting legislative competence to these sub-national legislatures the enabling statutes made clear that 'the power of the Parliament of the United Kingdom to make laws' at sub-national level was unaffected (see Section 28(7) of the Scotland Act; Section 5(6) of the Northern Ireland Act 1998; and Section 107(5) of the Wales Act 2006). In Bradley's (2011: 60) opinion, such provisions were 'legally unnecessary' and existed only 'for the avoidance of doubt, to assist readers of the Act[s] unfamiliar with Dicey's view of parliamentary sovereignty'. Alongside statutes devolving power in 1998, the same year saw the introduction of the Human Rights Act 1998, with the government once again reaffirming an orthodox Diceyan stance (see Cm 3782 1997: paras 2.10–2.13).

Thus, in the face of fundamental political change and constitutional innovations, successive governments have adhered resolutely to an absolutist legal notion of parliamentary sovereignty. Not surprisingly, this official view has been dismissed, especially in the context of a multi-level polity where challenges to the UK parliament's legal supremacy have been posed at both supranational and sub-national levels. In this context many analysts have come to share Barber's view (2011: 153) that 'the old absolutism of sovereignty is no longer viable'.

Membership of the European Union

Although the official view is unambiguous – that the UK's entry into the EEC in 1973 did not affect the ultimate legal sovereignty of the UK parliament – many public lawyers and political scientists maintain that, as long as the UK remains a member of the EU, then 'laws made by the supreme [UK] parliament must if necessary give way to the greater supremacy of Community law' (Bradley 2011: 56). By this view the European Communities Act 1972 imposed a substantive limitation on the UK parliament's legal supremacy (Bogdanor 2012: 186). Yet the extent of the 'substantive limitation' was only confirmed in 1991 with the *Factortame* rulings (for details see Loveland 2012: 402–7; Turpin and Tomkins 2011: 347–52). In 'disapplying' the provisions of UK primary legislation (the Merchant Shipping Act 1988), the final *Factortame* ruling by the European Court of Justice was deemed to have effectively recognised the overriding of the legislative intent of parliament.

The *Factortame* judgement had particular political resonance in that it constituted 'a black mark in the ledger of Euro-sceptic grievances – marking the point at which the courts suddenly entered public and political consciousness as the allies of Brussels and the upholders of a new constitutional-legal order against the old order of unquestioned parliamentary sovereignty' (Drewry 2007: 107). The sense of eurosceptic grievance was fuelled further by the 'Metric Martyrs' cases in 2002. The argument of the appellants, that EC law had become entrenched in the UK, was rejected. And it was reaffirmed by Lord Justice Laws that there was nothing in the 1972 Act that allowed any institution of the EU 'to touch or qualify the conditions of Parliament's legislative supremacy' (England and Wales High Court 195 2002: para 59). In reaching this conclusion, Laws made a distinction between 'ordinary' and 'constitutional' statutes. In setting out a 'hierarchy of Acts of Parliament' he argued that: 'Ordinary statutes may be impliedly repealed. Constitutional statutes may not' (England and Wales High Court 195 2002: para 63). In which case the 1972 Act, as a 'constitutional statute', could not be impliedly repealed and so could only be repealed by express provisions of an act of parliament (see McGarry 2012: 9–10). There was an underlying common law presumption in this argument.

When the draft European Union Bill was published in 2010 the accompanying Explanatory Notes made specific reference to Lord Justice Laws' argument in the 'Metric Martyrs' case (HC 633 2010: 33). The stated intention of section 18 of the EU Bill was to take the common law principle, enunciated by Laws in that case, that 'EU law takes effect in the UK through the will of Parliament and by virtue of an Act of Parliament' and to place it on a statutory footing (HC 633 2010: 33). In so doing it was claimed that 'clear authority' would be provided to reject the possible future contention that 'EU law constitutes a new higher autonomous legal order derived from EU Treaties of international law and principles which has become an integral part of the UK's legal system independent of statute' (HC 633 2010: 33 Appendix Explanatory Note 106).

Advertised as a 'sovereignty clause', section 18 of the EU Act was intended to set out 'categorically that directly applicable and directly effective European Union law takes effect in the UK by virtue of an Act of Parliament' and by 'putting the matter beyond speculation [would] assist the courts by providing clarity about Parliament's intentions' (HC 633 2010: Ev 41). Yet eminent public lawyers were not persuaded of the merits of such a section: it was simply a reaffirmation of established principles; it was not needed, as the legislative sovereignty of parliament was not under threat from EU law; and that, as with any other Act, the EU Act 2011 would apply until it was repealed. Thus section 18 would not limit any future parliament and so was 'unlikely to have much practical effect' (HC 633 2010: Q55, Q56). Indeed, the most compelling reason for the inclusion of section 18 in the EU Act was political. As Dougan pointed out: 'It is associated, in particular, with a Eurosceptic rhetoric lacking any persuasive evidential foundation' (HC 633 2010: Ev 11).

If, as the House of Commons European Union Scrutiny Committee concluded, legislative sovereignty was not currently under threat and therefore section 18 was 'not needed' (HC 633 2010: 30), the real significance of the EU Act 2011 for parliamentary sovereignty is perhaps to be found in Sections 2, 3, and 6 of the Act. These sections provide for 'referendum locks', which, paradoxically given the purpose of the EU Act, hold the potential for future parliaments to be bound by the provisions of that Act. These 'locks' will be considered below, but for now the further challenges posed to 'Diceyan orthodoxy' by devolution within the UK will be the focus of attention.

Devolution: Scotland, Northern Ireland, and Wales

The official position in relation to the legal sovereignty of the UK parliament is still absolutist in its adherence to the principle that the Westminster parliament retains the capacity to legislate across all policy fields over the entire territory of the UK, even to the extent of abolishing or suspending sub-national parliaments and assemblies (as it did before the Belfast Agreement in abolishing the Stormont Parliament in 1972; and in suspending the post-Agreement National Assembly on four occasions in its first four years). In practice, however, the sovereignty of the UK parliament is significantly constrained in each of the sub-national territories. In Northern Ireland the Belfast Agreement requires the UK government to exercise its powers in a manner consistent with the Agreement (which itself was a treaty with the sovereign state of Ireland). Moreover, Section 1 of the Northern Ireland Act 1998 contains the provision that: 'Northern Ireland in its entirety remains part of the United Kingdom and shall not cease to be so without the consent of a majority of the people of Northern Ireland voting in a poll held for the purposes of this section'. This is taken to be 'self-embracing sovereignty' in so far as the 1998 Act imposes an express statutory duty upon the UK government, in the event of a referendum outcome in favour of joining the Irish state, to facilitate such a transfer (Bogdanor 2009: 116; on self-embracing sovereignty see Hart 1994: 145–6; Loveland 2012: 34–5; Young 2009: 66–93). While this is taken as a 'severe limitation' on parliamentary sovereignty by Bogdanor, Goldsworthy (2012) still maintains that such a referendum requirement does not bind parliament in that it is not self-entrenched and so can be repealed or amended by ordinary legislation without a referendum being held. Goldsworthy reasserts Dicey's 'pristine theory' even in the context of political practice moulded by a 'violent past and the special circumstance of resolving a complex national issue. In particular there is the constitutionally interesting matter of factoring in the involvement of ... the Republic of Ireland and resolving a number of long-standing quarrels that have assumed constitutional status' (Anthony and Morison 2005: 191). How Goldsworthy's impeccable legal logic would fare in the event of the actual repeal or amendment of section 1 of the 1998 Act undoubtedly would not be a simple legal matter to be resolved between the courts and parliament, but would be an intensely political matter to be settled on the streets and recorded in the cemeteries of Northern Ireland.

The potential disjunction between legal and political conceptions of sovereignty has underpinned much of the analysis of devolution in Scotland since the founding referendum in 1998 (on the referendum see below). In strict legal interpretation, in conformity with Dicey, the UK parliament retains its sovereignty. Yet the political reality in Scotland is that the UK parliament recognises (through the 'Sewell Convention' and Legislative Consent Motions) that its ability to legislate on devolved matters is normally dependent upon the consent of the Scottish parliament. Moreover, on devolved matters 'whole swathes of policy-making has been removed from the purview of Westminster; nor would it be easy unilaterally to alter the devolution settlement' (Bogdanor 2009: 112). Even on reserved matters, under section 30 of the Scotland Act the Scottish parliament may be granted legislative competence. Just such an order, marking the agreement of both Houses of the UK parliament and the Scottish parliament, was used 'to allow a single-question referendum on Scottish independence to be held before the end of 2014. The Order [puts] beyond doubt that the Scottish Parliament can legislate for that referendum' (HM Government/Scottish Government 2012). This was a conferment of legislative power by the UK parliament, and so confirmed that the Scottish parliament was not itself sovereign (HL 263 2012: 7). Nonetheless, on an issue unambiguously designed by the SNP government in Edinburgh to fragment the unity of the kingdom, the UK parliament abrogated its unilateral right 'to make any law whatsoever'. This was in recognition of the divergence between the legal and political dimensions of parliamentary sovereignty: what was plausible in legal terms was implausible in political terms (Aughey 2010: 419; Loveland 2012: 432).

The centrality of parliamentary sovereignty to the practice and ideology of unionism in the UK has long been recognised, as, indeed, has the flexibility of that doctrine in allowing considerable variation in administrative and institutional configurations across the constituent nations without conceding the legal sovereignty of the UK centre (see Judge 1993: 161–79; Keating 2009: 38; Mitchell 2009: 13–15). The supreme incongruity arises therefore that insistence on the legal supremacy of the UK parliament allows for the possibility that the UK parliament may at some future stage repeal the Scotland Act 1998 and introduce a Scottish Independence Act. Thus the unionist logic underpinning this insistence also supports the legal possibility of agreed secession (Keating 2009: 82). In circumstances in which the prospect of independence were to become a political reality (measured for example by majority support in a referendum on independence in 2014), but in which subsequent agreement between the UK and Scottish government was not forthcoming over secession, then the legal notion of parliamentary sovereignty would provide only a hollow shell for resolution. An Act of the UK parliament would be required to effect Scottish independence. Failure to pass such an Act, or to introduce an Act with significant constraints upon the precise form of secession, would simply inflame nationalist sentiment within Scotland. This would be the exact opposite of what the UK government, in agreeing the Section 30 Order of 2012, sought to achieve. At this stage the shackles of political sovereignty would reveal the extent to which the UK parliament had become imprisoned by its absolutist interpretation of the doctrine of parliamentary sovereignty.

Human Rights Act 1998

The Acts creating the Scottish, Welsh, and Northern Ireland legislatures gave legal force to the European Convention on Human Rights. Such 'Convention rights' are directly enforceable in domestic law in those subnations, and hence the courts can set aside legislation that is contrary to those rights. This further underscores the distinction between the respective competences of devolved parliaments and assemblies and the UK parliament. Bogdanor (2009: 62) makes this distinction explicit in his observation that: 'the devolved bodies are, unlike Westminster, non-sovereign legislatures, and so giving judges the right of judicial review of legislation of the devolved bodies does not undermine the doctrine of the sovereignty of Parliament'.

Indeed, as noted above, the Labour government when introducing the Human Rights Act 1998 was insistent that the legal sovereignty of parliament would not be constrained by the Act (see Straw 2010a: 362, 2010b: 578; Young 2009: 3). The Human Rights Act 1998 introduced a general requirement that all legislation – past, present and future – should be compatible with the Convention. It was made unlawful for public authorities to act in a way that was incompatible with Convention Rights. Where legislation is deemed to be incompatible with Convention rights, superior courts may make a declaration of incompatibility (under section 4(2)). If a declaration of incompatibility is made it is then up to the government and Parliament to decide how to proceed. The government may decide to amend primary legislation, or not as the case may be (see Straw 2010a: 362).

In the strictest interpretation of the legal sovereignty of parliament the Human Rights Act has done little to infringe parliament's legislative supremacy. In practice, however, those strictures have been diluted (some would say dissolved) in the Act's effect of opening a dialogue between parliament and the courts. At one level this inter-institutional dialogue simply demonstrates the inter-relationship between the two institutions, and the manner in which the intent of parliament's Acts is filtered through the interpretation of the courts (Kavanagh 2009: 129; Young 2009: 11). At another level, however, it has been used to advance notions of dual or bipolar sovereignty. In these conceptions parliament is not accorded exclusive legal sovereignty; instead, parliament's will is expressed in the wording of its statutory provisions (Sedley 1995: 389). The courts are then tasked with interpreting legislation and determining whether parliament's particular intentions are met. As a result, 'sovereignty is best understood as shared between Parliament and the courts' (Young 2009: 11). The threat posed by such notions becomes apparent when claims are made that the judiciary, rather than parliament, is better placed to determine the scope and application of human rights (Bogdanor 2012: 192–3).

A more cautious view, however, was provided by the Attorney General, Dominic Grieve (2012): 'it cannot be ignored that in some cases the application of the Human Rights Act and the nature of the judgments which must be made in some human rights cases can be intensely political, and may stray into what Lord Justice Laws has previously described as areas of "macro-policy"'. Most particularly the 'macro-policy' issues of security and counter-terrorism in the post-9/11 era have caused fractious 'dialogue' between the courts and elected representatives. Declarations of incompatibility on issues, such as the indefinite detention without trial of foreign nationals (in the *Belmarsh* prison case), or the compatibility of control orders with the right to a fair trial, have shown that the courts 'can be an important and useful player in the constitutional politics surrounding national security in the UK' (Kavanagh 2011: 199; see also HL 86/HC 111 2010).

Some critics of the Human Rights Act, therefore, have argued that the interpretative powers of the courts under sections 3 and 4 of the Act have made it 'possible for the courts to give a dramatically different reading to legislation than Parliament intended it to have' (O'Cinneide 2012: 39). This was a view to which David Cameron subscribed before the general election of 2010, when he declared that a Conservative government would 'abolish the Human Rights Act and introduce a new Bill of Rights, so that Britain's laws can no longer be decided by unaccountable judges' (Cameron 2010). Even after the election, and despite the coalition agreement containing no such commitment, he reiterated that 'the problem is that the Human Rights Act, in my view, [has been] incorporated into British law in such a way that it's given the courts an ability to come up with a lot of very odd and perverse judgments' (Cameron *The Guardian*, 25 November 2011). Cameron's antipathy to the human rights rulings of 'unaccountable judges' was only heightened when the European Court on Human Rights ruled that a blanket ban denying prisoners the right to vote was a breach of the European Convention. This judgement questioned the domestic High Court's ruling that prisoners' voting rights was a matter for parliament to determine and not the courts (for details see White 2012). Thereafter, the tension between an absolutist version of UK parliamentary sovereignty and 'Strasbourg jurisprudence' was revealed in a protracted process of appeal by the UK government, further rulings by the European Court of Human Rights and its Grand Chamber, heated debate in the UK parliament, and a defiant vote (234 in favour versus 22 against) in support of a motion that 'legislative decisions of this nature should be a matter for democratically-elected lawmakers; and supports the current situation in which no sentenced prisoner is able to vote except those imprisoned for contempt, default or on remand' (HC Debates 10 February 2011: col 493). On 22 November 2012 the government did, however, publish a draft bill, the Voting Eligibility (Prisoners) Draft Bill, with three options: first, a ban on voting for all prisoners sentenced to four years or more; second, a ban for all prisoners sentenced to six months or more; and third a ban for all prisoners. The draft bill was sent for pre-legislative scrutiny to a joint committee of both Houses convened in May 2013. Notably, the committee began its work with the prime minister's earlier statement still resonating around Westminster: 'no one should be in any doubt: prisoners are not getting the vote under this Government' (HC Debates 24 October 2012: col 923).

Constitutional referendums

Dicey, as noted above, came to support the introduction of the referendum as a means of reflecting the 'political sovereignty' of the people alongside the 'legal sovereignty' of parliament. Dicey maintained that the two were conceptually distinct and that political sovereignty did not threaten the institutional boundaries of parliament. Whilst this conceptual distinction could be maintained if the institutional composition of parliament was deemed to be tri-partite – Monarch, House of Commons, and House of Lords – it would be challenged if it were deemed to be quad-partite – Monarch, House of Commons, House of Lords, and 'the people'. The danger identified by Dicey's critics was that the referendum would in practice lead to a redefinition of what parliament 'is' or a 'reconstitution' of its constituent elements. Lady Hale (then a member of the Court of Appeal and subsequently a member of the Supreme Court) explored such a 'redefinition' in her observation in the *Jackson* case:

> If the Sovereign Parliament can redefine itself downwards, to remove or modify the requirements for the consent of the Upper House, it may very well be that it can also redefine itself upwards, to require ... a popular referendum for particular types of measures. (UKHL 56 2005: para 163)

There are limits, however, to how far parliament can redefine itself without losing its institutional form as a representative institution. As Goldsworthy (2010: 139) concludes, the electorate cannot be deemed to be part of a parliament which has been elected to represent that very electorate. Moreover, in Dicey's terms, political sovereignty would overwhelm legal sovereignty and so puncture the hermetically sealed conceptual bubble of the legal supremacy of parliament.

While referendums were deemed to be advisory they could be accommodated within a pristine notion of parliamentary sovereignty: precisely because they were, formally, non-binding. This was the case with the devolution referendums in Scotland (1979, 1997), Northern Ireland (1978), and Wales (1997, 2011), as well as in London (1998) and North

East England (2004); and with the UK-wide referendum on continued membership of the EEC (1973). Yet even advisory referendums have been identified as steps towards popular sovereignty (McLean 2010: 140) and, by implication, steps away from absolutist notions of parliamentary sovereignty. Although not formally binding, the adverse political consequences of parliament not heeding the result of an advisory referendum would seem to undermine the logic of holding a referendum in the first place. As the House of Lords Constitution Committee noted: 'Despite referendums in the UK being legally advisory ... in reality referendums might be judged to be politically binding [in so far as] it would be difficult for Parliament to ignore a decisive expression of public opinion' (HL 99 2010: 45–6).

In instances where legislation contained 'binding' referendum requirements, however, the sovereignty of parliament would be directly challenged. As noted above, Section 1 of the Northern Ireland Act 1998 declares that the decision to remain or leave the UK requires the consent of a majority of the people of Northern Ireland voting in a referendum. Section 8 of the Parliamentary Voting System and Constituencies Act 2011 instructed ministers that in the event of a 'yes' vote in the AV referendum they '*must* make an order bringing into force' the provisions for the introduction of the Alternative Vote (emphasis added). Sections 2–4 and 6 of the European Union Act 2011 state that UK ministers could not ratify treaties amending or replacing the Treaty on European Union or the Treaty on the Functioning of the European Union, or take certain other decisions, if 'the referendum condition was met'.

Yet even in these instances an argument may still be advanced that parliamentary sovereignty is not impaired by a referendum requirement. Goldsworthy (2012) makes the case that such a requirement 'is perfectly consistent with ... parliamentary sovereignty, provided it is not self-entrenched and can therefore be repealed or amended, whether implied or expressly, by ordinary legislation'. Thus, in each case of a referendum requirement, parliament has not bound its substantive powers in any strict constitutional sense. Parliament would only be so bound if a referendum requirement were itself approved by a referendum: 'A future Parliament could then be said to be bound, not by an earlier will of no higher authority than its own will, but by an earlier will that does have such a higher authority – the expressed will of the people' (Goldsworthy HC 633 2010: Ev 32).

More sceptical analysts than Goldsworthy, however, point to the substantive restrictions imposed upon the scope of parliament's legislative supremacy. In essence, under the EU Act, parliament would remain sovereign to 'do anything it likes except amend a European Union treaty or transfer significant powers or competences to the Union without a referendum' (Bogdanor 2012: 190). Others have pointed to the irony of the EU Act seeking to safeguard parliamentary sovereignty from 'an entirely fictitious attack' from the EU or from UK judges while 'simultaneously launching a direct challenge to that very same principle of Parliamentary sovereignty ... by proposing a system of "referendum locks" which purport to limit the competence of future Parliaments to enact legislation relating to specified EU matters in various circumstances' (Dougan HC 633 2010: Ev 11). The pithiest assessment of this incongruity was perhaps provided by Bogdanor (HC 633 2010: Ev 29):

> The European Union [Act] declares that Parliament is sovereign. It then proposes to bind future parliaments through a referendum lock. Was it not the Queen, in Lewis Carroll's *Through the Looking Glass*, who declared that she had been able to believe in six impossible things before breakfast?

Conclusion

The prime focus of this chapter has been upon the Westminster model as a distinctive 'institutionalised arrangement' of representative government. The 'problems' of that model have been identified as: establishing the core elements of the model in the face of the numerous and diverse components that have been ascribed to it; reconciling a model which prescribes a legislative-centric mode of decision-making with, respectively, the practices of executive-centric government and of network governance; and of retaining a viable conception of parliamentary sovereignty in a complex inter-institutional matrix of elected representatives and non-elected judicial bodies at multi-levels, and heightened claims for popular sovereignty.

Whereas the Westminster model initially approximated to a 'standard model' of representative democracy in its idealised conception of a serial flow of popular authorisation and democratic control of government, a mutated 'power hoarding' version of representative government came to be accepted as a more accurate representation of the Westminster model. This acceptance was incongruous for several reasons: first, because of the inversion of the basic principles of the initial representative and responsible model from which it was derived; second, the claim to authenticity of the mutated version was offset by the actual practice of 21st century UK government that it was supposed to describe; third, that while that practice deprivileged electoral representative processes and institutions – and privileged networked governance – it still identified the Westminster model as a 'legitimising interpretation' which provided authorisation and democratic context for decision makers; and fourth, and coming full circle, this 'legitimating framework' was derived from the initial liberal model and not the 'power hoarding' model.

Parliamentary sovereignty, as the official statements of successive UK governments have made clear, is inhered into the heart of the Westminster model. Yet the general legal principle of parliamentary supremacy has been routinely questioned in inter-instititutional interactions with the courts in one direction and democratic transactions with 'the people' in the other direction. The incongruity arises, therefore, that although UK governments steadfastly assert the continued integrity of an absolutist version of parliamentary sovereignty, that version has been systematically challenged at supranational and subnational levels. Nowhere is the incongruity more apparent than in the EU Act 2011, which manages, simultaneously, to provide in statute that directly effective and directly applicable EU law would only take effect in the UK through the will of Parliament, while proposing a system of 'referendum locks' which would restrict the unilateral capacity of the UK parliament to enact legislation in relation to EU treaty amendment or transference of powers and competences from the UK to the EU. In this manner, the incongruities between the legal notion of parliamentary sovereignty and the democratic notion of popular sovereignty become manifest not only when Acts of Parliament stipulate positive popular consent for specified future constitutional changes, but also when 'advisory', 'non-binding' referendums transmute into 'politically binding' referendums given the prospect of an adverse popular response to the parliamentary negation of a decisive expression of public opinion. In this manner also, the 'problem of the people' re-emerges, but this time in direct participatory form. And it is the 'problem of participation' that is the focus of attention in Chapter 6.

6
The 'Problem' of Citizen Participation

The 'standard account' of representative democracy, as presented in Chapter 1, is premised upon a principal–agent relationship between citizens and their representatives. This relationship institutionalises a political division of labour between principal and agent at the moment of electoral decision and thereafter propagates periodised (until the next election) self-exclusion by citizens from public policy decision-making. In such an account the period between elections is something akin to a participatory black hole, illuminated only dimly and intermittently by institutions of representational transmission – primarily political parties and civil society organisations (see Chapter 3) – but otherwise for atomised citizens it is a participatory void. Dissatisfaction with this model, at a conceptual level, led to calls for a 'rethinking of electoral representation' to emphasise 'continuums of influence and power created by moments in which citizens can use the vote to select and judge representatives', but also to structure 'ongoing processes of action and reaction between [representative] institutions' (Urbinati and Warren 2008: 402). But dissatisfaction also led to exploration of conceptual frontiers beyond electoral representation and into novel territories of non-electoral claims, notions of self-authorised representatives, and 'citizen representatives' (Urbinati and Warren 2008: 405). Notably, the mapping of new conceptual territories was accompanied by a practical redrawing of the division of political labour through 'democratic innovations'. Smith (2009: 1) defines these innovations as 'institutions that have been specifically designed to increase and deepen citizen participation in the political decision-making process'.

These innovations are rooted in both contemporary democratic theory and political practice. The increased importance in recent years of theoretical perspectives that emphasise citizen participation and deliberation has, thus, been matched by practical attempts to reengage a disillusioned and disengaged citizenry through participatory processes. Unlike the radical participatory schemes of the 1960s and 1970s, however, proponents of current 'democratic innovations' tend to conceive of them as complements to, or supplements of, electoral representation and decision-making processes rather than challenges. However, as noted in Chapter 1, if these democratic innovations constitute a response to the perceived deficiencies of aggregative representative democracy and a search for a legitimate political order based upon participatory praxis, then rooting that order in an existing electoral representative frame holds the potential to generate fundamental conceptual and practical democratic incongruities. Not the least of these incongruities is the need to reconcile unmediated modes of participation with the mediation of electoral representative processes and institutions. Equally, the perceived legitimacy of democratic innovative institutions – rooted primarily in non-electoral legitimation claims – stand in a dialectical and incongruous relationship with the legitimation claims stemming from electoral representative institutions. This chapter traces these conceptual and practical incongruities as manifested in the 'democratic innovations' of deliberative democracy and 'mini-publics', referendums, e-petitions, and the broader experiences of e-democracy.

Deliberative democracy and deliberative initiatives

> Deliberative democracy, then, is meant to be a corrective for the instability, impossibility and ambiguity of aggregative democracy. (Chappell 2012: 101)

Both normatively and empirically deliberative democrats take as their starting premise that 'democracy ... is not just about the making of decisions through the aggregation of preferences' (Dryzek 2010: 3). At a normative level, deliberative democracy is essentially a theory of democratic legitimacy (Chappell 2012: 115; Dryzek 2010: 21; Mansbridge *et al.* 2012: 25). In this conception, in contrast to established liberal representative theories, a legitimate political order is achieved through the deliberative participation of those subject to a collective decision rather than through the public authorisation and accountability of decision makers effected through the medium of elections. At the theoretical core of deliberative democracy, therefore, is the claim that 'outcomes [of collective decisions] are legitimate to the extent they receive reflective assent through participation in authentic deliberation by all those subject to the decisions in question' (Dryzek 2010: 23). In this sense, in Chambers' (2003: 308) expressive phrase, 'talk-centric democratic theory replaces voting-centric democratic theory'. Yet the pithiness of Chambers' statement overemphasises the substitutive element for, as she proceeds to acknowledge, deliberative democracy is not normally thought of as an alternative to representative democracy: 'it is rather an expansion of representative democracy'. If deliberative democracy is seen as an improvement upon electoral democracy it 'still leaves intact the conventional institutional structures and political meaning of "democracy"' (Pateman 2012: 10; see also Crowley 2009: 1002; Nabatchi 2010: 385).

While deliberative democratic theory maps out the values of reciprocity, equality, inclusiveness, other-regardingness, and reason-giving as essentials for achieving collective consensus (Chappell 2010: 297), deliberative democratic innovations have struggled to embody these normative ideals in practice. In part this is because such innovations have been embedded in an existing system of representative democracy with all the 'assumptions, motivations, discourses and power structures of that system' (Parkinson 2006: 8). In part also it is because of a 'scale problem'. At its simplest, if the source of political legitimacy is deliberative participation by those affected by a collective decision (Dryzek 2001: 651, 2010: 22), then beyond all but the smallest of social groups not everyone can deliberate together to produce such outcomes (let alone not everyone may wish to do so or be capable of doing so) (Parkinson 2006: 147–8). The word 'outcome' is used deliberately here, as one of the issues to be examined shortly is whether processes of deliberation are designed for achieving collective decision or for collective consensus.

The scale problem has been addressed in two ways: first, to design small-scale deliberative initiatives and institutions; second, to nest micro-deliberative processes within a macro-deliberative system. The first stratagem was to design 'groups small enough to be genuinely deliberative, and representative enough to be genuinely democratic' (Goodin and Dryzek 2006: 22). Such groups have been termed 'mini-publics'. Mini-publics are characterised by face-to-face deliberation by citizens on closely defined issues and have taken such institutional forms as citizens' juries, deliberative polls, consensus conferences, and citizens' assemblies. Some of these forms, such as citizens' juries and consensus conferences, pre-date deliberative democratic theorisation; but mini-publics have featured in successive 'turns' following on from the initial 'deliberative turn' in democratic theory. Indeed, Dryzek

(2010: 6–8) has identified four further 'turns': institutional, systemic, practical, and empirical. In one way or another each of the institutional, practical, and empirical turns constitute 'working theories' (Chambers 2003: 307) in their respective attempts to design, introduce, or sustain deliberative institutions, or to study how deliberative theories inform the practice of deliberative institutional forms (Dryzek 2010: 6–9). Mini-publics serve to mitigate the tractability problems inherent in these 'turns' in so far as there are time-cost, resource-cost, and operational efficiencies to be derived from small-scale institutional design and empirical analysis. In other words, it is easier to design, establish, manage, and analyse empirically micro-deliberative forms than to do so for macro-deliberative institutions and processes. Perhaps understandably, therefore, micro-deliberation has been a primary focus of deliberative theorists and institutional innovators (Chappell 2012: 12).

Deliberative democratic theory has prompted a plethora of empirical studies designed to test its conceptual claims (for an overview see Ryfe 2005: 49–56). In particular, the internal dynamics of mini-publics have attracted much attention, especially the claims that deliberation can transform opinions and change preferences, with a series of quasi-experiments being used to examine how and why deliberators change their views (Chambers 2003: 318; Chappell 2012: 46–7, 113–15). Attention has been drawn to how the democratic goods of inclusiveness and considered judgement can be secured in mini-publics. Given the inherent small scale of mini-publics, ranging from 12 to 25 participants in citizens' juries or consensus conferences, through 100 to 160 in citizens' assemblies (though face-to-face discussion is facilitated in sub-groups), to 200 to 600 in deliberative polls, selection issues have featured prominently in theoretical and practical analyses. Equally, the organisational requirements for securing considered judgement – associated most closely with facilitation and internal decision rules and procedures – have attracted considerable attention (for an overview see Ryfe 2005: 49–71; Smith 2012: 90–111).

While micro-deliberation, in mini-publics at a local level, is often regarded by deliberative democrats as the most authentic form of deliberation (Chappell 2012: 39), it is not necessarily the most authentic form of democracy. If, as noted above, deliberative democracy is a theory of democratic legitimacy then, in its mini-public micro-deliberative form, it is confronted with a fundamental legitimation dilemma: 'By what right do the particular twenty people on some citizens' jury, or two hundred people involved in some deliberative poll, speak for all the rest of their fellow citizens?' (Goodin 2012: 807). In and of themselves the participants in mini-publics have no such right. The basic incongruity at the heart of deliberative democracy is, therefore, 'because the deliberation of *all* those subject to a decision or regime is impossible, deliberative democratic practices cannot deliver legitimate outcomes as [deliberative] theory defines them' (Parkinson 2006: 4; emphasis in original). The scale problem of deliberation, solved by mini-publics, fails to resolve the scale problem of democracy of securing the authorisation of those not included in micro-deliberation. To overcome this latter problem, some deliberative democratic theorists have moved away from treating mini-publics in isolation and have sought to locate them within a broader system of deliberation (Parkinson 2006: 6–8, 2012: 170; Mansbridge 1999b: 215).

Macro-deliberation and deliberative systems

The move to a systemic approach to deliberation, through recognition of the interconnectedness of micro- and macro-deliberation, might resolve the scale problem of democracy, but in turn might reopen the issue of what deliberation means in such a system (Boswell 2013: 628). If the intention of the 'systemic turn' in deliberative theory is 'to put the democracy back into deliberation' (Parkinson 2012: 152) it also raises the question of what remains deliberative about such a system. For, as Parkinson (2012: 152) notes, 'it has been thought for some time now that the deliberative and democratic desiderata pull in opposite directions, with deliberative criteria being maximized in small-scale settings and the democratic being maximized in large'. If reason-giving and public reasoning are, as noted earlier, at the heart of a deliberative system then it makes little sense to expect large groups of people, whether measured in hundreds, let alone thousands or millions, to 'reason together' (see Walzer 1999: 68). The way around this dilemma for those of a systemic disposition has been to loosen what it means to 'reason together'. In such a loosening 'reason' may be taken to mean 'narrating and claim-making in a way that is "decision-oriented"', and 'together' may be taken to mean 'on the same topic' and 'in the same, broad communicative system' (Parkinson 2012: 154). This opens up the possibility of conceiving of a deliberative ecological system in which a variety of formal and informal institutions, organisations, and deliberative venues interact and interconnect across multi-levels. In essence, different 'deliberative ecologies' can be identified in different contexts (see Mansbridge *et al.* 2012: 6–10).

If, as Goodin (2008: 2) argues, the deliberative democracy movement is distinctive in its 'concern with finding ways of putting the theory into practice', the challenge is to adapt and synchronise deliberative theory with existing democratic institutions. The problem in doing so is that 'simply bolting [micro-deliberative innovations] onto existing democratic institutions is not an adequate response' (Goodin 2008: 5). In this context the systemic 'turn' in deliberative democratic theory seeks to overcome this problem by positing deliberative contributions made by a large number of disparate actors in decision-making processes: what Goodin (2008: 186) terms 'distributed deliberation'. Goodin conceives of 'distributed deliberation' as sequenced deliberation linking micro-deliberation with macro-political decision-making, though he acknowledges that, in using existing frames of representative democracy, his model may resemble 'deliberative Schumpetarianism' (Goodin 2008: 202). From a deliberative point of view it might not be ideal, but in practice the contestation and deliberation of policy ideas in electoral, party, and parliamentary forums is 'probably the most to which we can realistically aspire' (Goodin 2008: 203).

Whilst Goodin's notion of 'distributed deliberation' is located at the restricted end of any conceptualisation of deliberative democracy, other theorists have envisioned broader, more participatory, systemic admixtures of micro-deliberative and macro-deliberative institutional forms. Indeed, as Dryzek (2010: 7) points out, the combination of micro-and macro- deliberation has 'actually been there all along' in the emphasis placed upon the significance of the 'public sphere' in constituting any deliberative democratic system. Habermas (1996: 306–8, 352–9) provided an early conceptualisation of a 'two-track model' of deliberation, in which opinion is formed in an informal public sphere of civil society and then transmitted to a formal public sphere of representative institutions as sites of decision-making (Parkinson 2006: 6–7). Leaving aside the intricacies of Habermas's ideas on discourse theory and ethics, and communicative rationality and action, the point of most relevance here is that the two-track model identifies a range of differentiated but interconnected deliberative venues – from 'every day talk' in private conversations, or discussions in workplaces, or civil society organisations, or in structured discourse in television and the print media, or in informal ICT and social networks through to formal discussion in bureaucracies and representative institutions at multi-levels both within and across states. The normative appeal of such a two-track model to deliberative democrats is that:

> It accommodates the messiness of debate in the public sphere, thus opening participation up to anyone affected by a decision. But it still

places emphasis on elite political institutions to ensure legitimacy and provide a source of democratic accountability. Meanwhile, mini-publics and more traditional mechanisms of citizen and stakeholder engagement are also seen to play a crucial role in linking these spaces. They provide a counter to the elitism of political institutions on the one hand, and the potentially distorted nature of the public sphere on the other. (Boswell 2013: 628).

The empirical appeal is less clear, however. Rummens (2012: 40) points to the potential for a deliberative system, composed of decentred deliberative sites connected to *ad hoc* publics dealing with specific problems as they arise, to lack adequate coherence and visibility. The problem becomes, to paraphrase Dewey ([1927] 1989: 187), 'there is too much public', with public deliberation being 'too diverse and scattered'. In this sense 'a multitude of fleeting publics focused on their own fleeting problems fails to provide sufficient integration to the democratic debate, and thus to democratic society' (Rummens 2012: 40). In other words, given the fragmented nature of a macro-deliberative system it is essentially unfeasible to hold a single conversation across a multitude of different venues (Boswell 2013: 628). Attempts to organise 'single conversations' by a corporatised, often 'tabloidised', and potentially manipulative, mass media bring in their wake their own democratic challenges. In these circumstances representative institutions become the default option for structuring 'single conversations' across micro- and macro-deliberative forums and for ensuring that the voices of ordinary citizens raised (and equally importantly the voices *not* raised) in deliberative venues are listened to when decisions are made.

Deliberation and decision-making

Early accounts of deliberative democracy were often criticised for their tenuous connection with decision-making (Parkinson 2012: 159). For Goodin (2012: 806) the central problem of deliberative democracy remains 'how to connect up to the "main game" politically ... how [to] have any genuinely consequential input into – get a grip on – the central decision-making processes [of public policy]'. It remains the case that the input of deliberative mini-publics in public policy processes has been primarily advisory or consultative, and sequenced before decision by electoral representatives. This leads Setälä (2011: 207) to raise the question of whether 'the basic idea of deliberative mini-publics is only about "re-inventing the wheel"' as elected representatives historically have engaged in 'deliberations that help to resolve epistemic problems and moral and political conflicts'. While deliberative democratic theorists have provided vibrant normative accounts on why and how mini-publics *should* be used in collective decision-making, they have been less successful in explaining why and how statal decision makers *would want* to use mini-deliberative forms. Relatively few formal decision makers would concede an 'obvious urgent need to make democracy more deliberative' (Chappell 2012: 136).

If, as noted above, deliberative democracy is a response to the deficiencies of aggregative representative democracy and constitutes a search for a legitimate political order based upon deliberative praxis, then rooting that order in macro-deliberative systems, which privilege electoral representative institutions, generates fundamental conceptual and practical democratic incongruities (Pateman 2012: 9–10; Setälä 2011: 204). These incongruities may be sidestepped if the processes of deliberation are prioritised above the products of deliberation. If deliberation is deemed of importance primarily for its processual impacts – upon preference formation, citizen reciprocity, the developmental potential for individual participants and for the broader political culture, the promotion of equality and inclusion, and the generation of cooperation and compromise within mini-publics – then its public policy impacts can be deemed to be of residual importance. Indeed, an emphasis upon these latter impacts may simply serve to undermine the dynamics of deliberation (see Smith 2012: 104–5). Where, however, it is held that deliberation should be 'consequential when it comes to affecting the content of collective decisions', then the incongruities of representation, authorisation, and accountability return to centre stage.

Before examining the 'consequentiality' of deliberation the democratic incongruities of mini-publics require some further elaboration. In the first instance the composition of mini-publics generates a series of dilemmas for democratic theorists. Various selection techniques – most particularly random or stratified sampling – have been deployed to ensure equality and inclusiveness of membership, or at least to reduce the systematic exclusion of segments of the populace (see Chappell 2012: 73–80; Fishkin 2009: 82–3). But in 'sampling', and in making non-electoral representative claims, the designers of mini-publics run up against the problems of accountability and authorisation (identified in Chapter 2). While mini-publics are 'driven by information gathering imperatives rather than decision-making ones' (Parkinson 2006: 34), or they 'continue to be nothing more than a fairly sophisticated method of public consultation' (Smith 2012: 105), or serve as a means of 'market testing' policy proposals (Goodin 2008: 25–8), or act as little more than focus groups (Pateman 2012: 9), the problems of accountability and legitimacy can be finessed. Once mini-publics assume a decision-making role, either directly or indirectly, through making recommendations to policy makers, they are forced to confront the legitimation dilemma specified by Goodin (noted above; 2012: 807). In these circumstances mini-publics lack the democratic legitimacy associated with electoral representation and with attendant mechanisms of formal authorisation and accountability (Elstub 2010: 310; Goodin 2008: 30; Parkinson 2006: 4; Smith 2012: 105). In themselves, mini-publics are unable to account for why non-participants should grant legitimacy to their deliberative outcomes (Parkinson 2006: 174). Ultimately, decisions have to be justified to those who were not present and did not deliberate (Dryzek 2010: 27), in which case, '[l]egitimacy in a deliberative system is still going to require the making, acceptance, or rejection of claims to representation and representativeness' (Dryzek 2010: 41). Whereas electoral claims of legitimacy have a basic intelligibility, claims made on behalf of deliberative legitimacy sometimes stray into abstruseness:

> Legitimacy can be sought instead in the resonance of collective decision with public opinions, defined in terms of the provisional outcome of the engagement and contestation of discourses in the public sphere as transmitted to public authority in empowered space. (Dryzek 2010: 40)

The 'average citizen', let alone the disadvantaged or dispossessed, might be somewhat bemused by such a definition of legitimacy. The academic analyst may also question the incongruity of deliberative institutional forms founded upon the 'deliberative participation of those subject to a collective decision' being validated on the basis of broader representative claims.

Mini-publics in practice in Britain

In a comparative review of the introduction of democratic innovations in Britain and the Netherlands between 1990 and 2010, Hendriks and Michels (2011) noted that citizens' juries had become an established method for public engagement in Britain over that period. New Labour, in government, had from the outset pledged to reinvigorate local democracy and to do so by promoting a broad range of democratic initiatives, including mini-publics of citizens' juries, focus groups, and citizens' panels, alongside deliberative opinion polls and citizens' forums (Department of the Environment, Transport and the Regions

1998: paras 4.12–4.17). Part of this reinvigoration strategy also entailed experimentation with participatory budgeting, designed to involve local people in local budgetary processes. While the origins of participatory budgeting in Porto Alegre in Brazil were rooted deeply in deliberative processes, in the UK, as in other European states, the public's deliberative inputs were more constrained, less 'democratically innovative', and often limited to the peripheries of budgetary policies (see Chappell 2012: 150–1; Davidson and Elstub 2013: 11–12; Pateman 2012: 10–12). Nonetheless, beyond participatory budgeting, mini-publics and other deliberative devices formed a consistent thread in New Labour's attempts, after 1998, at 'civic renewal' and 'community empowerment'. This thread was still clearly visible ten years later in the White Paper *Communities in Control* (Cm 7427 2008: 21), with its emphasis on 'empowerment' and 'passing more and more political power to more and more people, using every practical means available [including] public debates and citizens' juries' (Cm 7427 2008: 21).

In parallel to the deliberative initiatives in local government New Labour also promoted enhanced citizen engagement in the National Health Service (NHS). The NHS Act 2006 included new duties and responsibilities for health services in England to involve and consult users of those services. The Department of Health, in its accompanying guidance on the Act, suggested a range of engagement strategies and consultation techniques to fulfil these responsibilities, including health panels, citizens' juries, citizens' panels, and deliberative mapping (Department of Health 2008: 79–81). In fact, formal modes of citizen engagement in the NHS had been used in local health service planning from the 1970s (see Coe 2012: 266–7).

Though committed generally to the enhancement of deliberative involvement, the Department of Health did not keep track specifically, either before or after the 2006 NHS Act, of the number of occasions when citizens' juries, or other randomly selected panels, were convened (see HC Debates 12 January 2009: 141W; HC Debates 14 January 2010: 1083–4W). Nonetheless, citizens' juries continued to be convened in the NHS after the change of government in 2010: for example, the announcement by the Department of Health in 2011 of the creation of commissioning consortia for GP services as part of its radical reform of the NHS in England was accompanied by a number of deliberative projects (see, for example, Buckinghamshire NHS 2011). Indeed, the use of citizens' juries in the NHS was deemed to be a deliberative method that fitted well with the coalition government's 'Big Society' approach (Lynch and Young 2011: 8).

Building upon the experience of deliberative mechanisms at local level, the Brown government, as part of its programme for 'reinvigorating democracy', committed itself to the wider use of engagement mechanisms at national level, including the deliberative methods of citizens' juries and citizens' summits (Ministry of Justice 2008: 15–19). Michael Wills as Minister of State for Democratic Renewal was in no doubt that: 'It is important that we involve the British people in policy making between elections as well as at them ... [we] need to involve people in deliberative events to help formulate public policy' (HC Debates 21 July 2009: cols 749–50). The first citizens' juries commissioned by central government had been used a decade earlier by the Women's Unit of the Cabinet Office 'to inform' the development of a national childcare strategy; deliberative events were organised subsequently in 2006 in six regions to consider proposals made by the Pensions Commission; and in 2007 citizens' summits were held as part of the consultation on the draft Climate Change Bill and upon public service provision as part of the government's policy review (Maer 2007: 4–9). The Department of Health also convened five citizens' juries or panels in 2007–2008.

In 2007 Gordon Brown announced that a citizens' summit would be asked to formulate a British statement of values (Brown 2007), with Labour ministers continuing to insist, right up to the 2010 general election, that a British statement of values was emerging from a 'deliberative process' (Wills 2010). More specifically, in the context of the macro-governance of science and technology, the UK ranked highly in international comparisons in organising mini-publics to structure 'upstream dialogues' on policies in such fields as biotechnology, geo-engineering, and nanotechnology (Rask *et al.* 2012: 714). Given the contentious nature of policy making in these fields (in their interconnections with fundamental scientific, environmental, ethical, and economic concerns) mini-publics and other deliberative innovations were deemed to be of especial significance to the development of government and research council policies (Opinion Leader 2009: 9–14; Rask *et al.* 2012: 718).

While UK governments have actively promoted deliberative minipublics (and wider deliberative processes of people's panels, citizens' summits, deliberative polls (for an overview see Smith 2009)) as a method of informing decision-making and contributing to the formulation of public policies, the actual policy impact of mini publics remains indeterminate. In common with comparative assessments there is a broad consensus that the direct policy effects of the deliberations of mini-publics in the UK are limited at worst or ambiguous at best (see, for example, Biegelbauer and Hansen 2011: 594–5). At one end of the impact spectrum are assessments that maintain that national government-sponsored citizens' juries have had no impact on public policy (McLaverty 2009: 383). Many other assessments concede, however, that 'small scale carefully controlled deliberative events might have an impact on public policy' (Goodin 2012: 807), but the degree to which that impact is realised is difficult, if not impossible, to measure given the difficulties of isolating the specific contribution of mini-publics in a dynamic and variegated consultative process (Coe 2012: 274).

Indeed, mini-publics are frequently residualised in the policy process to something resembling focus groups (Beetham 2012: 60; Parkinson 2010: 10), with the attendant danger that 'technocrats have taken over and turned deliberative democracy into just another set of tools for researching, even manipulating, the "users" of public services' (Parkinson 2010: 15). An associated danger is the 'professionalisation' and 'commercialisation' of deliberative processes and the growth of a 'participation industry' of facilitators as public authorities outsource the organisation of deliberation (see Cooper and Smith 2012). Moreover, private companies have not only acted on behalf of public authorities but have been prepared to activate, on their own initiative, citizens' juries to 'engage in deliberative research that would complement the government's consultation activities' (PwC 2010: 2; see also PwC 2011). One of the identified advantages of such deliberative events was that they provided 'insight into which arguments work with the public and which frankly do not' (Institute of Government 2011). This was a direct echo of the value ascribed to mini-publics in their 'market testing' of government policy proposals (Goodin 2008: 25).

If the insights derived from citizens' juries are ignored, however, the danger is that the deliberative process might be devalued. Indeed, studies have repeatedly found that impact on policy was of overwhelming importance for jurors (see Coe 2012: 273–4; Gooberman-Hill *et al.* 2008: 279; Parkinson 2006: 157). Yet commissioning bodies rarely make explicit commitments to accept the recommendations of juries or integrate the findings of juries into the general policy process (McLaverty 2009: 381). This disjunction indicates 'a structural ambivalence within deliberative democracy about the relationship between talk and action' (Ryfe 2005: 61). This ambivalence relates directly to the legitimation dilemma noted earlier in this chapter: what right do mini-publics have to talk (or speak) for others or to act (or decide) on behalf of others? One answer is that they *should not* be allowed to decide public policy in a system of representative democracy (Beetham 2012: 61). This echoes

Goodin's (2012: 807–8) view that mini-publics, in and of themselves, have no intrinsic legitimacy: any policy impact/influence they might seek to exert is dependent upon acceptance by 'others who *do* have the genuine authority to make decisions – be they fellow citizens in the poll booths or duly elected officials in their representative capacity'. This is the fundamental democratic incongruity: of a talk-centric democratic theory being dependent upon vote-centric practice to legitimate its outputs.

Referendums

Whereas those democratic innovations that are focused upon deliberation in mini-publics have limited, often indeterminate, impacts upon policy outputs and also encounter problems of legitimation in relation to electoral representation, the 'innovation' of the referendum has both policy impact and intrinsic positive claims to legitimacy. Indeed, in an empirical study of 120 cases in 10 different representative democracies Michels (2011: 283–4) found that the policy impact of referendums was substantially greater than for deliberative innovations (including citizens' juries, citizens' conferences, consensus conferences, and planning cells). The general pattern of policy impact is that the voting outcomes of referendums have a direct effect on public policy, even in the case of non-binding referendums. In terms of legitimation, referendums have been found to have 'a special legitimising appeal amongst citizens' (Esaiasson *et al.* 2012: 803). In essence, this appeal is processual: 'a referendum is a straight vote, with each individual having a formally equal say, the decision often being made by simple majority' (Tierney 2012: 29; Butler and Ranney 1978: 14–15; Smith 2009: 113).

Referendums, in the opinion of their supporters, are held to encapsulate the democratic ideal of the direct participation of 'the people' in the making of policies that directly affect them, and hence are often subsumed under the label of direct democracy. But, as Smith (2009: 112) counsels, 'it is important to be careful about definitions'. There are a number of different types of referendums, just as there are also different types of other related 'direct democratic' innovations such as citizens' initiatives. Equally, there are a number of terminological differences, with meanings varying across types and across countries. Indeed, Smith draws a basic distinction between 'binding' referendums and initiatives, which he terms 'direct legislation' and which locate the final point of decision in a determinative vote of the citizenry, and 'advisory' referendums, where governments choose to put a proposition for vote by the citizenry but are under no compulsion to abide by the result of that vote. But the distinction between 'binding' and 'advisory' referendums is not clear-cut. In the UK, as noted in Chapter 5, despite referendums being advisory in strict legal terms (with the exception of the provisions of the Northern Ireland Act 1998 and the potential exception of the 'referendum locks' in the European Union Act 2011) they may be 'politically' binding in so far as 'a clear majority on a reasonably high turnout would leave Parliament with little option in practice other than to endorse the decision of the people' (HL 99 2010: Evidence 47).

Moreover, although referendums are often associated with the mobilisation of 'popular sovereignty' this is, in Tierney's (2012: 12) view, 'a category mistake'. Tierney draws a distinction between 'constitutive referendums', 'constitution-changing referendums', and 'ordinary legislative referendums'. Constitutive referendums are of such constitutional significance as to bring into existence a new state or a new constitutional order and so act as the supreme source of higher order constitutional law (2012: 296). In this sense they are associated with 'popular sovereignty', as 'the people' are engaged explicitly and directly in 'constituting power'. Thus for Tierney constitutive referendums are categorically distinct from 'constitution-changing referendums', which deal with, for example, issues related to the transference of state powers to supra-national or sub-national institutions, or issues related to substantive change or recalibration of state institutions (dealing with such matters as electoral reform, bicameral relations, or the status of the head of state). Equally they are distinct from 'ordinary legislative referendums' that address matters of 'first order law-making' or 'ordinary law-making' (Tierney 2009: 363–6). In making this distinction Tierney (2009: 364; original emphasis; see also Tierney 2012: 13) observes that:

> Legislative referendums do not impact upon the location and distribution of sovereign power within the state; rather they are constrained to play a role within mainstream *representative* democracy ... Therefore, even the categorisation of legislative referendums as an instance of *direct* as opposed to *representative* democracy is perhaps something of an over-simplification. ... they should perhaps more accurately be portrayed as being part of that representative system, since the effect given to the outcomes they produce is ultimately subject to the representative competence of constitutional institutions, most obviously legislatures, but also courts.

Indeed, beyond Tierney's constitutional law perspective, there is a broad agreement that 'the referendum serves not to *replace* the machinery of representative government, but only to *supplement* it' (Bogdanor 2009: 174; original emphasis). Referendums are thus best conceived as being 'intricately intertwined with the institutions and agents of representative democracy' (Mendelshon and Parkin 2001: 4; see also Newton 2012: 10–11).

Government-sponsored referendums

Certainly, given the number of government-sponsored referendums in the UK, 'there can be little doubt … that the [constitution changing] referendum has now become part of the British constitution' (Bogdanor 2009: 173). Since 1973 there have been a total of 11 constitution changing referendums: two at the UK national level (membership of the European Community, 1975; and the Alternative Vote (AV), 2011); and nine at sub-national/regional level (Northern Ireland 'Border Poll', 1973; Scottish devolution, 1979; Welsh devolution, 1979; Scottish devolution, 1997; Welsh devolution, 1997; Northern Ireland devolution 'Belfast Agreement', 1998; Greater London Assembly, 1998; North East England Elected Regional Assembly, 2004; and extended legislative powers for the Welsh National Assembly, 2011).

While proponents of the further 'democratisation' of the UK, through direct citizen participation, welcome the proliferation of referendums (see for example HL 99 2009: 13), the prime motivation of governments in their deployment of referendums has owed less to democratic altruism and more to political, often partisan, expediency. To date, most government-sponsored referendums in the UK have dealt with 'territorial politics where, so it seemed, the party system did not work very effectively in resolving them' (Bogdanor 1997: 128, 2009: 188). The referendums held and promised on the EU vividly illustrate this point. Intra-party divisions provide powerful explanatory variables for the actions of the Wilson Labour government in 1975, the Major Conservative government of 1996, and the Cameron Conservative-led coalition government in 2010 (in promising 'referendum locks'), and the Conservative prime minister announcing in January 2013, in order to placate Conservative eurosceptic MPs, a possible future referendum after the 2015 general election on the UK's continued membership of the EU. In contrast, inter-party variables help to account for promises made in 1997 and 2004, on occasions when the Labour party sought to decouple divisive EU issues – on the adoption of the euro and further EU constitutional change – from domestic UK party electoral competition (see Opperman 2013: 693–4).

Similarly, the 1979 referendums on devolution resulted in large part from the earlier 'shotgun conversion' (McLean 2010: 159) of the

Labour party to devolution in 1974, which left significant sections of the Labour party as reluctant 'converts'. As Bogdanor (2009: 185) concludes, the 1979 referendums were held largely because the governing party was divided on the issue. Equally, in 1997 partisan calculation was apparent in the decision to hold referendums in Scotland and Wales. By including a commitment to hold referendums in Labour's 1997 manifesto the Labour party recognised not only the legitimation advantages to be gained by prior public authorisation of its devolution legislation, but also the inter-party advantages to be derived from pre-empting opposition from an English-dominated Conservative party.

The AV referendum in 2012 was also the result of partisan calculations. The issue of electoral reform was central to the negotiations between the Conservatives and Liberal Democrats that preceded the formal coalition agreement. Cameron secured intra-party agreement to offer the Liberal Democrats a referendum on AV while leaving Conservatives free to campaign against AV (Kavanagh and Cowley 2010: 213–5). This agreement allowed the two parties in coalition to 'agree to differ' on an issue which divided them fundamentally. Indeed, Curtice (2013: 219) draws a direct parallel between the decision to hold a UK-wide referendum on AV and the first UK-wide referendum on continued membership of the EU: 'Now, thirty-five years later, British politicians once again found holding a referendum a convenient way of papering over deep divisions that otherwise threatened the ability of the government to cohere'.

In each of these cases of 'constitution-changing' referendums held in the UK the clear verdict was that the referendum was 'a weapon for the political class, not the people' (Bogdanor 2009: 196). Although speaking specifically of the referendum on AV, Curtice's (2013: 222) conclusion that the UK's experience 'is unlikely ever to be widely regarded as a model of democratic practice' has wider resonance. Far from being an unmediated form of democracy, referendums in the UK have been subject to the mediation of, and manipulation by, existing institutions – particularly political parties – at the core of representative politics in the UK.

Referendums at local level

Alongside the constitution-changing referendums sponsored by UK national governments, a number of referendums have been held on institutional change at local level, specifically on the introduction (and removal) of directly elected mayors. After the first referendum in London in 1998, 40 referendums were held under the provisions of the

Local Government Act 2000, ten followed the Localism Act 2011, and a further three were held to remove mayors. By 2012 these referendums had resulted in the establishment of 14 elected mayors (alongside three mayoral posts created without a referendum), and the removal of two elected mayoral positions.

While referendums on directly elected mayors have attracted most public and academic attention, local 'ordinary referendums' have been a feature of local government since the early 1970s. The Local Government Act 1972 enabled parish councils in England (the lowest tier of local government) to hold non-binding parish polls (referendums) on any question arising at a parish council. Subjects covered by such polls have ranged widely, from opposition to airport expansion (at Lydd in Kent in April 2007), to greater use of village playing fields (Wellow in Somerset in January 2013), to opposition to EU treaty reforms (several parish councils held referendums on the Lisbon Treaty in 2008 which led to the Audit Commission advising parish councils that such subjects did not constitute 'parish affairs' within the meaning of the 1972 Act and so might be deemed unlawful).

Other 'ordinary referendums' had also been initiated by higher-tier local authorities, even before the provisions of Labour's Local Government Act 2003 conferred specific powers on local authorities to hold advisory referendums on matters relating to local services, expenditure on those services, or the 'promotion of well-being' in their areas. These provisions followed from the pledge in the 1998 White Paper *Modern Local Government: In Touch with the People*, 'that councils should use referendums as an important tool to give people a bigger say' (Cm 4014 1998: para 4.8). Thus, in 2005, Edinburgh City Council held a referendum on congestion charging, and in 2008 Greater Manchester Council asked the local electorate whether a public transport investment package, which included a congestion charge, should be introduced.

The experience of these local referendums did little, however, to support Labour's belief that they would act as 'an important tool to give people a bigger say'. In fact, in analysing the experience of these ordinary local referendums in the UK, Laisney (2012: 654) reached the conclusion that '[i]n none of the cases reviewed has the local referendum genuinely been designed to widen public participation'. Pragmatic and partisan tactical considerations prevailed over democratic or participatory motivations in prompting referendums. As one policy advisor involved in the decision to hold the Greater Manchester referendum noted: 'we only went down the referendum route because we had to, because political pragmatism required that was where we had to go' (quoted in Laisney 2012: 654). The variables of local inter-party competition, or inter-institutional policy contestation across central and local government levels, therefore provide more explanatory power for the use of local referendums than variables of citizen participation and local involvement in decision-making processes.

Nonetheless, in introducing its proposals for decentralisation and localism after the 2010 general election the coalition government echoed and emphasised Labour's 1998 commitments to 'give people a bigger say': 'Local voters therefore need more opportunities in which to make their voices heard' (Department for Communities and Local Government 2010: 11). An integral part of the coalition government's proposed Localism Bill's 'package of democratic reforms' was, therefore, its provisions for referendums to be held on directly elected mayors, council tax increases and on 'any local issue' that local residents instigated through a petition. However, this latter provision for citizen initiative did not survive the passage of the Bill, being removed in the House of Lords in the face of opposition from the Local Government Association (the representative organisation of over 400 local authorities) owing to its cost and its potential to disrupt established consultation processes.

The provision to hold council tax referendums was retained in the Localism Act. A duty was placed on local authorities to determine whether the basic amount of council tax set for a financial year was 'excessive' (as defined by principles determined by central government). Any authority proposing to set an excessive council tax then triggered a referendum. While the Secretary of State for Communities and Local Government, Eric Pickles (2010), identified this provision as 'a radical extension of direct democracy', Clive Betts, a former local council leader and chairman of the House of Commons Communities and Local Government Select Committee, pointed out the democratic flaw in a provision which allowed 'only for a one-way referendum if a Secretary of State thinks that a council tax might be excessive as defined by him' (HC Debates 17 January 2011). Similarly Jones and Stewart (2010: 9) questioned both the localist democratic credentials of council tax referendums and their compatibility with the existing system of local electoral democracy:

> The local budget is the result of a process of balancing expenditure priorities, which cannot be expressed in a simple yes/no question. It damages representative democracy since it destroys the whole point of local elections, if elected councillors see their judgments

based on their electoral promises overturned in a referendum called by a minister.

The Localism Act 2011 also created a new neighbourhood planning system in England. 'A core principle' of the new system was that 'the community should be in the driving seat of planning the future of their areas'. A referendum at the end of the process was deemed to be integral to ensuring that 'communities have the final say' in neighbourhood planning and development (Department for Communities and Local Government 2011). These provisions were effected through the Neighbourhood Planning (Referendums) Regulations 2012 and the first referendum on a neighbourhood plan was held in Upper Eden in East Cumbria in March 2013. However, the Local Government Association opposed these regulations on the grounds that planning referendums would be 'time-consuming, complex and wasteful'. Enforced local referendums by central government decree were deemed to run counter to the democratic logic of localism; and the stark either/or choice inherent in referendum questions held the potential to divide communities rather than facilitate consensus-building and deliberative decision-making (see Local Government Association 2012; HL Debates 23 July 2012: cols. GC194–5).

e-petitions

According to the House of Commons' Procedure Committee, petitions have the potential to be 'an important means of engaging with the public' (HC 513 2007: 7). Indeed, there is a long history in the UK of petitions being used by citizens to inject their demands into parliamentary deliberations – whether for action or for redress of grievance. Whereas petitions are identified historically, and contemporarily, as 'a different means for the public to access representative institutions' (Bochel 2013: 799), they also highlight, both historically and contemporarily, the pragmatic constraints placed upon such access by UK executives (see Judge 1978: 391–4).

There has been renewed interest in parliamentary petitioning since the introduction of e-petitioning systems in a number of legislatures in recent years (including, in the UK, the Scottish parliament, Welsh National Assembly, and, internationally, the German Bundestag, and in the Queensland and Tasmanian legislatures in Australia (see HC 513 2007: 17–18; Hough 2012: 485–6; Lindner and Riehm 2009)). The e-petitioning system adopted at UK level in August 2011 was not, however, a 'parliamentary system' as such. The Hansard Society (2012b: 7) has described the system as 'an usual hybrid, straddling a constitutional no-man's land: it is neither fully a parliamentary nor a government system'. As the Procedure Committee (HC 1706 2012: 5), in reviewing the new system, noted ruefully: 'It is worth noting ... that the petitions hosted on the Government's website are petitions to Government, and not to Parliament'.

The origins of this hybrid system can be traced back to the introduction of an e-petitioning website by the UK prime minister in 2006. Before its closure in 2010, by the incoming coalition government, the Number 10 website had accepted 33,058 e-petitions with over 12 million signatures (and rejected a further 38,263 petitions). When launching the website the Blair government had promised to respond to petitions with 200 signatures, which it did – but in a largely formulaic manner. A default response was often adopted, of 'signposting' the policy objectives of the government and the measures taken to achieve those objectives (Miller 2009: 165–7). Indeed, when 1.8 million signatures were attached to an e-petition opposing the government's proposals on road pricing in 2007, the PM's email response explained 'the problems the country faces and why I believe road charging is surely part of the answer here as it is in many other countries' (Blair 2007). The PM's hope (ultimately forlorn) was that: 'the more people understand the nature and scale of the problems, the more likely we will as a country reach the right decisions on the way forward'. In contrast, the Transport Minister, who was left with the difficult task of progressing the policy in the face of such tangible opposition, was less convinced of success but utterly convinced, reportedly, that 'whoever came up with this idea [of e-petitions] must be a prat' (*The Guardian* 17 February 2007).

Partly as a result of the experience of the Number 10 website and the antipathy of Gordon Brown as PM to his predecessor's e-petitions initiative, the Labour government after 2007 willingly encouraged proposals for the development of a parliamentary e-petitions system. It did so on the basis that 'it would be more appropriate for the House of Commons than for the Executive to be the forum to which many national petitions are presented' (Cm 7193 2007: 6; for the House of Commons proposals see HC 513 2007: 18–20; HC 136 2008: 14–17; HC 493 2009: 5–8; HC 1117 2009: 71–3). Underpinning the proposals developed within the House of Commons for the introduction of a parliamentary e-petitioning system was the elemental belief that 'Parliament should be the primary recipient of petitions from the public' (HC 513 2007: 18;

HC 136 2008: 14). The Conservative party's 2010 manifesto appeared to support this belief:

> People have been shut out of Westminster politics for too long ... So, with a Conservative government, any petition that secures 100,000 signatures will be eligible for formal debate in Parliament. The petition will enable members of the public to table a Bill eligible to be voted on in Parliament.

While the commitment on the tabling of bills was dropped, the debate trigger was subsequently included in the 'political reforms' listed in the coalition agreement (Cabinet Office 2010b: 27). In July 2011 the government announced that a new e-petitions website was to be launched on the DirectGov portal. The website duly went live on 4 August 2011 – and immediately crashed under the weight of 1,000 visitors per minute trying to access the site (*Financial Times*, 4 August 2011). In the first 17 months of its existence the e-petitions website received some 40,000 petitions with over eight million signatures (HC Debates 17 January 2013: col 1046), with 11 reaching the 100,000 signature threshold. Yet, despite parliamentary pressure, the government in 2013 still had not brought e-petitions 'fully in-House, so that people are aware that they are petitioning Parliament and not the Government' (Natasha Engel, Chair of the Backbench Business Committee HC Debates 17 January 2013). Indeed, this was symptomatic of the government's reluctance to engage with parliamentary authorities in devising, launching, and administering the scheme (see HC 1706 2012: Q29).

Yet the government's stated intention in introducing the e-petitions system was to build 'a bigger and stronger bridge between this house and those we represent' (HC Debates 11 January 2010: col 434). Moreover, it resolutely maintained later that 'e-petitions have been a success in building a bridge between people and Parliament' (HC 1902 2012: 1). Despite these assertions, parliamentarians were less convinced that the government-inspired e-petitions system had been an unalloyed success. Although, as noted above, the initial commitment, to the introduction of an 'initiative' process through the tabling of bills via e-petitions, was dropped, MPs still had reservations that the government was offering a 'false prospectus' in claiming, on the original DirectGov website, that 'e-petitions is an easy way for you to influence government policy in the UK' and that e-petitions with more than 100,000 signatures 'will be eligible for debate in the House'. As the Procedure Committee noted tersely, e-petitions 'are not, and should not be claimed to be, an easy way *to change* Government policy or legislation' (HC 1706 2012: 11 emphasis added). Moreover, there was no automaticity following from reaching the signature threshold and the scheduling of a debate in the Commons. On both counts, the Procedure Committee recommended a redrafting of the statements on purpose and possible outcomes – a recommendation that the government partially, and grudgingly, accepted when in 2012 it changed the wording on the DirectGov webpage to 'e-petitions are an easy, personal way for you to influence government and Parliament', and 'if you collect 100,000 signatures your e-petition could be debated in the House' (http://epetitions.direct.gov.uk).

Perhaps not surprisingly therefore the initial verdict on the e-petitioning system from beyond Westminster was that:

> If all that is sought is a 'finger in the wind' exercise to determine the depth of public feeling on a range of issues then the system meets this test. But it is not, in its current form, a means to empower them through greater engagement in the political and specifically parliamentary process and it affords only limited opportunity for deliberation on the issues raised. (Hansard Society 2012b: 9)

This echoed concerns within Westminster that: 'At the moment engagement is not engagement ... it is very one-sided' (HC 1706 2012: Q4). Of equal concern were 'process' deficiencies. These included: problems arising from indirect access and the fact that a debate on an e-petition could not be initiated solely on the volition of the Backbench Business Committee but also required an MP to request such a debate, and the ring-fencing of time in Westminster Hall for e-petition-inspired debates which, although it provided a 'time-allocation' solution, ran the 'risk that petitioners regard themselves as shunted off away from the main arena' (Hansard Society 2012b: 17) as well as simultaneously removing the possibility of holding a vote by confining debate to a simple 'take note' motion.

Such process deficiencies are not simply of technical concern but go to the heart of the petitioning process, for, as Carman (2010: 736 original emphasis) observes, 'the *process* by which petitions are considered is vitally important'. What matters above all is that the process is perceived to be 'politically neutral and potentially influential'. An assessment of the fairness of the petitioning process not only affects the petitioners' willingness to accept the outcomes of that process but also influences more broadly their perceptions of the efficacy of parliament as an institution (Carman 2014: 158). The danger for the e-petitioning process instituted by the coalition government was that it 'may leave petitioners feeling that their participation is not valued' or that, for petitions that fall below the signature threshold, 'petitioners may justifiably feel that their participation is a waste of their time' (Bochel 2013: 804). The further danger, following from Carman's research, is that these negative perceptions of the petitions process might well spill over into perceptions of the efficacy of the UK parliament more broadly.

Carman's data was derived from the experience of the e-petitioning system introduced by the Scottish parliament in 2004. The Welsh National Assembly also introduced an e-petitions system in 2008. Both allowed petitioners (from anywhere in the world) direct access to the legislature on any matter within the competence of the respective parliament/assembly. Both processed petitions through Public Petitions Committees, which have broad-ranging powers to seek information from devolved governments, to refer a petition to ministers, to report to the parliament/assembly, to request a debate in the chamber, or 'to take any other action which the committee considers appropriate' (Scottish Parliament standing order 15.6; National Assembly of Wales standing order 28.8). Both devolved legislatures believe that their petitioning processes have resulted in greater engagement of the public with their activities, greater public awareness of their representative roles, and greater impact on public policies (see National Assembly of Wales 2012: 12; Scottish Parliament 2013: 5; see also Bochel 2013: 805). Yet Carman's detailed analysis of the Scottish petitioning system reaches a more cautious assessment of the achievements of the e-petitioning process. He concluded that, in terms of public engagement, 'surprisingly few people in Scotland actually claim to know anything about the Scottish Parliament's public petitions system', and overall 'it seems that the unique experiment in public engagement may not have lived up to expectations' (Carman 2014: 152; see also Carman 2010: 747). Moreover, while many petitioners in Scotland, after their experience of the petitioning process, retained a belief in the fairness of that system, they also reported 'high levels of belief that their petitions did not receive due consideration' (Carman 2010: 741).

In addition to the e-petition systems introduced by the UK parliament, the Scottish Parliament, and the Welsh National Assembly, e-petitioning systems have been developed at local authority level. In England in 2004 Bristol City Council and the London Borough of Kingston upon Thames piloted online petitioning systems alongside their traditional written petitioning procedures, and these pilots were later extended to a number of other local authorities (see Panagiotopoulos and Elliman 2012: 86–7). Indeed, as part of its 'empowerment agenda' the Labour government's 2008 White Paper *Communities in Control* (Cm 7427 2008: 65) proposed a new duty for councils to respond to petitions and to take them into account in decision-making. While the government was 'not proposing government by petitions, nor are we suggesting that the role of elected representatives in taking difficult decisions should be undermined', it did believe 'that stronger petition powers will enable more people to have their voice heard and help elected representatives do their jobs better' (Cm 7427 2008: 64). The Local Democracy, Economic Development and Construction Act 2009 subsequently included requirements for English and Welsh local authorities to 'make, publicise and comply with a scheme for handling both paper and electronic petitions', to acknowledge, to respond, and to debate petitions and call certain officers to account if a signature threshold was reached. One obvious democratic incongruity was that central government sought to impose upon other democratically elected tiers of local government a requirement to introduce and maintain a system where 'power is exercised by citizens ... directly through petitions' (Cm 7427 2008: 14).

A further, subsequent, incongruity arose when the coalition government, which had the avowed objective of promoting decentralisation and democratic engagement (Cabinet Office 2010b: 11), used the Localism Act 2011 (Section 46) to repeal the Local Democracy, Economic Development and Construction Act 2009 and its provisions for mandatory e-petitions schemes. In the event, even after the 2011 Act, many local authorities continued to maintain e-petition schemes, in part because the start-up costs had already been met and it was relatively cost-free to maintain electronic access for petitioners, and in part also because, even under the mandatory schemes, the impact of petitioning was at best mixed and normally limited. There appeared to be little enthusiasm for those schemes either on the part of local authorities or on the part of citizens. Thus, in a detailed study of 353 local authority websites in 2011, Panagiotopoulos *et al.* (2011: 212) discovered that most local authorities had 'allocated the minimum possible effort and resources' needed to comply with the 2009 Act; and that citizens had seemingly reciprocated by submitting very few petitions. Indeed, over 75 per cent of local authority websites recorded no petitions (either open or closed) (Panagiotopoulos and Elliman 2012: 88).

Overall, the experiences of e-petitioning in the UK reveal a series of incongruities. Comparative analysis of e-petitioning suggests that it 'represents a safe "playing field" from the perspective of established political institutions' inasmuch as e-petition systems are 'highly compatible with the principles of representative democracy, and [their] transformative potential is very moderate' (Lindner and Riehm 2009: 10). In the UK, the restricted transformative potential of e-petitions at national level has certainly been acknowledged. Bochel (2013: 804), for example, has concluded that e-petitions 'afford citizens with the opportunity to air their views, but with little or no "real" participation or empowerment'. On the other hand, while the 'safety' of e-petitions for representative institutions remains largely unquestioned in principle, in practice 'process issues', in Carman's terms, may pose dangers for representative institutions in the UK. Thus, at the UK level, an e-petitioning system was introduced with the stated purpose of 'bridging the gap between the House and the country' (Leader of the House, HC Debates 2 December 2010: col 977), but which interposed a government entry portal and an executive filtering process between parliament and the people. Once access had been gained, the Commons' procedures for processing e-petitions, most notably in the requirement for an MP to sponsor debate in the House and in the timetabling restrictions placed upon debates on petitions, led to widespread criticism – including thousands of 'angry e-petitioners sending emails' to the Chair of the Backbench Business Committee (see HC 1706 2012: Q5). Potentially, therefore, the greatest incongruity is that a system designed to enhance public engagement with parliament might 'risk reputational damage to the House of Commons ... and an exacerbation of public disillusionment with the political system in the long-term' (Hansard Society 2012b: 5). Moreover, the statutory imposition of an e-petitioning system on elected local authority representatives by elected UK government representatives, in the Local Democracy etc. 2009 Act, and the almost instant reversal of that requirement in the Localism Act 2011 points to the further incongruity of one democratic tier of government determining the nature of e-petitioning linkages at a lower level tier of government through executive fiat.

e-democracy

The discussion of e-petitions serves as an introduction for a broader consideration of e-democracy, if for no other reason than e-petitions have been adjudged to be 'the closest the UK has come to implementing any form of e-democratic facility at the national level' (Millard *et al.* 2012: 2); and that the Number 10 e-petition website, in particular, has been identified as 'one of the most successful e-democracy projects of all time' (Chadwick 2009: 33). E-democracy itself is a nebulous term and may include, variously, notions of e-participation, e-campaigning, e-voting, e-consultation, and crowdsourcing, with some commentators also willing to include aspects of e-government (when ICT is used to enhance the transparency and accountability of governing institutions beyond simple improvement and facilitation of service delivery). From early utopian, often deterministic, claims that new information technologies would serve to 'revolutionise' political and social interactions, more cautious assessments of 'politics as usual' or of a 'normalized revolution' came to temper these initial claims (for an overview see Wright 2012). Indeed, the concept of 'normalized revolution' usefully captures the complexity of the relationship between technological innovation and democratic practices. On the one hand, the internet has brought about significant behavioural changes in how citizens interact with each other and with political institutions; on the other hand, however, social and political power relationships have not been fundamentally restructured. As Wright (2012: 253 original emphasis) suggests: 'The key factor with a normalized revolution is, thus, that significant power still rests with elected representatives, but that new technology can help to create stronger *representative* democracy'. Importantly, in this perspective, the effects of technological change are conditional: they may serve to enhance democratic processes, but their actual impacts are uncertain. While interactive, digital media have a potential to facilitate communication and more direct modes of participation, ultimately that 'potential is vulnerable' (Coleman and Blumler 2009: 11). At present, the capacity of citizens 'to make a difference through the public expression and debate of arguments' and 'to arrive at legitimate, fair and consequential resolutions' leaves the democratic potential of ICT both unfulfilled and assailable (Coleman and Blumler 2012: 147–8).

Not surprisingly, the deliberative potential of electronic communication, particularly in its 'web 2.0' form, have attracted the attention of deliberative democrats (see for example Fishkin 2009: 169–75). Indeed, Chadwick (2009: 14) maintains that 'the ideal of the deliberative public sphere is probably the most influential concept in the scholarly writing on e-democracy'. Conceptually, e-democracy affords a space, occasionally referred to as a 'third space' (Chadwick 2009: 30; Wright 2011: 254–5), for online discussion. Such a virtual space allows for asynchronous discussion across time and spatial borders in 'arenas of virtual co-presence' (Coleman and Blumler 2009: 28). The inherent macro-deliberative nature of such open, unregulated cyberspace appeared initially to offer the prospect of the realisation of something approximating to a Habermasian 'public sphere'. Yet a public sphere in this sense continued to be unrealised in the web 2.0 era (Chadwick 2009: 13–14; Papacharissi 2009: 236–7). At one level, social networking sites and discussion forums appear to offer the opportunity for relatively open, flexible, self-governing, autonomous, and unconstrained 'conversations' to occur. Although often focused on 'everyday' social interactions, rather than directly or specifically focused on political discussion, nonetheless these sites provide 'space' for 'political talk'. Indeed, analysis of such informal discussion of political issues in online 'non-political' forums suggests that 'where it occurs it is largely deliberative in nature' (Wright 2012: 8; Graham 2008: 32). At another level, and paradoxically, however, these deliberative interactions take place within 'a private media environment located within the individual's personal and private space' (of individual Facebook pages, Twitter accounts, blogs, or atomised online discussion forums) (Papacharissi 2009: 244). Papacharissi goes so far as to characterise such interactions as 'civically motivated narcissism', whereby political engagement is framed in a private sphere of self-reflection, expression, and behaviour.

The challenge for e-democrats is twofold: first, how 'to interpret and integrate the distributed deliberation already taking place online' into broader public interactions and public discourses, and, second, how to find ways 'of acknowledging and representing these discourses ... in policy formation, and political decision-making' (Moss and Coleman 2013: 15). This second, more delimited, challenge has tended to preoccupy decision-makers rather than the broader macro-deliberative aspirations associated with the first challenge. The future ambition remains to link 'third space' discourses with 'the resources and power invested in representative institutions, [to] link civic society with the political sphere' and to do so in a manner 'beyond just a crude and reductive vision of democracy as majoritarian head counting' (Moss and Coleman 2013: 15). The present reality, however, is somewhat different. Comparative studies have revealed that electronic linkage between citizens and representative institutions tends towards the 'crude and reductive' pole of the e-democratic spectrum – in its unidirectionality and its informative rather than interactive nature – rather than the sophisticated and engaged pole (see for example Griffith and Leston-Bandeira 2012: 510; Ostling 2012: 297). Studies of the electronic linkage of citizens and decision makers in the UK likewise have pointed to the fact that 'web 2.0 has not revolutionised the representative process' (Jackson and Lilleker 2009: 259; see also Davidson and Elstub 2013: 14).

Elected representatives and the internet

Studies of electronic connectivity between elected representatives and citizens in the UK have tended to reveal limited interactivity and restricted citizen engagement in representative processes and institutions. This is so at local level (Pratchett 2012: 125–6) and national level (Williamson 2009: 6), but marginally less so at sub-national level (particularly in Scotland) where e-democratic initiatives have gained more traction than elsewhere in the UK (see Seaton 2005). In the specific case of linkage between MPs and citizens, while there has been willingness, both individually and collectively, on the part of representatives to explore ICT opportunities the emphasis has been upon reinforcement of existing interactions rather than a recalibration of the representative relationship. In fact, MPs still retain a preference for the web 1.0 platform of email when interacting with their constituents. Email usage by MPs is ubiquitous and, although inward communication is enhanced by email, MPs still privilege its outward communication and information dissemination aspects (see Norton 2012: 414–15; Williamson *et al*. 2010: 17). Even so, web 2.0 usage has increased rapidly, to the extent that by early 2013 the vast majority of Westminster MPs had a web presence with, for example, only 5 per cent of Labour MPs not having a website. Perhaps in recognition of the growing importance of MPs' websites an e-petition was launched in February 2013 calling for the 'centralisation' of MPs' websites to facilitate ease of access for the public (http://epetitions. direct.gov.uk/petitions/45638). Yet successive studies have shown that MPs tend to use websites 'to disseminate material rather than encourage a dialogue with constituents' (Norton 2012: 145, 2013: 276). In this respect, as Griffith and Leston-Bandeira (2012: 503) note, parliamentarian websites are 'essentially one-way modes of communication'.

Whereas web 1.0 platforms are at the passive end of web-based media, web 2.0 platforms, including blogs, social network sites, and Twitter, have been identified as 'an important new frontier' (Williamson 2009: 6) for interaction between representative and represented. Web 2.0 applications allow for greater citizen connection with politicians' online presences (Jackson and Lilleker 2009: 238). Thus blogs, for example, provide elected representatives not only with an electronic voice to amplify their opinions, but also with a means for citizens to respond and echo their own voices through feedback posts. Yet surveys of local politicians in 2007 revealed that less than 5 per cent of councillors chose to blog, and, when they did, they had little idea about who their audience was, in part because they received very few posts in response. Even when feedback posts were received they were often ignored (Wright 2009: 162–4). Similarly, at the UK level, MPs' use of blogs has been limited, with fewer than one in ten blogging in 2008 and with only 42 MPs (6 per cent) identified as having 'sticky' blogs (in the sense of evident updating of these blogs (Jackson and Lilleker 2009: 244)). While the number of MP bloggers increased after the 2010 election, blogging remained a minority activity at Westminster (Norton 2012: 415). As a medium of interaction, blogging conformed to the top-down, one-way self-promotional pattern observable in web 1.0 platforms. In essence, although blogging provides MPs with a platform to address a wide virtual audience, 'there is limited evidence that they listen to what is said to them in reply' (Jackson and Lilleker 2009: 258). In part, this is because of negative perceptions of blogs held by some MPs. The unregulated realm of the blogosphere holds reputational dangers for MPs, with scope for virtual abuse and personal attacks from citizens; as well as holding a potential for the amplification of basic 'yah-boo' partisan tribalism (see Williamson 2009: 18). At least one MP, however, was prepared to accept such dangers in the more positive spirit that: 'we live in the age of anti-politics and as politicians we isolate ourselves in the Westminster bubble and we get what we deserve and the internet brings it home to us ... blogs are probably a much more accurate reflection on what people actually think' (quoted in Williamson 2009: 18).

Beyond blogs, MPs have been more receptive to participation in social networking sites (such as Facebook, Myspace, and Bebo) and to the use of Twitter. Indeed, the number of MPs with Twitter accounts rose rapidly from 10 per cent in 2009 to 62 per cent in early 2013 (68 per cent of Labour MPs and 56 per cent of Conservative MPs (http://tweetminster.co.uk/mps)). While the number of tweeting MPs has increased significantly, the efficacy of their tweeting activities has been questioned. A survey of usage in September 2013 concluded, for instance, that not only was there a wide disparity of usage among MPs but there was also a massive difference in the success rates of individual MPs in attracting followers (Parliament Street 2013). Whereas the average number of followers was 6,624 per MP, for the top ten MP tweeters the average was 32,269 followers, with Labour MP Tom Watson amassing over 130,000 by late-2013. However, in comparison with other prominent public figures, the average number of followers for MPs has been adjudged to be 'dismally low' (Parliament Street 2012).

In common with many other users of Twitter, MPs' tweets serve largely for 'impression management' through self-promotion (Jackson and Lilleker 2011: 97–8). Self-promotion often conveys the implicit message: 'look at me, I'm working really hard' (Jackson and Lilleker 2011: 100). Yet the most effective parliamentarian tweeters combine such strategic narcissism with humour and insights into their personal 'hinterland' beyond their formal political activities. Importantly, active MP tweeters are also more prone to value the interactivity of Twitter and the opportunities of engaging in 'authentic conversations' with their followers. Indeed, some analysts are willing to declare already that, through the use of Twitter, '[w]e can see citizens inter-acting with their MPs and trust being re-established' (Margaretten and Gaber 2012). Others express hopes that microblogs such as Twitter may yet 'incorporate a more participatory platform of engagement' (Jackson and Lilleker 2011: 101). However, given the experience of ICT usage by MPs to date, such hopes may yet prove to be wishful thinking. Nonetheless, there is an almost missionary zeal on the part of some of the most active MP tweeters to demonstrate the scope for two-way interaction, engagement, and authentic conversations between representatives and the represented. In this they share in Coleman and Blumler's (2009: 38 original emphasis) less than revolutionary ambition 'to settle *for more deliberative democracy*'. A 'more deliberative democracy' would factor the fragmentary and informal conversations conducted via Twitter and social networking into the broader consultative and epistemic networks of routine governmental decision-making.

Representative institutions and the internet

Beyond the use of web 2.0 platforms by individual representatives, representative institutions in the UK have been proactive in developing their online presence. The UK parliament has professionalised its web and social media activities through the work of the Parliament Web and Intranet Service (WIS). The House of Commons' Corporate Business Plan 2012–13 to 2014–15 (House of Commons 2012: 29) identified as a key priority '[giving] the public the information needed to understand and appreciate the work of the House and its Members, to engage constructively and to have an input into parliamentary processes'. In terms of disseminating information about its activities as they happen, through its Facebook, Twitter, Flickr, and YouTube pages and podcasts via iTunes, the UK parliament has been 'ahead of the game compared to many legislatures across the globe' (Hansard Society 2010b: 6). In terms of 'constructive engagement', however, the UK parliament has not been at the forefront of developing a coherent and interactive strategy for consultation of, and deliberation with, citizens.

Although there was a brief flurry of committee-based e-consultations in the 2005–10 parliament there was little evidence thereafter of public engagement through online forums. One notable exception was the online forum used as part of the Justice Committee's investigation into court language services in 2012 (though this was as much an effort to encourage 'stakeholders' to submit evidence under the anonymity afforded by non-identifiable user names as it was an attempt to involve the public in the committee's deliberations). The Education Committee conducted an online consultation in 2011, in association with an external student website, on youth services; and used its Twitter feed in 2012 (#AskGove) to 'crowdsource' questions for a scrutiny session with the Education Secretary, Michael Grove (HC 1786-I 2012). Some 5,000 tweets were received. This latter exercise was deemed to be 'one of the most successful question crowdsourcing exercises ever carried out on twitter in the UK' (HC 697 2012: Ev w72). In April 2013 the Energy and Climate Change Committee used its twitter feed to source questions from the public in its inquiry into Energy Prices, Profits and Poverty. Nonetheless, as noted above in relation to e-petitions, the expectations of the public as to the impact of such electronic engagement exercises upon parliamentary outputs might be at variance with the practical limitations imposed by parliamentary procedure, intra-institutional rivalries and inter-institutional processes (Coleman and Blumler 2009: 97; HC 697 2012: Ev w66). The incongruity remains, therefore, that the potential of parliamentary electronic engagement with citizens still exceeds the practice (Norton 2012: 417).

In addition to parliamentary sponsored e-democracy initiatives, a number of external 'parliamentary informatics' projects – designed to improve the accountability and transparency of representative institutions – have also been initiated (for an overview see Ostling 2012). One of the most prominent informatics projects in the UK has been TheyWorkForYou (TWFY). The TWFY website (http://www.theyworkforyou.com/) provides an intuitive searchable interface to debates, public bills, and questions and statements in the UK parliament (coverage of proceedings in the Northern Ireland Assembly has been less comprehensive, and has been non-existent for the National Assembly of Wales and also, since 2011, for the Scottish Parliament). The UK site is interactive to the extent that it allows for the annotation of MPs' speeches and reproduces citizens' comments alongside the original speeches. In turn, other citizens are able to make further comments on the annotations. In essence such sites are 'monitorial', providing the citizenry with ready access to data and information about the activities of their representatives with which to evaluate their performance. In this monitory form, parliamentary transparency might be enhanced by parliamentary informatics (see Hazell *et al.* 2012: 907), but there is no guarantee of enhanced interactivity. Indeed, as Ostling (2012: 297) concludes, there are few observable instances of parliamentary informatics projects, including TWFY, having 'any impact' in terms of parliamentary responsiveness or of MPs' closer interaction with citizens (see also Moss and Coleman 2013: 9).

Political parties and the internet

The common theme running through the discussion in this chapter thus far, of the seemingly exponential potential for web-based citizen engagement yet the limited realisation of that potential in practice, continues to be threaded through empirical analyses of the ICT strategies of the major UK political parties. UK parties have avidly adopted digital media both as internal organisational and management tools to connect party leaders to networks of members and supporters (see Williamson 2010: 58) and as tools for more differentiated and professionalised marketing and for campaign mobilisation (Gibson 2013: 2). Successive studies have revealed that the major parties in the UK have used the internet primarily for promotional purposes, and have created 'interactive spaces' to the limited extent of enabling members to join, donate, download information resources, participate in polls, or link to associated social networks. What these studies tend to confirm is that the adoption of web 2.0 tools by political parties to facilitate 'some new kind of interactive, discursive [relationship with citizens] can be discounted' (Lee 2012: 11; see also Lilleker and Jackson 2010; Lilleker *et al.* 2010: 111). After the 2010 UK election Lilleker and Jackson (2010: 93) concluded that the campaign did 'not support evidence of a clear win-win zone where politically interested people can engage with parties. Rather, what exists at present is a share-share zone, where the process of communication exists, but the results do not yet justify any significant changes'. Gibson's (2013: 8) research also found that in the 2010 campaign 'parties were more likely to offer [web] tools for supporters to cooperate in distribution of the party message rather than its creation'. Overall therefore not only have the major UK parties deployed the interactive features of web applications to varying degrees, they have done so more sparingly than other major parties in EU states (Lilleker and Jackson 2010: 89). In large part this a reflection of the organisational hierarchies of the major UK parties (noted in Chapter 3). Party leaders have been unwilling to relinquish control over the formulation of party policies, the dissemination of the party message, and the management of election campaigns. In this respect electronic 'interaction with the wider public cannot override the importance of the formal internal policy making processes [of political parties]' (Lilleker *et al.* 2010: 111).

Crowdsourcing

As noted above, there have been a few notable examples of the use of 'crowdsourcing' by House of Commons committees to inform their scrutiny of departmental activities. Yet 'crowdsourcing' in its original meaning was a mode of decentralised decision-making. As the originator of the term noted:

> A diverse group of problem solvers will almost always beat a homogeneous group of problem solvers ... And when you have a crowd, because you have the power of large numbers, there are times that taken as a whole, they excel because they are trying so many different things all at once. (Howe 2008)

The attraction of such an approach for UK central government was that it held out the prospect of decentralised information-gathering and consultation, leading to enhanced deliberation and the identification of preferred solutions. Whereas consultations conducted through online platforms do not differ fundamentally from traditional consultation exercises, crowdsourcing exercises hold the potential for greater deliberation and 'authentic conversation' online (Lodge and Wegrich 2012: 8). In the run-up to the 2010 general election the Conservative party observed: 'In the post-bureaucratic age, new technologies make it easier than ever before to involve the public in the legislative process and harness the wisdom of crowds to improve legislation and spot potential problems before a Bill is implemented. This is a Big Society approach to improving legislation' (Conservative Party 2010). It was little surprise, therefore, that immediately after the election the coalition government launched two crowdsourcing or 'smart crowd' websites: *Your Freedom* (Gov.uk 2010) and *Spending Challenge* (HM Treasury 2010).

The *Your Freedom* website offered the opportunity for members of the public to suggest ideas on restoring lost civil liberties, repealing 'unnecessary laws', and reducing the regulation of businesses and charities. The *Spending Challenge* website encouraged members of the public, along with public sector employees, to submit 'ideas on how government could spend money more effectively, how it could save money by stopping some activities, and where it could reduce waste by taking practical steps to improve efficiency'. Both websites promised that users would be able 'to comment on and rate their favourite ideas and relevant departments [would] then respond to the most popular workable ideas' (Gov.uk 2010). The *Your Freedom* website received over 15,000 individual proposals. The *Spending Challenge* website received 48,000 suggestions from the public and over 63,000 from public sector workers, with 8 per cent and 46 per cent of responses respectively being deemed 'non-compliant' by the Treasury. While these initial exercises attracted a significant public response, the extent to which they conformed to the initial conception of 'crowdsourcing' or of 'smart crowds' has been questioned. First, the logic of crowdsourcing dissipates when confronted by issues that are 'complex and inescapably eristic' (Moss and Coleman 2013: 13) – in fact, precisely the type of issues under consideration in *Your Freedom* and *Spending Challenge*. Not surprisingly, therefore, Moss and Coleman (2013: 13) maintain that these issues were not suitable for crowdsourcing; and that the simple ranking of ideas in a limited consultative exercise did not meet the deliberative and conversational aspirations of e-democrats.

Following from the *Your Freedom* and *Spending Challenge* exercises, a more ambitious attempt at crowdsourcing was instigated by the Cabinet Office in April 2011. This was the *Red Tape Challenge* (RTC). The accompanying website announced that: 'This site is designed to promote open discussion of ways in which the aims of existing regulation can be fulfilled in the least burdensome way possible' (Cabinet Office 2011b). The first phase of the RTC, from April 2011 until March 2013, saw the publication – in phased 'spotlight' sequences – of regulations grouped into 28 themes. The views of members of the public were then sought as 'to which regulations are working, which are not, what should be scrapped, what should be simplified, and what can be done differently'. At the end of the 'spotlight' period the responsible departments were required to respond by collating and analysing the public responses. Proposals for scrapping, reducing, or improving regulations were then produced before being subjected to intra-departmental and extra-departmental 'challenges' (for details of the process see Cabinet Office 2012). Without assessing the impact of RTC on the regulatory profile of central government, it is worth noting, in accordance with Moss and Coleman's observations, that the logic of crowdsourcing for more intelligence and more deliberation was undermined by the framing of the issue and by the limits of the consultative process. The issue was framed in terms of 'getting rid of unnecessary red tape' with crowdsourcing being viewed by the designers of RTC as a means of unleashing popular frustration with regulation and burdensome legislation. In the event, however, most of the posted comments in the first phase of RTC were broadly more in favour of keeping regulations than of scrapping them (Lodge and Wegrich 2012: 18–19). Yet still the coalition government persisted with its commitment 'to abolish or reduce at least 3,000 of the 6,500 substantive regulations being examined by the Red Tape Challenge' (Cabinet Office 2013). Crowdsourcing did not legitimate this persistence. Instead, the political agenda within the coalition government drove the process of regulatory change. The outcome was little influenced by 'deliberation' between 'the crowd' and decision makers in Whitehall. In fact, there was 'very little evidence of deliberation [even as] defined in the minimal sense of someone responding to another message' (Lodge and Wegrich 2012: 21). At best Lodge and Wegrich's (2012: 21) analysis reveals that 'in many ways the crowdsourcing exercise resembled more traditional consultation exercises ... However, in some ways, the [RTC] exercise proved to be worse than analogue consultation exercises as [public posts] were largely anonymous and ill-targeted'. As with other crowdsourcing initiatives deployed by the coalition government the deliberative potential of RTC, and the propagation of extensive participatory problem-solving networks, remained unfulfilled.

Conclusion

The 'problem' of citizen participation in representative democracy is not simply that there is too little, as critics of the exclusionary DNA of electoral representation claim, but that 'democratic innovations', when implanted within this genetic frame, have their participatory stem cells transmuted. The 'problem', therefore, is not a lack of theorisation of citizen participation or a failure of political will to enact participatory and deliberative initiatives. In fact, as this chapter has revealed, there has been a proliferation of 'democratic innovations', ranging from deliberative experiments with citizens' juries, citizens' surveys, deliberative forums, and mini-publics, through direct citizen involvement in the use of referendums, to ICT-facilitated modes of e-participation, e-petitions, and electronic linkage of non-electoral and electoral processes and institutions of representation. All of these have been designed to enhance citizen participation, to supplement, or to complement existing aggregative modes of electoral representation. Yet, if the underpinning theories of these democratic innovations are, in essence, theories of democratic legitimacy – legitimacy derived variously from processes of deliberation, or unmediated citizen participation, or from the wisdom of electronic crowds – they directly confront the legitimation claims of elected representatives. It is one thing to assert that democratic innovations 'expand' representative democracy; it is another to demonstrate that this is the case when these 'ideas are in action'.

A basic contention of this chapter has been that notions of expanding/enhancing representative democracy give rise to a series of ideational and practical incongruities. In the case of deliberative innovations their legitimation claims ultimately distil into the incongruous proposition that, to address the shortcomings of the electoral representative system, citizens are required to act in some sense as representatives of other citizens. Yet, when located on the conceptual terrain of representation, deliberative innovations are confronted with the same legitimation dilemmas faced by other forms of non-electoral representation. If deliberation is deemed of importance primarily for its processual impacts, then this dilemma may be sidestepped by claiming that public policy impact is a second-order consideration. If, however, deliberative processes are to be connected to the 'main game politically', to have 'consequential' impacts on public policy, then the democratic incongruities of representation, authorisation and accountability inherent within those processes become manifest. As argued above, in the 'main game' of public policy decision-making, talk-centric deliberative theory is ultimately dependent upon vote-centric representative practice to legitimate its outputs.

Similarly, in the case of popular participation through referendums, theories of unmediated citizen engagement become rapidly entangled in mediated processes and institutions of representative democracy. Experience in the UK has revealed the incongruity that, far from providing evidence of modes of unmediated participation, referendums reveal starkly the constricting force of mediated institutions and processes of electoral representation. Thus, although conceived as 'supplements' to existing representative processes and institutions, referendums become subsumed, and so changed, by those processes and institutions.

The inclusion–exclusion paradox of representative democracy captures the institutionalised self-exclusion of the bulk of the population from systematic involvement in decision-making, yet this paradox also finds reflection in analyses of the participatory credentials of e-democracy. On the one hand, e-democracy holds the potential to facilitate communicative interaction, popular deliberation, and more direct modes of political participation and so, in Wright's words noted above, to 'create stronger representative democracy'. Democratic theorists thus hold out the beguiling prospect of linking 'third space discourses' to the macro-deliberative frame provided by electoral representation. On the other hand, however, experience of e-democracy has led to a scaling down of the democratic ambitions of the technological revolution to a 'normalised political revolution': where the exclusionary 'normality' of representative democracy overrides the inclusionary 'revolutionary' potential of e-participation. If anything, the creation of virtual, deliberative 'third spaces' and the rapidity of information flows and opinion formation through social media reinforces the exclusionary tendencies of representative democracy. These spaces remain largely decoupled and delinked from electoral processes of representation and formal representative institutions designed 'to couple' and 'to link' citizens to decision makers. In this sense, e-democracy comes to reflect the exclusionary tendencies of 'actually-existing' representative democracy.

7
The 'Problem' of 'Post-': Post-Representative, Post-Parliamentary, Post-Democracy

Introduction

The multi-national UK state has provided the territorial focus for the analysis of representative democracy in this book. Indeed, the complex linkages between nations and state in the UK have long found reflection in the term 'multi-level governance', both in the practice of representative democracy and in academic discourse. Equally, however, the term points to other complex linkages, not only within the state (to interactions with non-electoral representatives beyond the electoral arena), but also to linkages beyond the state (to networks of supranational institutions, international organisations, and the trans-border interconnections of civil society organisations and social movements). These linkages and interconnections have not gone unnoticed in earlier chapters of this book: in the expanding electoral marketplace of elections for sub-national, national, and supra-national representative institutions (Chapter 2); in the intricacies of party systems in the UK, and the multi-level strategies of civil society organisations and social movements and the trans-boundary nature of many of their non-electoral representative claims (Chapter 3); in the challenges posed to the Westminster model by notions of network governance, differentiated polity, and asymmetric power, and in the confrontation of legal notions of parliamentary sovereignty by the daily practice of decision-making in the broader context of devolution and the European Union (Chapter 5); and in the expansion of spatially liberated 'democratic innovations' and e-democracy (Chapter 6). However, the 'problem' to be considered in this chapter is the extent to which these developments undermine 'old expressions of representative democracy' (Bevir 2010: 2).

At its extreme, the problem posed is whether representative democracy has been undermined to the extent that 'it is difficult to dignify it as democracy itself' (Crouch 2004: 21) and that 'post-democracy', 'post-parliamentary democracy', or 'post-representative democracy' provide more accurate descriptors of UK democracy in the 21st century. In posing the problem in this manner, and in searching for answers to this question, a fundamental incongruity is exposed in so far as representative democracy as a normative frame and as an institutional system is not replaced, but rather is displaced, in 'a move beyond democracy' (Crouch 2004: 20). In this 'move', electoral representation – as process and institutional form – continues to provide formal legitimation of state outputs, but is 'supplemented', yet simultaneously and incongruously 'degraded', by informal non-electoral modes and institutions of representation.

Post-democracy

'Post-democracy' as conceived by Crouch is an exaggeration. In specifying post-democracy as a polar opposite of active public participation Crouch's (2004: 4) declared intention is to include 'enough elements [that] are recognizable in contemporary politics to make it worth while asking where our political life stands on a scale [between these poles]'. In answering this question his basic contention is that 'we are moving towards the post-democratic pole'.

Post-democracy is characterised by complexity: it is 'post-' in the sense that 'strong traces' of pre-existing democratic modes and institutions remain, but, at the same time, 'something new has come into existence' and, hence, post-democracy is different from these democratic residues (Crouch 2004: 20). It is not 'non-democracy' or 'anti-democracy' because of the continued linkages between politicians and citizens. In fact, the formal electoral institutions and components of democracy survive virtually intact within post-democracy. Thus, elections 'certainly exist and can change governments', but most citizens play only a 'passive, quiescent, even apathetic part' in politics (2004: 4). Faced with growing voter apathy and declining public engagement with political parties, politicians have sought, incongruously, to encourage 'the maximum level of minimal participation' (2004: 112). Yet, behind this 'spectacle of the electoral game', public policies are made 'in private by interaction between elected governments and elites' (2004: 4). Hence, 'while the forms of democracy remain fully in place – and today in some respects are actually strengthened – politics and government are increasingly slipping back into the control of privileged elites in the manner characteristic of pre-democratic times' (2004: 6). Crouch expects, therefore, further 'entropy of democracy' (2004: 12).

Crouch's basic argument is that 'post-democracy' has arrived and cannot be reversed, but that it should not simply be accepted. At one (political) level elected decision makers are now subject to increased scrutiny, greater transparency, and less deference from citizens and the media, and as a result are 'so worried about the views of a subtle and complex electorate that they have to devote enormous resources to discovering what it thinks, and then respond anxiously to it' (2004: 13). Indeed, demands for more open government and constitutional reform, designed to enhance government responsibility to the people, have had an impact. Furthermore, the activities of social movements and civil society organisations, and the deliberative opportunities provided by the internet, alongside the contemporary importance ascribed to non-electoral representative claims, all point to 'a far richer democracy' (2004: 15).

Offsetting these 'political' gains, however, has been an economic imperative of 'economic globalization', wherein large corporations have often outgrown the governance capacity of individual nation states. Increasingly, 'the global firm' has become the 'key institution of the post-democratic world' (2004: 30). In somewhat deterministic mode, Crouch (2004: 122) maintains that 'the claims made by global firms that they will not be able to operate profitably unless freed from regulations and subordination to criteria of welfare and redistribution will continue to trump all polite democratic debate'. Indeed, he identifies the growing political power of the firm as accelerating the advance of post-democracy. As concentrations of power, firms (and their associated corporate elites) not only dominate the economy but also come to 'dominate the running of government' (2004: 44). In this politico-economic world, post-democratic politics 'is neither *representative*, nor *participatory*, nor indeed *responsible*. On the contrary, the post-democratic fusion of populism and corporate dictates gives rise to highly irresponsible government' (Blühdorn 2007: 308 original emphasis).

Nonetheless, Crouch holds out the hope that the entropy of democracy (which at various points he describes as 'inevitable') can be countered in a 'new disruptive creativity' (2004: 116) fashioned in a 'vigorous, chaotic, noisy context of movements and groups' (2004: 120). Yet if this is the 'main hope for the future' (2004: 116), the institutional residues of the past cannot be ignored because, as Crouch (2004: 114) concedes, 'support for cause movements cannot replace the political party'. Nor for that matter are electoral institutions replaced. Indeed, in the face of 'difficult and disruptive new demands' raised by movements and groups, elected politicians continue to assert that 'they themselves constitute the embodiment of democratic choice' (2004: 116). Therein lies the incongruity, for if, as Crouch maintains (2004: 122), 'post-democratic politics works through lobbies', then it is electoral institutions (primarily at national level and in the form of political executives) that are still being lobbied by global firms and civil society movements and organisations alike (admittedly with asymmetrical outcomes).

Post-parliamentary democracy

Several of the general tendencies identified in the discussion of 'post-democracy' had earlier informed the discussion of 'post-parliamentary democracy' in Britain. Among the earliest and the most insistent proponents of the view that the British policy process was best conceived as being 'non-parliamentary' were Jordan and Richardson. Their description of the segmentation of policy-making and the development of policy communities residualised electoral representation and led them to conclude that 'the traditional model of cabinet and party government is a travesty of reality' (Richardson and Jordan 1979: 191). Throughout their joint work, therefore, Jordan and Richardson contrasted the 'clear-cut and traditional principles of parliamentary and party government' (Richardson and Jordan 1979: 74), 'traditional notions of democracy, accountability and parliamentary sovereignty' (Jordan and Richardson 1987: 288), and 'traditional notions of parliamentary and electoral democracy' (Jordan and Richardson 1987: 289) with the reality and practice of governance in Britain. In so setting this practice against the theory of parliamentary democracy Richardson and Jordan characterised the British system of government as 'post-parliamentary'. Indeed, this characterisation came to find reflection in other important commentaries (see for example Marquand 1988: 182–6), with other pioneering UK network analysts also identifying the claims of 'self-authorised' networks 'to make policy free from the "irritating" constraint of political, especially electoral, legitimacy' (Rhodes and Marsh 1992c: 200). Since the time of these early studies 'the increased political science focus on governance, policy communities and networks' has, in the view of Jordan at least, only served to confirm that 'the parliamentary focus is further marginalised' (Jordan and Cairney 2013: 248).

Analyses of multi-level governance certainly appeared to reinforce this view. Not only did they identify a system of differentiated, disaggregated, and networked governance at multi-levels, and so served to substantiate claims that the UK itself had become a differentiated polity (see Chapter 5); but they also identified the broader context of the EU, within which the UK polity was nested, as 'an instance of *post-parliamentary governance* where the direct "influence of the people" through formal representative democracy has a marginal place' (Andersen and Burns 1996: 227 original emphasis). New modes of networked governance were perceived to be 'more technically effective and flexible than the forms of representative democracy' with the consequence that 'they tend *to replace and crowd out* the latter' (Andersen and Burns 1996: 231 emphasis added). In which case the 'post-parliamentary' trajectory of domestic UK politics was simply steepened by corresponding developments within the EU. Not surprisingly, similar trajectories, often termed 'deparliamentarisation' were also observable in other EU member states (see for example Rasmussen 2012: 99–100; Rittberger 2005: 198–9; Schüttemeyer 2009: 9). And these conjoined trajectories at national and EU levels served to produce a 'frustrating and delegitimising gap between representative democracy's responsibility and its lack of structural capability and control' (Andersen and Burns 1996: 243). In this gap, alternative forms of legitimacy – most notably 'output' and 'throughput' legitimacy – served to challenge or even to displace 'input' legitimacy derived from electoral representation and 'majoritarian' institutions.

Input legitimacy, as Schmidt (2013: 7) points out, is dependent upon citizens 'expressing demands institutionally and deliberatively through representative politics while providing constructive support via their sense of identity and community'. In the case of the EU the expression of demands and the provision of support (in an Eastonian sense) are often so diffuse as to be vacuous. Even the notion of 'dual legitimacy' based, first, upon electoral representation and institutions in member states and, second, upon direct elections to the European Parliament (EP) struggles to counteract the image of post-parliamentarism. Indeed, as Lord and Pollok (2010: 122) point out: 'Representative institutions – with equally legitimate claim to representativeness – may only block one another and thus produce "joint-decision traps"'. Thus, in the absence of a single European *demos*, or a European party system, or a European government, notions that the two levels of 'input' legitimation may be aggregated – of adding EU representative democracy onto existing national processes of representation – give rise to counter, and paradoxical, notions that 'dual legitimation' may result in the disaggregation of legitimacy. Whereas the EP draws upon notions of a 'direct' transnational linkage of EU citizens to the EU's legislative processes;

national parliaments invoke ideas of the 'indirect' authorisation of EU legislative outputs through the negotiations of national governments at EU level and their ultimate accountability to their own domestic parliaments. As a result, citizens in member states may only elliptically authorise EU policies made on their behalf and only effect a restricted and mediated form of political accountability and responsibility through the election of national representatives. On both counts – of authorisation and accountability – policy-making in the EU is deemed to be deficient when contrasted to a standard model of representative democracy: hence the ubiquity of notions of 'democratic deficit' in analyses of the EU (see Bellamy and Kröger 2013: 477–97; Judge and Earnshaw 2008: 68–89). One consequence of the dysfunctionality of notions of electoral authorisation and accountability in the EU is that, if citizens' preferences are not adequately reflected and if their elected national representatives are only tenuously accountable for the outcomes of EU policy, then opposition to EU policies can turn into opposition of the EU polity itself (Bellamy and Kröger 2011: 16). Another consequence is, in Bellamy and Kröger's (2011: 16) words: 'in the absence of channels of reasonable disagreement on EU matters, one risks getting unreasonable disagreement'.

A related incongruity associated with notions of EU 'input' legitimacy is that the democratic 'inputs' required to legitimate EU policies are primarily rooted in national-level representative processes: first, in nationally organised 'second-order' elections focused primarily upon the salience of national issues and with national party contests serving as proxies for EU representation; and, second, in the accountability of national executives, for their contributions to EU policy making, effected through national representative institutions and representative processes. This is reflected in the nature of deliberative discourse in the EU:

> Discourse comes largely by way of national political actors speaking to national publics in national languages reported by national media and considered by national opinion. ... The institutional input reality [is] that without a European-wide representative politics to focus debate, European political leaders have little opportunity to speak to the issues and European publics have little ability to deliberate about them or to state their conclusion directly, through the ballot box. (Schmidt 2013: 13)

In these circumstances standard 'input' models of democratic legitimation have been seen to be, at best, 'distorted' or 'attenuated' or, at worst, largely irrelevant when applied to the EU (see Bellamy 2010: 7; Scharpf 2012: 20). Such views have led to a search for alternative non-majoritarian or non-electoral models of legitimation. In this search, 'output' legitimation has provided the most sustained non-electoral alternative.

'Output' legitimacy assumes a distinction between legitimation derived from the ability of EU institutions to provide effective policy outcomes *for* the people and legitimation derived from political participation *by* the people. In making this distinction Majone (2005: 37) has pointed to the growing importance of non-majoritarian institutions in all democratic states as a clear indication that 'for many purposes reliance upon qualities such as expertise, professional discretion, policy consistency, fairness, or independence of judgment is considered to be more important than reliance upon direct democratic accountability'. This is particularly the case in the EU, where, by virtue of the relative importance of regulatory policies in the EU in comparison to member states, non-majoritarian institutions are major policy actors. They are deemed to have 'a distinctive institutional competence' which emphasises accountability by result, and which serves to 'generate and maintain the belief of being, of all feasible institutional arrangements, the most appropriate one for solving a certain range of problems' (Majone 2005: 38). In this sense their legitimacy stems from their 'problem-solving capacity', expertise, and Pareto-improving policy outputs (see also Christiansen 2013: 109). What is of particular importance for an analysis of post-parliamentary democracy is that these non-majoritarian institutions '*by design*, are not directly accountable to the voters or their elected representatives' (Majone 2005: 37; emphasis added). The expansion of non-majoritarian institutions and modes of governance in the EU beyond the Commission, the European Central Bank, and the European Court of Justice – to include, variously, regulatory agencies, 'high-level' consultative and advisory committees, non-legislative rule making, along with the Open Method of Coordination – simply appears to further insulate EU policy-making from electoral institutions and processes of representative democracy. Indeed, in this expansion, the initial 'post-parliamentary' claims of Andersen and Burns (1996: 244) appear to resonate more profoundly some two decades later: 'Monitoring, overview, investigation, deliberation, decision-making is far beyond the capacity of parliament[s] (and their membership)'.

Monitory democracy

The notion of 'post-parliamentary democracy' finds particular prominence in Keane's (2009, 2011) conception of 'monitory democracy'.

Indeed, Keane (2011: 212) starts from the premise that there has been 'an historic sea change'; and that 'from roughly the mid-twentieth century representative democracy began to morph into a new historical form of "post-parliamentary democracy"'. This new form was 'monitory democracy', a form in which the rapid, almost exponential growth of extra-parliamentary, power-scrutinising mechanisms – combined with the growth of 'multi-media saturated societies', symbolised by the communicative plenitude and possibilities of the internet – produced a latticed, networked pattern of power monitoring. The distinctiveness of monitory democracy for Keane (2009: 695; original emphasis) was thus to be found in: 'the way *all fields of social and political life* come to be scrutinised, not just by the standard machinery of representative democracy but a whole host of *non-party, extra-parliamentary and often unelected bodies*, operating within and underneath and beyond the boundaries of territorial states'. Such was the degree of difference and complexity of this new democracy that it 'demands a headshift, a break with conventional thinking' to encompass 'the deepest and widest system of democracy ever known' (2011: 218).

Keane (2011: 231) maintains, therefore, that the 'simple spatial metaphors' inherited from representative democracy are incapable of describing the dynamics of monitory democracy. In particular, the notion of the 'sovereignty' of national parliaments is 'just too simple', as monitory democracy is 'no longer confined to the territorial state' (Keane 2009: 697). Instead, this new form 'pulverises' the distinctions between 'domestic' and 'foreign' and 'local' and 'global' (Keane 2011: 225). The complexity of monitory democracy is to be found in the growth of new types of extra-parliamentary, power-scrutinising institutions 'unknown to previous democrats' (2011: 213). Indeed, Keane identifies over 100 such institutions that have developed since 1945, ranging from deliberative innovations of citizens' juries, citizens' assemblies, deliberative polls, and chat rooms; through consultative mechanisms of online petitions, public consultations, and focus groups, as well as consumer councils and consumer testing councils; to global watchdog organisations, international criminal courts, global social forums, international non-governmental organisations, and transnational social movements; and new forms of protest movements – both virtual (wiki-induced) and social media facilitated ('designer', 'occupy', and 'Arab-spring'-type protests). Although diverse and disjointed, these new modes of participation are defined 'by their overall commitment to strengthening the diversity and influence of citizens' voices and choices in decisions that affect their lives – *regardless of the outcome of elections*'

(Keane 2009: 693; 2011: 216 emphasis added). In particular, they are concerned to scrutinise and control the activities of decision-makers (in both public and private organisations, and electoral and non-electoral institutions). For Keane's critics, this means in practice that monitory democracy provides 'an essentially negative view of politics', and that 'power is being siphoned away from the traditional institutions of representative democracy (that were at least mandated and legitimized through electoral mechanisms) and transferred to a new activist elite' (Flinders 2011: 609). In this critical view, monitory democracy is thus 'something to *fear* rather than celebrate' (Flinders 2011: 608 original emphasis). The specific fear is that the politicisation of accountability through the activities of monitory institutions serves to eviscerate public trust and confidence in elected politicians and electoral processes. Yet, in outlining a linear causality between the rise of monitory institutions and the residualisation of representative institutions, Flinders both simplifies Keane's argument and underplays the incongruities at the core of a post-parliamentary conception of monitory democracy. Indeed, for Keane, monitory democracy is 'post-parliamentary' but is not non-parliamentary or anti-parliamentary (see below).

Globalisation, post-representative politics, and post-post-representative (cosmopolitan) democracy

Notions of multi-level governance have been deemed to 'represent a transnational version of the familiar network ideas employed to understand the domestic level of governance' (Peters and Pierre 2004: 81). In this version, sub-national, national, and transnational governance networks are intermeshed in an interactive vortex, increasingly energised by instantaneous digital communication, which challenges traditional models of state-delimited representative democracy. Indeed, for Held and McGrew (2002: 18) multilayered regional and global governance has come to epitomise 'the present era of global politics'. Certainly, a complex pattern of transnational institutional interconnectedness is evident in the activities of international policy-making forums such as the United Nations, World Trade Organisation, World Bank, International Monetary Fund, Group of Eight (G8), or Group of Twenty (G20), and international regulatory agencies; the informal deliberative forum of international elites of the World Economic Forum; and the emergence of international legal institutions associated with 'cosmopolitan law' (on human rights, the environment, and the conduct of war). Moreover, the emergence of a global or transnational civil society has been discerned in the rapid spread of international non-governmental organisations (sometimes referred to as social movement organisations) and international social movements (see Colás 2013). These interrelated developments, of exponential increases in socio-economic transactions across state borders and associated transnational governance responses, leads to 'an increasing incongruence between social and political spaces' (Lavenex 2013: 107). Out of this spatial incongruence arises a further political incongruence that as network governance at supra-state levels comes to replicate the post-parliamentary/post-representative tendencies at state level – of the privileging of non-electoral representation, non-majoritarian institutions, and output legitimation over electoral representation, majoritarian institutions, and input legitimacy – there is an amplification of calls for the 'democratisation' of transnational networks. In the absence of a system of 'metagovernance of multi-level governance' (Torfing *et al.* 2012: 96), or of an authentic transnational civil society, these calls, however, are still fundamentally conditioned by existing conceptions of representation and representative democracy – despite heroic attempts to provide alternative conceptualisations in 'cosmopolitan democracy' or 'global stakeholder democracy'.

The blurring of the boundaries between the nation-state level and trans-state/transnational levels, in relation to civil society, political agendas, legal and administrative regimes, policy-making institutions, and governance networks, has highlighted a central incongruity of globalisation that – while governance has become increasingly multi-layered and transnational – political representation and democratic legitimation have remained rooted in the practice of nation-states (Held and McGrew 2002: 121). To overcome this incongruity, cosmopolitan democratic theorists have offered schemes designed to provide citizens with political representation in 'assemblies parallel to and independent from those of their national political institutions' (Archibugi and Held 2011: 446). For such theorists the most efficacious way to achieve this objective would be to 'create a world parliamentary assembly ... to allow global citizens to deliberate on common issues' (Archibugi and Held 2011: 446–7). Such deliberation is deemed necessary at global level as '[o]nly when citizen and business interests work together within an overarching representative body can they achieve policy accommodations that will be seen as legitimate' (Falk and Strauss 2001: 216). Global representative assemblies would recognise, therefore, the 'importance of nonterritorially bounded political communities composed of individuals with common interests' (Archibugi and Held 2011: 448) and reflect the growing importance of a global civil society above and beyond national civil societies (see Kuper 2004: 122–7).

Indeed, notions of a global civil society have underpinned other prospective global representative institutional designs based on non-state and non-electoral modes of representation (Kuper 2004: 165; Macdonald 2010: 113–5). Macdonald (2008: 6), for example, has envisaged a global stakeholder democracy based upon the non-electoral, and often non-national and non-territorial, representative claims of NGOs (though the claims of transnational corporations and international organisations may also be accommodated within her model (2008: 224–6)). Indeed, to substantiate these claims, NGOs have to 'invoke a conception of representation that does not rely on the formal mechanisms of *electoral* authorization and accountability' (2008: 7 original emphasis). In so doing, these conceptions have to 'establish legitimate representative agency' through alternative institutional mechanisms capable of delivering authorisation and accountability (2008: 15; 165). Yet, in attempting to specify the nature of these alternative mechanisms, Macdonald is forced to retreat into a 'generalized theoretical account of these institutional mechanisms' (2008: 177) and 'some speculative discussion of how such democratic representation could plausibly work in relation to NGOs' (2008: 193). Nonetheless, such a prospective institutional framework would be non-state, non-electoral, and non-parliamentary and, in Macdonald's opinion, 'could more feasibly be applied to existing structures of global public power than could conventional electoral institutions' (2008: 220). In this sense, global stakeholder democracy is doubly 'post-parliamentary': at both state level and supra-state levels. Yet Macdonald (2008: 221) is confronted by an extant representational reality in which 'at the present time ... most practices of NGO authorization and accountability fall short of the democratic standards [required for stakeholder representation]' (Macdonald 2008: 193). Not surprisingly, therefore, global stakeholder democracy 'is not yet up and running in any real world context' (2008: 193), and is unlikely to be realised in the near future (2008: 5).

More damningly, Macdonald concedes that her model might very well 'to some degree further erode the strength of democratic institutions within states' (2008: 227). In fact, she accepts that there would be tensions between global representative institutions and state-based democratic institutions (2008: 227). In part, these tensions arise from the distinctiveness of the legitimation claims of electoral and non-electoral representation (see Chapter 3); with electoral representation recognised as facilitating the resolution of contentious decisions (2008: 116); allowing for conjoined authorisation and accountability of representatives (2008: 190); and, when set within the context of the state, providing for aggregative processes of decision-making (2008: 121). Ultimately, Macdonald (2008: 161) has to concede that: 'multi-stakeholder representation will usually need to be implemented in conjunction with a representative framework that is underpinned by the liberal individualist ideal, to provide a basis for legitimate aggregative procedures'. The essence of the liberal individualist ideal is the equal opportunity of individuals, afforded through a vote of equal weight, to influence the outcome of decisions made by their representatives. In its own right multi-stakeholder representation is unable to guarantee such processual equality (2008: 218), or to make the simultaneous linkage between authorisation and accountability, or for that matter to provide an aggregative frame within which plural stakeholder interests can be reconciled and accommodated. In these circumstances Macdonald (2008: 162) contemplates 'a hybrid representative model' in which multi-stakeholder representatives would have 'a voice but not a vote'. In other words, electoral representation would trump non-electoral representation, and state-based representation would prevail over transnational representation.

In reaching this point in the analysis of post-parliamentary democracy the discussion starts to circle back to the issues raised initially in Chapters 1, 3, and 5, and to demand further consideration of the extent to which electoral representative democracy has been displaced, rather than supplemented or complemented, in 'post-representative', 'post-parliamentary', or 'post-democracy' models. The following sections outline, therefore, the incongruities that are associated with claims that democracy has moved beyond, or is distinctly different from, traditional notions and modes of electoral representation while also, simultaneously, maintaining that these traditional ideas and institutions underpin new democratic models.

Complementing, supplementing, or displacing?

A common feature of analyses of 'post-democracy', or variants of 'post-parliamentary', 'post-representative', 'monitory', or 'cosmopolitan' democracy, is a shared belief that existing modes of electoral representation, and the associated institutions of parties and parliaments, remain intact. This is captured succinctly in Crouch's (2004: 20) exposition of the notion of 'post-' as implying 'that something new has come into existence to reduce the importance of X by going beyond it in some sense ... However, X will still have left its mark; there will be strong traces of it still around. ..."Post-" periods should therefore be expected to be very complex'.

This complexity is captured, in relation to 'post-parliamentary democracy', when network governance analysts acknowledge that '[o]verlooking the role of parliaments in [network] analyses of policy making is ... a great mistake' (Daugbjerg and Marsh 1998: 63). Daugbjerg and Marsh (1998: 62) are ultimately willing to allow, therefore, that: 'Since representative democracy is the major form of governance in Western societies, it does not make sense simply to argue that parliaments are excluded from influence because we cannot observe the direct effects upon the policy outcome'. This view is reinforced by Andersen and Burns (1996: 227) who, while convinced that the EU is an instance of post-parliamentary governance, are at pains to point out that their characterisation of governance 'does not claim that parliamentary democracy has become largely meaningless, or has no future role to play' (1996: 228). In particular, in normative terms, 'popular sovereignty/representation' still remains 'part of the sacred core' of western democracy (1996: 240). And in the pragmatics of the legislative and policy making processes, formal responsibility still resides in 'the system of representative democracy' and in the 'institutions of representative democracy' (1996: 238). In many respects, therefore, Andersen and Burns acknowledge that 'formal democratic arrangements, in particular parliaments, still remain essential' (1996: 246).

Similarly, Keane, while being adamant that monitory democracy 'operates in ways greatly at variance with textbook accounts of "representative", "liberal" or "parliamentary democracy"' (Keane 2009: 706; 2011: 221), insists repeatedly that 'legislatures neither disappear, nor necessarily decline in importance' (Keane 2011: 213), that 'monitory democracies depend upon legislatures' (2011: 218), and that 'institutions like periodic elections, multi-party competition and the right of citizens to voice their public approval or disapproval of legislation remain familiar fixtures in the life of democracies' (Keane 2009: 706).

Equally, representative assemblies at global level, whether of a world parliament, or a network of regional parliaments, or a United Nations Parliamentary Assembly, have been conceived primarily as complements to, rather than replacements for, representative institutions at state and sub-state levels (Held 2006: 305). Indeed, Archibugi and Held (2011: 446) maintain that cosmopolitan democracy 'advocates giving citizens political representation in assemblies parallel to and independent from those of their national political institutions'. Even the more radical representational propositions envisaged in notions of global stakeholder democracy still conceive of new modes of representation operating in conjunction with an extant representative framework rooted in electoral democracy at state level (Macdonald 2008: 162).

Distinctiveness of electoral representation

At this point it is worth re-emphasising the distinctiveness of electoral representation and remembering the significance of 'systemic' notions of political representation. In Chapter 1 it was noted that democratic legitimation, effected through elections, rested not only on principles of formal political equality, authorisation, accountability, and temporality of decision-making capacity, but also on an assumption that, as a process of adjudication, conflicting claims could be reconciled within an articulation of some common interest. In this sense, there was an institutionalised capacity for communal judgement of the articulation of such collective claims. In Pitkin's (1967: 217) words, decision-making processes rooted in political representation, had the capacity to resolve 'the conflicting claims of the parts, on the basis of the common interest in the welfare of the whole'. As a process of adjudicating amongst, and reconciling, conflicting claims representative democracy requires the construction of some common interest. Historically, it has been state representative assemblies that have claimed priority in formulating a 'national interest' out of the rival claims of interests and localities within the state, and it is for this reason that representation has 'most commonly [been] ascribed to the legislature' (Pitkin 1967: 227).

Where the recent discussion has moved on from Pitkin's position, however, is in the recognition of legitimate representative claims beyond the institutional configurations of elections and representative assemblies (Urbinati and Warren 2008: 391) and beyond state boundaries. Yet, as noted above, even theorists of non-electoral, claims-based representation recognise the formulative/unifying capacity of parliamentary institutions to provide an answer to the basic political question: who resolves issues when they are contested? Thus, Saward (2010: 91) acknowledges that, in the case of liberal democracies, it is a state's legislature that 'brings the nation together symbolically under one roof'.

While non-elected representatives may wish to claim that they too speak for a 'higher level' national interest (or in the case of multi-stakeholder representation for even 'higher levels' beyond the state), what differentiates their claim from that of elected representatives, is the manner in which the visions of the collective interest is constructed. In essence, elected representatives in parliaments in modern representative democracies can be conceived as 'not simply facilitators of collective decision-making. Their decisions are taken in the name of the collective, and on its behalf' (Runciman 2007: 105). This point is echoed in Eriksen and Fossum's (2011: 5) statement that parliaments enjoy a special status, they embody 'the idea of joint self-determination in that an elected body of responsible citizens is there to legislate in the name of all. ... The rationale of parliament rests on a "dynamic-dialectic" of argument and counter-argument, of public debate and discussion. Deliberation is intrinsic to the mode of representation that parliaments are based on, and enables government by discussion'. This statement implicitly accepts the 'unitarity' of the claim of elected representatives to act 'in the name of all' and links this claim to an institutionalised determination of the 'public will'. As Urbinati (2006: 134) maintains, 'citizens have to see and understand that they have something in common that unifies them' and political representation in parliament provides a 'unifying process'. A prime purpose of parliaments, therefore, is to subject the conception of an aggregated national interest held by political representatives to what Manin (1997: 191) calls 'the trial of discussion'. In this view representative democracy and representative government are systems in which 'everything has to be justified in debate'.

This process of justification, and hence of legitimation, serves to differentiate collectively accountable (and collectively authorised) electoral representatives and representative institutions from 'self-authorised' non-electoral representatives and institutions. This point has been recognised, somewhat obliquely, by governance analysts in the argument that while states have become less hierarchical there continues to be a central role for state governments in 'setting the ground rules and context within which governance takes place' (Fawcett and Daugbjerg 2012: 198). The concept of the 'shadow of hierarchy' has been invoked in governance studies to acknowledge the capacity of the state (in its electoral, governmental institutional form) to impose, explicitly or implicitly, a legislative or regulatory framework for network activity. This 'shadow' hangs over network participants to the extent that 'their cost-benefit calculations [are weighted] in favor of a voluntary agreement closer to the common good rather than to particularistic self-interests' (Börzel and Risse 2010: 116). Ultimately, it is state actors who retain the capacity for taking and enforcing collective decisions. In other words, this capacity 'takes the form of authoritative decisions with claims to legitimacy' (Börzel and Risse 2010: 116). As such 'a functioning shadow of hierarchy not only serves to increase the effectiveness of governance involving non-state actors but also provides a "horizon of legitimacy"' (Börzel and Risse 2010: 116). This 'horizon' is the point of intersection with 'the common good', because unlike non-electoral network participants, elected governments are held accountable through democratic procedures (Börzel and Risse 2010: 116). There is thus a growing recognition of the importance of legitimation afforded by electoral representative processes in the practice of network governance. This recognition resonates with Judge's long-held view (1990, 1993, 2005) that networks are nested in processes of parliamentary representation and legitimation. For him, new modes of governance were not as insulated from electoral representative processes as network analysts made out (see Judge 1993: 120–30; 2005: 106–114). Indeed, as revealed in Chapter 5, in Britain the legitimating frame provided by the Westminster model is now widely recognised as being of elemental importance, even by those intent on demonstrating that political practice does not correspond to the political prescriptions of a standard model of representative democracy.

The 'horizon of legitimacy' came into plain sight after 2008 as the global financial crisis and the sovereign debt (eurozone) crisis, along with the post-Lisbon constitutional settlement, brought the incongruities of representative democracy in the EU into stark relief. As noted earlier in this chapter, there has been a widespread perception that, in the context of a decentred EU polity, 'conventional parliamentary approaches' or 'classic parliamentary forms' are inapplicable (Magnette 2005: 176; Shaw 1999: 581). This view culminates in the characterisation of the EU as a form of 'post-parliamentary governance' in which post-parliamentary institutional forms and processes displace electoral representative institutions, and in which output legitimation encapsulates 'the belief that the common good is better served by authorities that are not under the direct control of parliaments and governments exposed to electoral accountability and the temptation of partisan politics' (Scharpf 2012: 20). Such conceptions of the EU as a supranational regime based upon non-electoral notions of output legitimacy had long been subject to theoretical contestation, but came under sustained criticism as the institutional and policy responses to the eurozone crisis after 2010 were accompanied by a rapid withdrawal of public trust and support for those very responses. Thus although non-electoral, depoliticised, and technocratic processes continued to underpin the EU's attempts to manage the eurozone crisis, notions of output legitimacy suffered a 'real blow' (Smismans 2013: 351); with Scharpf (2012: 26) going so far as to argue that '[o]utput-orientated justifications' of EU rescue measures during the crisis had 'lost most of their plausibility'.

In these circumstances, the handling of the crisis marked a move away from existing non-majoritarian emphases of EU governance and the diminishing credibility of 'output-orientated justifications'. An institutional turn towards enhanced 'input legitimation' through electoral institutions was mapped out, but, notably, in an intergovernmental rather than a supranational direction. In this manoeuvring the European Parliament was largely confined to the sidelines (see Bellamy and Castiglione 2013: 215; Beukers 2013: 25). While this is not the place to examine the complexities of the EU's crisis responses, what is of immediate relevance are the democratic incongruities revealed in this intergovernmental 'turn'. On the one hand, within the Eurogroup, national governments were accorded primary responsibility for managing the crisis – with asymmetric fiscal effects evident between 'creditor states' (primarily Germany and to a lesser extent France) and 'debtor states' (most particularly Greece, Portugal, Spain, and Cyprus). In turn, national parliaments were called upon to 'endorse the European decisions of their governments and simultaneously to sell the sacrifices to their constituents' (Puntscher Riekmann, and Wydra 2013: 565). Thus, national parliaments bore the full brunt of popular opposition to EU fiscal policies (often being the institutional and physical target of protest) while also being asked to legitimate, through parliamentary debates and votes on bailout conditions, the very EU policies heightening national distress. In more positive vein Bellamy and Kröger (2012: 1) argued that:

> The Euro crisis has brought to the fore the continued significance of domestic democratic legitimation of European policy initiatives. In particular, it has revealed the importance of national parliaments (NPs) in this process. Bailout packages have required ratification by all NPs, which have reasserted their right to monitor government budgetary decisions notwithstanding the provisions of the new fiscal compact. NPs have also begun to exercise the new powers within the EU's political system that they acquired in the Lisbon Treaty.

Certainly, national parliaments, recently empowered by the Lisbon Treaty, sought more active involvement in EU decision-making processes, through pre-legislative 'subsidiarity checks' and enhanced monitoring and control of national executives (see Judge and Earnshaw 2008: 274–6; Hefftler and Wessel 2013: 9). This has led Bellamy and Kröger (2011: 2) to claim that 'national representative institutions are back in the game' and that 'the continued importance of domestic representative institutions – parliaments and parties – in EU matters is undeniable'. Perhaps in recognition of the extent to which '[a]nachronistically, more than 50 years after the foundation of the European Union the crisis ... appears to be reinstating the constraining power of national borders', the European Commission (2012: 10) reiterated the 'meta-standard' of the EU, found in the Lisbon Treaty, that the Union shall be 'founded on representative democracy' and that both the European Parliament and national parliaments – directly and indirectly – are essential to the good functioning of the Union (see Bellamy and Kröger 2011: 1; Kröger and Friedrich 2013: 158; Lord and Pollok 2010: 126).

Attempts to manage the eurozone crisis in the post-Lisbon constitutional context thus prompted official reaffirmation of the importance of representative democracy, electoral institutions, input legitimacy, and a need to promote further 'parliamentarisation' of the EU. The UK, although not a Eurogroup member state, has not been insulated from this reaffirmation of the meta-standard of representative democracy, nor has it sought to discourage the intergovernmental turn, nor has it been hesitant in promoting notions of state-based input legitimation. Yet, in the frame of EU multi-level governance, domestic legitimation of governments through national electoral processes does not automatically transmute into transnational legitimation of EU-level outputs. In other words, 'no dynamic relationship exists between [national] representatives and those they represent when it comes to European issues' (Bellamy and Castiglione 2013: 220). In the absence of EU majoritarian inputs (in the form of a directly elected EU government), or of the 'constructive preconditions' of a European *demos* or a common European identity, input legitimation is still associated primarily with the level of the member state (Schmidt 2013: 9). A mismatch, an incongruity, is thus apparent between the kind of representative democracy deemed normatively legitimate at national level and the supranational conception of input legitimacy associated with EU governance.

Such a mismatch is even more apparent in prospective institutional schemas for global democracy. Clearly this is not the place to embark upon a detailed consideration of global democracy other than to draw out themes that have been evident in the discussion thus far of postnational electoral representation. Archibugi (2010: 85) makes clear that 'any form of democracy at the post-national level could not, and should not, be just a replica of the forms of democracy we have experienced at national level'. As noted earlier, advocates of cosmopolitan global democracy propose an extension of electoral representation in parallel to, but independent of, the national political franchise. In this extension, however, the incongruities at the centre of existing supranational governance arrangements (as noted above in relation to the EU) are magnified. While cosmopolitan theorists may wish to conceive of 'overlapping communities of fate' that transcend national boundaries, notions of 'collective representation remain under-theorized by cosmopolitan democrats' (Weale 2007: 240). The result is that the legitimation claims of parallel bases of representation – of states (and national governments) and transnational communities (and 'cosmopolitan citizens' and social movements) – remain counterposed. While cosmopolitan theorists may 'assume that if global politics become more accountable and representative, this may also have an important effect on domestic politics' (Archibugi and Held 2011: 434), the effect might just as easily be conceived as mutually fractious as mutually convergent. Indeed, advocates of global democracy are aware that states and national representative processes will continue as the main 'depositories of legitimacy' (Archibugi 2010: 85). In the absence of some global conception of collective interest or public good, states will continue to articulate and aggregate the preferences of citizens within their boundaries and nest their claims to legitimacy within territorially delimited representative processes. Nowhere was this more evident than in the post-2008 global financial crisis. Despite sustained arguments about the emergence of a global economy, and the erosion of the capacity of individual states and governments to regulate transborder transactions, capital flows, and financial spillovers – seemingly epitomised in the global financial crisis – there is strong evidence that in the first phase of crisis, the so called 'banking crisis', 'governments in liberal democratic states sought to bring matters under their direct control, revealing the degree to which they might still seek to regulate globalized markets if they chose to do so' (Dryzek and Dunleavy 2009: 318). This does not minimise the extent of transnational policy response, but simply points to the continuing capacity of individual states to take relatively unfettered action. In this respect, the UK state is no exception. Indeed, Johal *et al.* (2012a: 71) go so far as to argue that 'what is remarkable about this crisis is the limited impact it [had] on the practice of politics in Britain'. If anything, the central governing institutions in the UK remained pivotal to crisis management, reasserting the core executive's role in financial regulation and greatly strengthening 'a highly traditional nexus of power in the Westminster governing system' (2012a: 74; see also Kickert 2012: 175; Serricchio *et al.* 2013: 60).

'Return home': Representative democracy in the UK

If the responses of UK governments to the financial crisis after 2008 reveal the continuing importance of national political action in a globalising economy, they also serve to confirm that the '"hollowed out" [UK] state is a myth' (Johal *et al.* 2012a: 71). Moreover, they reveal the long-term importance of 'the arena of democratic politics' and electoral representative institutions and their continuing capacity to 're-politicise' supposedly depoliticised issues (in this specific case of financial sector regulation (see Froud *et al.* 2012: 56; Johal *et al.* 2012b)).

In this 'return home' to a focus on the UK state, and in acknowledging the limitations of post-national notions of meta-governance – and the mismatch between new forms of transnational governance (and their claims to output legitimacy) and traditional national representative processes and institutions (and their claims to input legitimacy) (see Vorländer 2013: 81) – the incongruities of domestic representative democracy are brought back into stark relief. As preceding chapters have revealed these incongruities are many and varied. Yet what links these diverse incongruities is a contestation of the very notion of democratic legitimacy. Indeed, a 'meta-incongruity' can be discerned between the legitimation claims based upon electoral representation and alternative legitimation claims – derived variously and disparately from deliberative, unmediated participatory, non-electoral, or output theories. This is not to deny that legitimation is a multi-dimensional concept, nor is it a reductionist argument that equates legitimation simply with electoral representation. Instead, it is a contention that electoral representation provides a holistic framework of authorisation and accountability, and a 'presumption' of generality and processual equality, within which public policies may be made. Ultimately, alternative legitimation claims come to be nested within this frame; and, hence, ideas about democratic innovation, notions of non-electoral representation, concepts of governance (at multi-levels), and even theories of post-parliamentary and post-representative politics, routinely pre-suppose the continuing centrality of processes and institutions of representative democracy.

Yet to argue that electoral representation is somehow to be supplemented or enhanced, by non-electoral representation or non-parliamentary modes of decision-making, generates the incongruity that in the process of supplementation the legitimation claims of the former would be challenged. Yet, these alternative forms of representation and governance presuppose the very 'input legitimacy' of representative processes and institutions that their own bases of 'perceived legitimacy' contest.

This point is neatly captured in the phrase: 'Any effort to enhance representation also alters representation'. This identifies a dialectical process whereby, on the one side, the simple serial flow of aggregated power, from represented to elected representatives mapped out in a standard model of representative democracy, becomes mediated in buffered, or segmented, or disjointed linkages between citizens and decision-makers. In the other direction, if legitimation claims based upon modes of 'self-authorised', non-electoral representation are seen to question standard models of representative democracy then, as noted in Chapters 3, 5, and 6, conceptual and practical incongruities arise in the nesting of these alternative modes within a model of electoral representation which serves as the 'received' ideational frame of democratic decision-making.

In coming full circle, back to a 'standard account' of representative democracy as the ideational frame within which public policy decision-making is still conceived and legitimated in the UK, the elemental incongruity remains of a model, which is deemed to be deficient by theorists and practitioners alike, continuing to structure official discourse. In this discourse the inclusion–exclusion paradox of representative democracy is resolved in favour of the self-exclusion of citizens from unmediated engagement in public policy decision-making. Beyond the point of election, however, citizen participation becomes mediated through a range of alternative representative institutions and processes each with their own legitimation claims (whether electoral or non-electoral) and each privileging the 'inclusionary' dimension of democracy.

Out of this paradox emerge the fundamental political incongruities of UK governance: of the tensions between exclusionary notions inhered within the Westminster model and inclusionary notions inhered within democratic innovation and enhancement. While successive governments have adopted the inclusionary rhetoric of democratic innovators – in designs for engagement with citizens in deliberative initiatives, e-petitions, and crowdsourcing experiments – the reforming rhetoric has been offset by a wider official discourse emphasising the legitimate exclusion of citizens at the point of decision. In this discourse elected representatives alone constitute the legitimate decision-makers, or more precisely 'power is exercised by the ... Government, which has a democratic mandate to govern' (Cabinet Office 2011a: 2). Citizen preferences may be articulated, aggregated, and advanced through alternative modes and channels of representation and participation, but, in the last instance, these are modes of transmission rather than decision. Hence democratic reformers have remained disappointed by the degree to which democratic innovations have been connected up to the 'main game' of decision-making and have had consequential effects upon decision-making processes. The notion of 'democratic drift' still characterises UK representative democracy, as the 'power-sharing reforms' that have been introduced have been 'designed and implemented within the contours of what remains a power-hoarding democracy' (Flinders 2010: 287; see Chapter 6). In these circumstances the inclusionary logic of the former is transmuted in the exclusionary logic of the latter. Practical attempts to reengage a disillusioned citizenry in the processes of representative democracy have been framed conceptually as complements to or supplements of those processes. Yet this is a frame that continues to assert the legitimation claims of mediated electoral representation over the claims of unmediated non-electoral participation.

There has been no shortage of counterclaims of unmediated legitimation. Indeed, such claims have been the essence of notions of deliberative democracy, referendum democracy, and radical notions of e-democracy. As such they have been posited as alternative models of decision-making, where legitimation stems from the participation of those subject to a collective decision rather than from the public authorisation and accountability of decision makers subject to election. In this guise these models have a conceptual clarity. Yet this clarity becomes clouded, and debilitating incongruities emerge, when the ideas of unmediated engagement of citizens are translated into practical designs for citizens to inform decision-making and contribute to the formulation of public policies.

So democratic incongruity in the UK arises not from a failure to recognise the 'disconnect' between citizens and their elected representatives, nor from a failure to introduce democratic innovations and implement institutional change designed to address this fractured linkage (though there has been a profound mismatch between intention and result). Instead, for many critics, the incongruity arises from the failure of UK governments to provide a 'new narrative', or 'discernable alternative conceptions', or an 'overarching theory', or 'any singular set of values or philosophy' distinct from the standard account of representative democracy built into the foundations of the 'Westminster model' (see, for example, Diamond 2011: 68; Diamond and Richards 2012: 191; Flinders 2010: 285; Garland 2013: 7; Hazell 2007: 18–19). In itself this criticism is incongruous in expecting UK governments, as the beneficiaries of an exclusionary model, to propagate a radical alternative inclusionary model. In the absence of official acceptance of an alternative narrative, the core incongruity will remain: attempts to enhance, strengthen or expand representative democracy through privileging citizen inclusion will impact upon the exclusionary capacities of the Westminster model, and so alter that model. This is the declared objective of democratic innovators and democratic designers (Smith 2012; Stoker 2011) and as such does not constitute an internal incongruity in innovative designs, as the inclusion–exclusion paradox would be resolved in favour of inclusion. The incongruity arises, however, when the legitimation claims of unmediated inclusion are voiced within the frame of the legitimation claims of mediated exclusion of the Westminster model. In this case the inclusionary dynamic is subverted, and hence changed, by the institutional and process inertia of existing models of representative democracy.

References

Aldrich, J. H., Montgomery, J. M. and Wood, W. (2011) 'Turnout as Habit', *Political Behavior*, vol. 33, no. 4, pp. 535–63.

Alexander, D. T., Barraket, J., Lewis, J. M. and Considine, M. (2012) 'Civic Engagement and Associationalism: The Impact of Group Membership Scope versus Intensity of Participation', *European Sociological Review*, vol. 28, no. 1, pp. 43–58.

Allen, P. (2013) 'Linking Pre-Parliamentary Political Experience and Career Trajectories of the 1997 General Election Cohort', *Parliamentary Affairs*, vol. 66, no. 4, pp. 685–707.

Allern, E. H. and Bale, T. (2012) 'Political Parties and Interest Groups: Disentangling Complex Relationships', *Party Politics*, vol. 18, no. 1, pp. 7–25.

Alonso, S., Keane, J. and Merkel, W. (2011) 'Rethinking the Future of Representative Democracy', in S. Alonso, J. Keane and W. Merkel (eds) *The Future of Representative Democracy* (Cambridge: Cambridge University Press).

Amenta, E., Caren, N., Chiarello, E. and Su, Y. (2010) 'The Political Consequences of Social Movements', *Annual Review of Sociology*, vol. 36, pp. 287–307.

Andersen, S. S. and Burns, T. (1996) 'The European Union and the Erosion of Parliamentary Democracy: A Study of Post-Parliamentary Governance', in S. S. Andersen and K. A. Eliassen (eds) *The European Union: How Democratic Is It?* (London: Sage).

Anderson, C. J., Blais, A., Bowler, S., Donovan, T. and Listhaug, O. (2005) *Losers' Consent: Elections and Democratic Legitimacy* (Oxford: Oxford University Press).

Andeweg, R. B. and Thomassen, J. J. A. (2005) 'Modes of Political Representation: Toward a New Typology', *Legislative Studies Quarterly*, vol. 30, no. 4, pp. 507–28.

Anthony, G. and Morison, J. (2005) 'Here, There and (Maybe) Here Again: The Story of Law Making for Post-1998 Northern Ireland', in R. Hazell and R. Rawlings (eds) *Devolution, Law Making and the Constitution* (Exeter: Imprint Academic).

Archibugi, D. (2010) 'The Hope for a Global Democracy', *New Political Science*, vol. 32, no. 1, pp. 84–91.

Archibugi, D. and Held, D. (2011) 'Cosmopolitan Democracy: Paths and Agents', *Ethics and International Affairs*, vol. 25, no. 4, pp. 433–61.

Arzheimer, K. and Evans, J. (2012) 'Geolocation and Voting: Candidate-Voter Distance Effects on Party Choice in the 2010 UK General Election in England', *Political Geography*, vol. 31, no. 5, pp. 301–10.

Ashe, J., Campbell, R., Childs, S. and Evans, E. (2010) '"Stand by Your Man" Women's Political Recruitment at the 2010 UK General Election', *British Politics*, vol. 5, no. 4, pp. 455–80.

Aughey, A. (2010) 'British Questions: A Non-Instrumentalist Answer', *Parliamentary Affairs*, vol. 63, no. 3, pp. 407–24.

Bache, I. and Flinders, M. (2004) 'Multi-Level Governance and British Politics', in I. Bache and M. Flinders (eds) *Multi-Level Governance* (Oxford: Oxford University Press).

Baggot, R. (1995) *Pressure Groups Today* (Manchester: Manchester University Press).

Bale, T. (2011) *The Conservative Party from Thatcher to Cameron* (Cambridge: Polity).

Barber, N. W. (2011) 'The Afterlife of Parliamentary Sovereignty', *International Journal of Constitutional Law*, vol. 9, no. 1, pp. 144–54.

Bardi, L. and Mair, P. (2008) 'The Parameters of Party Systems', *Party Politics*, vol. 14, no. 2, pp. 147–66.

BBC. (1999) 'The Elections in Quotes', *BBC News*, 7 May, http://news.bbc.co.uk/1/hi/uk_politics/337405.stm (accessed 29 March 2012).

BBC. (2001) 'Turnout at 80 Year Low', *BBC News: Vote 2001*, http://news.bbc.co.uk/news/vote2001/hi/english/newsid_1376000/1376575.stm (accessed 27 April 2012).

BBC. (2003) 'Millions Join Global Anti-War Protests', *BBC News*, 17 February, http://news.bbc.co.uk/1/hi/world/europe/2765215.stm (accessed 10 May 2012).

BBC. (2012) 'Denis MacShane Urges "All Working Class" MP Shortlists', *BBC News*, 25 July 2012, http://www.bbc.co.uk/news/uk-politics-18969789 (accessed 11 August 2012).

Beetham, D. (2012) 'Evaluating New vs Old Forms of Citizen Engagement and Participation', in J. Parkinson and J. Mansbridge (eds) *Deliberative Systems* (Cambridge: Cambridge University Press).

Bellamy, C. (2011) 'The Whitehall Programme and After: Researching Government in Time of Governance', *Public Administration*, vol. 89, no. 1, pp. 78–92.

Bellamy, R. (2010) 'Democracy Without Democracy? Can the EU's Democratic "Outputs" be Separated from the Democratic "Inputs" Provided by Competitive Parties and Majority Rule?', *Journal of European Public Policy*, vol. 17, no. 1, pp. 2–19.

Bellamy, R. and Castiglione, D. (2013) 'Three Models of Democracy, Political Community and Representation in the EU', *Journal of European Public Policy*, vol. 20, no. 2, pp. 206–23.

Bellamy, R. and Kröger, S. (2011) *Europe Hits Home: The Domestic Deficits of Representative Democracy in EU Affairs*, UCL European Institute, Working Paper 2/2011 (London: University College London European Institute).

Bellamy, R. and Kröger, S. (2012) 'Domesticating the Democratic Deficit? The Role of National Parliaments and Parties in the EU's System of Governance', *Parliamentary Affairs*, Advance Access, DOI: 10.1093/pa/gss045.

Bellamy, R. and Kröger, S. (2013) 'Representation Deficits and Surpluses in EU Policy-Making', *Journal of European Integration*, vol. 35, no. 5, pp. 477–97.

Berelson, B., Lazarsfeld, P. and McPhee, W. (1954) *Voting: A Study of Opinion Formation in a Presidential Campaign* (Chicago: University of Chicago Press).

Berger, B. (2009) 'Political Theory, Political Science, and the End of Civic Engagement', *Perspectives on Politics*, vol. 7, no. 2, pp. 335–50.

Beukers, T. (2013) 'The Eurozone Crisis and the Legitimacy of Differentiated Integration', in B. de Witte, A. Héritier and A. H. Trechsel (eds) *The Euro Crisis and the State of European Democracy* (Florence: European Union Democracy Observatory, European University Institute).

Bevir, M. (2010) *Democratic Governance* (Princeton: Princeton University Press).

Bevir, M. (2012) 'A History of Modern Pluralism', in M. Bevir (ed.) *Modern Pluralism: Anglo-American Debates Since 1880* (Cambridge: Cambridge University Press).

Bevir, M. and Rhodes, R. A. W. (2003) *Interpreting British Governance* (London: Routledge).

Bhatti, Y. and Hansen, K. M. (2012) 'The Effect of Generation and Age on Turnout to the European Parliament – How Turnout Will Continue to Decline in The Future', *Electoral Studies*, vol. 31, no. 2, pp. 262–72.

Biegelbauer, P. and Hansen, J. (2011) 'Democratic Theory and Citizen Participation: Democracy Models in the Evaluation of Public Participation in Science and Technology', *Science and Public Policy*, vol. 38, no. 8, pp. 589–97.

Birch, A. H. (1964) *Representative and Responsible Government* (London: Unwin).

Birch, A. H. (1971) *Representation* (London: Macmillan).

Blair, T. (2007) 'The e-petition Shows that My Government is Listening', *The Observer*, 18 February.

Blais, A. and Rubenson, D. (2013) 'The Source of Turnout Decline: New Values or New Contexts?', *Comparative Political Studies*, vol. 46, no. 1, pp. 95–117.

Blondel, J. (1968) 'Party System and Types of Government in Western Democracies', *Canadian Journal of Political Science*, vol. 1, no. 2, pp. 180–203.

Blühdorn, I. (2007) 'The Third Transformation of Democracy: On the Efficient Management of Late-Modern Complexity', in I. Blühdorn and U. Jun (eds) *Economic Efficiency – Democratic Empowerment Contested Modernization in Britain and Germany* (Plymouth: Lexington Books).

Blyth, M. and Katz, R. (2005) 'From Catch-All Politics to Cartelisation: The Political Economy of the Cartel Party', *West European Politics*, vol. 28, no. 1, pp. 33–60.

Bochel, C. (2013) 'Petitions Systems: Contributing to Representative Democracy?' *Parliamentary Affairs*, vol. 66, no. 4, pp. 798–815.

Bogdanor, V. (1997) *Power and the People: A Guide to Constitutional Reform* (London: Victor Gollancz).

Bogdanor, V. (2009) *The New British Constitution* (Oxford: Hart Publishing).

Bogdanor, V. (2011) *The Coalition and the Constitution* (Oxford: Hart Publishing).

Bogdanor, V. (2012) 'Imprisoned by a Doctrine: The Modern Defence of Parliamentary Sovereignty', *Oxford Journal of Legal Studies*, vol. 32, no. 1, pp. 179–95.

Börzel, T. A. and Risse, T. (2010) 'Governance without a State: Can it Work?', *Regulation and Governance*, vol. 4, no. 2, pp. 113–34.

Boswell, J. (2013) 'Why and How Narrative Matters in Deliberative Systems', *Political Studies*, vol. 61, no. 3, pp. 620–36.

Bradley, A. (2011) 'The Sovereignty of Parliament – Form or Substance', in J. Jowell and D. Oliver (eds) *The Changing Constitution* (7th edn.) (Oxford: Oxford University Press).

Brandenburg, H. and Johns, R. (2013) 'The Declining Representativeness of the British Party System, and Why it Matters', *Political Studies*, Early View, DOI: 10.1111/1467-9248.12050.

Brown, G. (2007) *Speech to the National Council of Voluntary Organisations 3 September*, http://webarchive.nationalarchives.gov.uk/20071003115008/http://number10.gov.uk/page13008 (accessed 29 January 2013).

Buckinghamshire NHS. (2011) *Buckinghamshire Citizen's Jury Learning and Outcomes Report: Dementia Services* (Amersham: Buckinghamshire Health Care NHS Trust).

Budge, I. (2012) 'Implementing Popular Preferences: Is Direct Democracy the Answer?', in B. Geissel and K. Newton (eds) *Evaluating Democratic Innovations: Curing the Democratic Malaise* (London: Routledge).

Bühlmann, M. and Kriesi, H. (2013) 'Models for Democracy', in H. Kriesi, S. Lavenex, F. Esser, J. Matthes, M. Bühlmann and H. D. Bochsler (eds) *Democracy in the Age of Globalization and Mediatization* (Houndmills: Palgrave Macmillan).

Burke, E. ([1780] 1801) 'Speech at Bristol at the Conclusion of the Polls', in *Works*, vol. 4 (London: Rivington).

Burstein, P. (1998) 'Interest Organizations, Political Parties, and the Study of Democratic Politics', in A. N. Costain and A. S. McFarland (eds) *Social Movements and American Political Institutions* (Lanham, MD: Rowman & Littlefield).

Butler, D. and Ranney, A. (1978) *Referendums: A Comparative Study of Practice and Theory* (Washington, D.C.: American Enterprise Institute Press).

Cabinet Office. (2010a) *Ministerial Code, May 2010* (London: Cabinet Office).

Cabinet Office. (2010b) *The Coalition: Our Programme for Government* (London: Cabinet Office).

Cabinet Office. (2011a) *The Cabinet Manual: A Guide to the Laws, Conventions and Rules on the Operation of Government* (London: Cabinet Office).

Cabinet Office. (2011b) *Red Tape Challenge,* http://www.redtapechallenge.cabinet office.gov.uk/home/index/ (accessed 2 February 2013).

Cabinet Office. (2012) *Red Tape Challenge – Decision Map,* http://www.red tapechallenge.cabinetoffice.gov.uk/wp-content/uploads/2012/02/Red-Tape-Challenge-Decision-Map.pdf (accessed 2 February 2013).

Cabinet Office. (2013) *The Red Tape Challenge and the Wider Government Deregulation Agenda is Yielding Real Benefits for Business,* http://www.red tapechallenge.cabinetoffice.gov.uk/2013/02/15-02-13-red-tape-challenge-achievements-to-date/ (accessed 4 February 2013).

Cairney, P. (2007) 'The Professionalisation of MPs: Refining the "Politics-Facilitating" Explanation', *Parliamentary Affairs*, vol. 60, no. 2, pp. 212–33.

Cameron, D. (2010) 'Rebuilding Trust in Politics', 8 February (London: University of East London).

Campbell, R., Childs, S. and Lovenduski, J. (2010) 'Do Women Need Women Representatives?', *British Journal of Political Science*, vol. 40, no. 1, pp. 171–94.

Campbell, R. and Cowley, P. (2013) 'What Voters Want: Reactions to Candidate Characteristics in a Survey Experiment', *Political Studies*, Early View, DOI: 10.1111/1467-9248.12048.

Carman, C. (2010) 'The Process is the Reality: Perceptions of Procedural Fairness and Participatory Democracy', *Political Studies*, vol. 58, no. 4, pp. 731–51.

Carman, C. J. (2014) 'Barriers are Barriers: Asymmetric Participation in the Scottish Public Petitions System' *Parliamentary Affairs*, vol. 67, no. 1, pp. 151–71.

Castiglione, D. and Warren, M. E. (2006) 'Rethinking Democratic Representation: Eight Theoretical Issues', Paper Prepared for 'Rethinking Democratic Representation, Centre for the Study of Democratic Institutions, University of British Columbia, 8–19 May.

Celis, K. and Childs, S. (2008) 'Introduction: The Descriptive and Substantive Representation of Women: New Directions', *Parliamentary Affairs*, vol. 61, no. 3, pp. 419–25.

Celis, K. and Childs, S. (2012) 'The Substantive Representation of Women: What to do with Conservative Claims?', *Political Studies*, vol. 60, no. 1, pp. 213–25.

Celis, K., Childs, S., Kantola, J. and Krook, M. L. (2008) 'Rethinking Women's Substantive Representation', *Representation*, vol. 44, no. 2, pp. 99–110.

Chadwick, A. (2009) 'Web 2.0: New Challenges for the Study of E-Democracy in an Era of Informal Exuberance', *I/S Journal of Law and Policy for the Information Society*, vol. 5, pp. 9–41.

Chambers, S. (2003) 'Deliberative Democratic Theory', *Annual Review of Political Science*, vol. 6, pp. 307–26.

Chappell, Z. (2010) 'A Tension Between Ideal and Practice: Re-Evaluation of Micro and Macro Models of Deliberation', *Representation*, vol. 46, no. 3, pp. 295–308.

Chappell, Z. (2012) *Deliberative Democracy: A Critical Introduction* (Houndmills: Palgrave Macmillan).

Childs, S. and Cowley, P. (2011) 'The Politics of Local Presence: Is there a Case for Descriptive Representation?', *Political Studies*, vol. 59, no.1, pp. 1–19.

Childs, S. and Krook, M. L. (2009) 'Analysing Women's Substantive Representation: From Critical Mass to Critical Actors', *Government and Opposition*, vol. 44, no. 2, pp. 125–45.

Childs, S. and Lovenduski, J. (2013) 'Political Representation', in G. Waylen, K. Celis, J. Kantola and L. Weldon (eds) *The Oxford Handbook of Gender and Politics* (Oxford: Oxford University Press).

Childs, S., Webb, P. and Marthaler, S. (2010) 'Constituting and Substantively Representing Women: Applying New Approaches to a UK Case Study', *Politics & Gender*, vol. 6, no. 2, pp. 199–223.

Christiansen, T. (2013) 'European Governance', in M. Cini and N. Pérez-Solórzano Borragán (eds) *European Union Politics* (Oxford: Oxford University Press).

Christoforou, A. (2011) 'Social Capital Across European Countries: Individual and Aggregate Determinants of Group Membership', *American Journal of Economics and Sociology*, vol. 70, no. 3, pp. 699–728.

Clark, A. (2012) *Political Parties in the UK* (Houndmills: Palgrave Macmillan).

Clarke, H. D., Sanders, D., Stewart, M. C. and Whiteley, P. (2004) *Political Choice in Britain* (Cambridge: Cambridge University Press).

Clarke, H. D., Saunders, D., Stewart, M. C. and Whiteley, P. (2009) *Performance Politics and the British Voter* (Cambridge: Cambridge University Press).

Cm 3782. (1997) *Rights Brought Home: The Human Rights Bill* (London: Stationery Office).

Cm 4014. (1998) *Modern Local Government: In Touch with the People* (London: Stationery Office).

Cm 5291. (2001) *The House of Lords: Completing the Reform* (London: Stationery Office).

Cm 7193. (2007) *The Governance of Britain – Petitions: The Government's Response to the Procedure Committee's First Report, Session 2006–07, on Public Petitions and Early Day Motions* (London: Stationery Office).

Cm 7427. (2008) *Communities in Control: Real People Real Power* (London: Stationery Office).

Cm 7824. (2010) *Government Response to the Speaker's Conference Report* (London: Stationery Office).

Cm 8208. (2011) *Political Party Finance: Ending the Big Donor Culture*, Thirteenth Report, Committee on Standards in Public Life (London: Stationery Office).

Coe, N. L. (2012) 'Health Panels: The Development of a Meaningful Method of Public Involvement', *Policy Studies*, vol. 33, no. 3, pp. 263–81.

Colás, A. (2013) *International Civil Society: Social Movements in World Politics* (Cambridge: Polity).

Cole, M. (2006) *Democracy in Britain* (Edinburgh: Edinburgh University Press).

Coleman, S. and Blumler, J. G. (2009) *The Internet and Democratic Citizenship: Theory, Practice and Policy* (Cambridge: Cambridge University Press).

Coleman, S. and Blumler, J. G. (2012) 'The Internet and Citizenship: Democratic Opportunity or More of the Same?', in H. A. Semetko and M. Scammell (eds) *The SAGE Handbook of Political Communication* (London: Sage).

Committee on Standards in Public Life. (2011) *Survey of Public Attitudes Towards Conduct in Public Life in 2010* (London: Committee on Standards in Public Life).

Conservative Party. (2010) *Big Ideas to Give Britain Real Change*, http://www.con servatives.com/News/News_stories/2010/04/~/media/Files/Downloadable%20 Files/Big%20ideas%20to%20give%20Britain%20Real%20change.ashx (accessed 2 February 2013).

Cooper, E. and Smith, G. (2012) 'Organizing Deliberation: The Perspectives of Professional Participation Practitioners in Britain and Germany', *Journal of Public Deliberation*, vol. 8, no. 1, Article 3, pp. 1–39.

Coppedge, M., Gerring, J., Altman, D., Bernhard, M., Fish, S., Hicken, A., Kroenig, M., Lindberg, S. I., McMann, K., Paxton, P., Semetko, H. A., Skaaning, S-E., Staton, J. and Teorell, J. (2011) 'Conceptualizing and Measuring Democracy: A New Approach', *Perspectives on Politics*, vol. 9, no. 2, pp. 247–67.

Cosgrove, R. A. (1980) *The Rule of Law: Albert Venn Dicey, Victorian Jurist* (Houndmills: Macmillan).

Cowley, P. (2002) *Revolts and Rebellions: Parliamentary Voting Under Blair* (London: Politico's).

Cowley, P. (2005) *The Rebels: How Blair Mislaid His Majority* (London: Politico's).

Cowley, P. (2010) 'The Most Rebellious Parliament Ends', *Election 2010 Blog*, http://electionblog2010.blogspot.co.uk/2010/04/most-rebellious-parliament-ends.html (accessed 11 July 2012).

Cowley, P. (2013) 'Why Not Ask the Audience? Understanding the Public's Representational Priorities', *British Politics*, vol. 8, no. 2, pp. 138–63.

Cowley, P. and Stuart, M. (2005) 'Parliament', in A. Seldon and D. Kavanagh (eds) *The Blair Effect 2001–5* (Cambridge: Cambridge University Press).

Cowley, P. and Stuart, M. (2010) 'Party Rules, OK: Voting in the House of Commons on the Human Fertilisation and Embryology Bill', *Parliamentary Affairs*, vol. 63, no. 1, pp. 173–81.

Cowley, P. and Stuart, M. (2012) 'The Coalition's Wobbly Wings: Backbench Dissent in the Commons since May 2010', in H. Kassim, C. Clarke and C. Haddon (eds) *The Coalition: Voters, Parties and Institutions* (London: Institute for Government).

Cowley, P. and Stuart, M. (2013) *Cambo Chained: Dissension Amongst the Coalition's Parliamentary Parties 2012–13* (Nottingham: University of Nottingham).

Cracknell, R. (2012) *Ethnic Minorities in Politics, Government and Public Life*, Standard Note SN/SG/1156 (London: House of Commons Library).

Crouch, C. (2004) *Post-Democracy* (Cambridge: Polity).

Crowley, K. (2009) 'Can Deliberative Democracy Be Practiced? A Subnational Policy Pathway', *Politics & Policy*, vol. 37, no. 5, pp. 995–1021.

Curtice, J. (2007) 'Elections and Public Opinion', in A. Seldon (ed.) *Blair's Britain 1997–2007* (Cambridge: Cambridge University Press).

Curtice, J. (2013) 'Politicians, Voters and Democracy: The 2011 UK Referendum on the Alternative Vote', *Electoral Studies*, vol. 32, no. 2, pp. 215–23.

Daalder, H. (1983) 'The Comparative Study of European Parties and Party Systems: An Overview', in H. Daadler and P. Mair (eds) *Western European Party Systems: Continuity and Change* (London: Sage).

Dahl, R. A. (1998) *On Democracy* (New Haven: Yale University Press).

Dahl, R. A. (2005) 'What Political Institutions Does Large-Scale Democracy Require?', *Political Science Quarterly*, vol. 120, no. 2, pp. 187–97.

Dahlerup, D. (2009) 'What Constitutes Successful Substantive Representation of Women? Theoretical and Methodological Problems in the Study of "Women's Substantive Representation" ', Paper Presented to the International Political Science Association World Congress, Santiago de Chile, 11–16 July.

Dalton, R. J. (1985) 'Political Parties and Political Representation: Party Supporters and Party Elites in Nine Nations', *Comparative Political Studies*, vol. 18, no. 3, pp. 267–99.

Dalton, R. J. (2004) *Democratic Challenges, Democratic Choices* (Oxford: Oxford University Press).

Dalton, R. J., Farrell, D. M. and McAllister, I. (2011) *Political Parties and Democratic Linkage: How Parties Organize Democracy* (Oxford: Oxford University Press).

Dalton, R. J. and Gray, M. (2003) 'Expanding the Electoral Marketplace', in B. E. Cain, R. J. Dalton and S. E. Scarrow (eds) *Democracy Transformed? Expanding Political Opportunities in Advanced Industrial Democracies* (Oxford: Oxford University Press).

Darcy, R., Welch, S. and Clark, J. (1994) *Women, Elections and Representation* (2nd edn.) (Nebraska: University of Nebraska Press).

Daugbjerg, C. and Marsh, D. (1998) 'Explaining Policy Outcomes: Integrating the Policy Network Approach with Macro-Level and Micro-Level Analysis', in D. Marsh (ed.) *Comparing Policy Networks* (Buckingham: Open University Press).

Davidson, S. and Elstub, S. (2013) 'Deliberative and Participatory Democracy in the UK', *British Journal of Politics and International Relations*, Early View, DOI: 10.1111/1467-856X.12001.

Davis, A. (2011) 'The 99%: A Community of Resistance', Comment is Free, *The Guardian*, 15 November.

Della Porta, D. and Diani, M. (2006) *Social Movements: An Introduction* (2nd edn.) (Oxford: Blackwell).

Delli Carpini, M. and Keeter, S. (1996) *What Americans Know About Politics and Why it Matters* (New Haven: Yale University Press).

DeNardo, J. (1985) *Power in Numbers: The Political Strategy of Protest and Rebellion* (Princeton, NJ: Princeton University Press).

Denemark, D. and Niemi, R. G. (2012) 'Political Trust, Efficacy and Engagement in Challenging Times: An Introduction', *Australian Journal of Political Science*, vol. 47, no. 1, pp. 1–9.

Denver, D. (2007) *Elections and Voters in Britain* (2nd edn.) (Houndmills: Palgrave Macmillan).

Denver, D. (2010) 'The Results: How Britain Voted', *Parliamentary Affairs*, vol. 63, no. 4, pp. 588–606.

Denver, D. (2011) 'Elections and Voting', in R. Heffernan, P. Cowley and C. Hay (eds) *Developments in British Politics 9* (Houndmills: Palgrave Macmillan).

Denver, D., Carman, C. and Johns, R. (2012) *Elections and Voters in Britain* (3rd edn.) (Houndmills: Palgrave Macmillan).

Department for Communities and Local Government. (2010) *Decentralisation and the Localism Bill: An Essential Guide* (London: Department for Communities and Local Government).

Department for Communities and Local Government. (2011) *Introduction to Neighbourhood Planning* (London: Department for Communities and Local Government).

Department of Health. (2008) *Real Involvement Working with People to Improve Health Guidance for NHS Organisations on Section 242(1B) of the NHS Act 2006, the Duty to Involve and Good Involvement Practice* (London: Department of Health).

Department of the Environment, Transport and the Regions. (1998) *Modernising Local Government Local Democracy and Community Leadership Paper* (London: Department of the Environment, Transport and the Regions).

Detterbeck, K. (2005) 'Cartel Parties in Western Europe?', *Party Politics*, vol. 11, no. 2, pp. 173–191.

Dewey, J. ([1927] 1989) *The Public and Its Problems* (Athens, OH: Ohio University Press).

Diamond, P. (2011) 'Beyond the Westminster Model: The Labour Party and the Machinery of the British Parliamentary State', *Renewal*, vol. 19, no. 1, pp. 64–74.

Diamond, P. and Richards, D. (2012) 'The Case for Theoretical and Methodological Pluralism in British Political Studies: New Labour's Political Memoirs and the British Tradition', *Political Studies Review*, vol. 10, no. 2, pp. 177–94.

Diani, M. (2012) 'Interest Organizations in Social Movements: An Empirical Exploration', *Interest Groups and Advocacy*, vol. 1, no. 1, pp. 26–47.

Dicey, A. V. ([1885] 1959) *An Introduction to the Law of the Constitution* (10th edn.) (Houndmills: Macmillan).

Dicey, A. V. (1894) 'The Referendum', *National Review*, vol. 23, March, pp. 65–72.

Dicey, A. V. ([1915] 1982) *An Introduction to the Law of the Constitution* (8th edn.) (Indianapolis: Liberty Fund).

Douglass, R. (2013) 'Rousseau's Critique of Representative Sovereignty: Principled or Pragmatic?', *American Journal of Political Science*, vol. 57, no. 3, pp. 735–47.

Dovi, S. (2002) 'Preferable Descriptive Representatives: Will Just Any Woman, Black or Latino Do?', *American Political Science Review*, vol. 96, no. 4, pp. 729–43.

Drewry, G. (2007) 'The Jurisprudence of British Euroscepticism: A Strange Banquet of Fish and Vegetables', *Utrecht Law Review*, vol. 3, no. 2, pp. 101–15.

Driver, S. (2011) *Understanding British Party Politics* (Cambridge: Polity).

Dryzek, J. S. (2001) 'Legitimacy and Economy in Deliberative Democracy', *Political Theory*, vol. 29, no. 5, pp. 651–69.

Dryzek, J. S. (2010) *Foundations and Frontiers of Deliberative Governance* (Oxford: Oxford University Press).

Dryzek, J. S. and Dunleavy, P. (2009) *Theories of the Democratic State* (Houndmills: Palgrave Macmillan).

Dubnik, M. J. (2011) 'Move Over Daniel: We Need Some "Accountability Space"', *Administration and Society*, vol. 43, no. 6, pp. 704–16.

Durose, C., Gains, F., Richardson, L., Combs, R., Broome, K. and Eason, C. (2011) *Pathways to Politics* (London: Equality and Human Rights Commission).

Duverger, M. (1964) *Political Parties: Their Organization and Activity in the Modern State* (3rd edn.) (London: Methuen).

Dyzenhaus, D. (2013) 'Austin, Hobbes, and Dicey', in M. Freeman and P. Mindus (eds) *The Legacy of John Austin's Jurisprudence* (London: Springer).

Easton, D. (1965) *A Systems Analysis of Political Life* (New York: Wiley).

Electoral Commission. (2010) *What was the Turnout at Recent Elections?* http://www.electoralcommission.org.uk/faq/elections/turnout-general-elections (accessed 16 April 2012).

Electoral Commission. (2011) *UK General Election 2010, Campaign Spending Report* (London: Electoral Commission).

Eleftheriadis, P. (2009) 'Parliamentary Sovereignty and the Constitution', *Canadian Journal of Law and Jurisprudence*, vol. 22, no. 2, pp. 267–90.

Elstub, S. (2010) 'Linking Micro Deliberative Democracy and Decision-Making: Trade-offs between Theory and Practice in a Partisan Citizen Forum', *Representation*, vol. 46, no. 3, pp. 309–24.

England and Wales High Court 195. (2002) *Thoburn v Sunderland City Council*, England and Wales High Court (Administrative Court) Decisions (London: Supreme Court of Judicature, Queen's Bench Division).

Eriksen, E. O. and Fossum, J. E. (2011) 'Representation Through Deliberation: The European Case', *RECON Online Working Paper 2011/14*, (Oslo: ARENA), http://www.reconproject.eu/main.php/RECON_wp_1114.pdf?fileitem=5456472 (accessed 2 June 2013).

Esaiasson, P., Gilljam, M. and Persson, M. (2012) 'Which Decision-Making Arrangements Generate the Strongest Legitimacy Beliefs? Evidence from a Randomised Field Experiment', *European Journal of Political Research*, vol. 51, no. 6, pp. 785–808.

Eurobarometer. (2013) *Public Opinion in the European Union: May 2013*, Standard Eurobarometer 79, Table of Results (Brussels: European Commission).

European Commission. (2012) *A Blueprint for a Deep and Genuine Economic and Monetary Union: Launching a European Debate*, COM(2012) 777 final/2 (Brussels: European Commission).

Evans, E. (2012) 'From Finance to Equality: The Substantive Representation of Women's Interests by Men and Women MPs in the House of Commons', *Representation*, vol. 48, no. 2, pp. 183–96.

Evans, G. and Tilley, J. (2012) 'How Parties Shape Class Politics: Explaining the Decline of the Class Basis of Party Support', *British Journal of Political Science*, vol. 42, no. 1, pp. 137–61.

Falk, R. and Strauss, A. (2001) 'Toward Global Parliament', *Foreign Affairs*, vol. 80, no. 1, pp. 212–20.

Fawcett, P. and Daugbjerg, C. (2012) 'Explaining Governance Outcomes: Epistemology, Network Governance and Policy Network Analysis', *Political Studies Review*, vol. 10, no. 2, pp. 195–207.

Fieldhouse, E., Trammer, M. and Russell, A. (2007) 'Something About Young People or Something About Elections? Electoral Participation of Young People: Evidence from a Multilevel Analysis of the European Social Survey', *European Journal of Political Research*, vol. 46, no. 6, pp. 797–822.

Fisher, J. (2009) 'Hayden Phillips and Jack Straw: The Continuation of British Exceptionalism in Party Finance', *Parliamentary Affairs*, vol. 62, no. 2, pp. 298–317.

Fisher, J., Fieldhouse, E. and Cutts, D. (2013a) 'Members Are Not the Only Fruit: Volunteer Activity in British Political Parties at the 2010 General Election', *British Journal of Politics and International Relations*, Early View, DOI: 10.1111/1467-856X.12011.

Fisher, J., Johnston, R., Cutts, D., Pattie, C. and Fieldhouse, E. (2013b) 'You Get What You (Don't) Pay for: The Impact of Volunteer Labour and Candidate Spending at the 2010 British General Election', *Parliamentary Affairs*, Advance Access, DOI: 10.1093/pa/gst006.

Fisher, J., van Heerde, J. and Tucker, A. (2010) 'Does One Trust Judgement Fit All? Linking Theory and Empirics', *British Journal of Politics and International Relations*, vol. 12, no. 2, pp. 161–88.

Fisher, J., van Heerde, J. and Tucker, A. (2011) 'Why Both Theory and Empirics Suggest There is More than One Form of Trust: A Response to Hooghe', *British Journal of Politics and International Relations*, vol. 13, no. 2, pp. 276–81.

Fishkin, J. S. (2009) *When The People Speak: Deliberative Democracy and Public Consultation* (Oxford: Oxford University Press).

Flanagan, C., Finlay, A., Gallay, L. and Kim, T. (2012) 'Political Incorporation and the Protracted Transition to Adulthood: The Need for New Institutional Inventions', *Parliamentary Affairs*, vol. 65, no. 1, pp. 29–46.

Flinders, M. (2002) 'Shifting the Balance? 'Parliament, the Executive and the British Constitution', *Political Studies*, vol. 50, no. 1, pp. 23–42.

Flinders, M. (2008) *Delegated Governance and the British State: Walking Without Order* (Oxford: Oxford University Press).

Flinders, M. (2010) *Democratic Drift: Majoritarian Modification and Democratic Anomie in the United Kingdom* (Oxford: Oxford University Press).

Flinders, M. (2011) 'Daring to be Daniel: The Pathology of Politicized Accountability in Monitory Democracy', *Administration and Society*, vol. 43, no. 5, pp. 595–619.

Franklin, M. and Hobolt, S. (2011) 'The Legacy of Lethargy: How Elections to the European Parliament Depress Turnout', *Electoral Studies*, vol. 30, no. 1, pp. 67–76.

Franklin, M., Lyons, P. and Marsh, M. (2004) 'Generational Basis of Turnout Decline in Established Democracies', *Acta Politica*, vol. 39, no. 2, pp. 115–51.

Franklin, M. and Wessels, B. (2002) 'Learning (Not) to Vote: The Generational Basis of Turnout Decline in Established Democracies', Paper Delivered at the Annual Meeting of the American Political Science Association, Boston MA, 29 August – 1 September.

Frazer, E. and Macdonald, K. (2003) 'Sex Differences in Political Knowledge in Britain', *Political Studies*, vol. 51, no. 1, pp. 67–83.

Froud, J., Nilsson, A., Moran, M. and Williams, K. (2012) 'Stories and Interests in Finance: Agendas of Governance Before and After the Financial Crisis', *Governance*, vol. 25, no. 1, pp. 35–59.

Fuks, M. and Casalecchi, G. A. (2012) 'Trust and Political Information: Attitudinal Change in Participants in the Youth Parliament in Brazil', *Brazilian Political Science Review*, vol. 6, no. 1, pp. 70–89.

Galligan, Y. (2007) 'Gender and Political Representation: Current Empirical Perspectives', *International Political Science Review*, vol. 28, no. 5, pp. 557–70.

Gamble, A. (1990) 'Theories of British Politics', *Political Studies*, vol. 37, no. 3, pp. 404–20.

Garsten, B. (2009) 'Representative Government and Popular Sovereignty', in I. Shapiro, S. C. Stokes, E. J. Wood and A. S. Kirshner (eds) *Political Representation* (Cambridge: Cambridge University Press).

Gauja, A. (2013) *The Politics of Party Policy: From Members to Legislators* (Houndmills: Palgrave Macmillan).

Gay, O. (2005) 'MPs Go Back to Their Constituencies', *Political Quarterly*, vol. 76, no. 1, pp. 57–66.

Gibson, R. K. (2013) 'Party Change, Social Media and the Rise of "Citizen-Initiated" Campaigning', *Party Politics*, Early View, DOI: 10.1177/1354068812472575.

Gibson, R. K. and McAllister, I. (2011) 'How the Internet is Driving the Political Knowledge Gap', Paper Presented at the American Political Science Association Meeting, Seattle, 31 August–4 September.

Giger, N., Rosset, J. and Bernauer, J. (2012) 'The Poor Political Representation of the Poor in Comparative Perspective', *Representation*, vol. 48, no. 1, pp. 47–61.

Godefroy, R. and Henry, E. (2011) *Voter Turnout and Fiscal Policy*, http://ssrn.com/abstract=1960551 (accessed 16 April 2012).

Goldsworthy, J. (1999) *The Sovereignty of Parliament: History and Philosophy* (Oxford: Oxford University Press).

Goldsworthy, J. (2010) *Parliamentary Sovereignty: Contemporary Debates* (Cambridge: Cambridge University Press).

Goldsworthy, J. (2012) 'Parliamentary Sovereignty's Premature Obituary', *UK Constitutional Law Group*, http://ukconstitutionallaw.org/2012/03/09/jeffrey-goldsworthy-parliamentary-sovereigntys-premature-obituary/ (accessed 10 November 2012).

Gooberman-Hill, R., Horwood, J. and Calnan, M. (2008) 'Citizens' Juries in Planning Research Priorities: Process, Engagement and Outcome', *Health Expectations*, vol. 11, no. 3, pp. 272–81.

Goodin, R. E. (2008) *Innovating Democracy: Democratic Theory and Practice After the Deliberative Turn* (Oxford: Oxford University Press).

Goodin, R. E. (2012) 'How Can Deliberative Democracy Get a Grip', *Political Quarterly*, vol. 83, no. 4, pp. 806–11.

Goodin, R. E. and Dryzek, J. S. (2006) 'Deliberative Impacts: The Macro-Political Uptake of Mini-Publics', *Politics & Society*, vol. 34, no. 2, pp. 219–44.

Gov.uk. (2010) *Your Freedom*, http://www.number10.gov.uk/news/your-freedom/ (accessed 2 February 2013).

Graham, T. (2008) 'Needles in a Haystack: A New Approach for Identifying and Assessing Political Talk in Non-Political Discussion Forums', *Javnost – The Public*, vol. 15, no. 2, pp. 17–36.

Grant, W. (2000) *Pressure Groups and British Politics* (London: Macmillan).

Grieve, D. (2012) 'Parliament and the Judiciary', *Speech to BPP Law School*, 25 October, http://www.attorneygeneral.gov.uk/NewsCentre/Speeches/Pages/AttorneyGeneralSpeechtoBPPLawSchool.aspx (accessed 10 November 2012).

Griffith, J. and Leston-Bandeira, C. (2012) 'How are Parliaments Using New Media to Engage with Citizens?', *Journal of Legislative Studies*, vol. 18, no. 3–4, pp. 496–513.

Groves, J. (2012) 'Increase in "Professional Politicians" Means One in Seven MPs Have Never Done a Real Job', *Daily Mail*, 19 July 2012.

Habermas, J. (1996) *Between Facts and Norms: Contributions to a Discourse Theory of Law and Democracy* (Cambridge, MA: MIT Press).

Hackett, P. and Hunter, P. (2010) *Who Governs Britain? A Profile of MPs in the New Parliament* (London: Smith Institute).

Hain, P. (2012) 'Refounding British Labour to Win', *Social Europe Journal*, http://www.social-europe.eu/2012/03/refounding-british-labour-to-win/ (accessed 24 July 2012).

Hajnal, Z. and Trounstine, J. (2005) 'Where Turnout Matters: The Consequences of Uneven Turnout in City Politics', *The Journal of Politics*, vol. 67, no. 2, pp. 515–35.

Hall, M. (2011) *Political Traditions and UK Politics* (Houndmills: Palgrave Macmillan).

Hansard Society. (2005) *Audit of Political Engagement 2* (London: Hansard Society).

Hansard Society. (2007) *Audit of Political Engagement 4* (London: Hansard Society).

Hansard Society. (2010a) *Audit of Political Engagement 7* (London: Hansard Society).

Hansard Society. (2010b) *Lessons from Abroad: How Parliaments Around The World Engage With Their Public* (London: Hansard Society).

Hansard Society. (2011) *Audit of Political Engagement 8* (London: Hansard Society).

Hansard Society. (2012a) *Audit of Political Engagement 9* (London: Hansard Society).

Hansard Society. (2012b) *What Next for e-Petitions?* (London: Hansard Society).

Hansard Society. (2013) *Audit of Political Engagement 10* (London: Hansard Society).

Harman, H. (2006) *A New Deal for Democracy*, Speech to the Hansard Society, 16 January, http://www.harrietharman.org/a_new_deal_for_democracy (accessed 10 April 2012).

Hart, H. L. A. (1994) *The Concept of Law* (2nd edn.) (Oxford: Oxford University Press).

Hay, C. (2007) *Why We Hate Politics* (Cambridge: Polity Press).

Hayward, C. R. (2009) 'Making Interest: On Representation and Democratic Legitimacy', in I. Shapiro, S. C. Stokes, E. J. Wood and A. S. Kirshner (eds) *Political Representation* (Cambridge: Cambridge University Press).

Hazell, R. (2007) 'The Continuing Dynamism of Constitutional Reform', *Parliamentary Affairs*, vol. 60, no. 1, pp. 3–25.

Hazell, R., Bourke, G. and Worthy, B. (2012) 'Open House? Freedom of Information and its Impact on the UK Parliament', *Public Administration*, vol. 90, no. 4, pp. 901–21.

HC 96. (2012) *Post-Legislative Scrutiny of the Freedom of Information Act 2000*, Justice Committee, First Report, Session 2012–13 (London: Stationery Office).

HC 136. (2008) *e-Petitions*, Procedure Committee, First Report, Session 2007–08 (London: Stationery Office).

HC 239. (2010) *Speaker's Conference (on Parliamentary Representation)*, Final Report (London: Stationery Office).

HC 330. (2012) *Sitting Hours and the Parliamentary Calendar*, Procedure Committee, First Report, Session 2012–13 (London: Stationery Office).

HC 337. (2007) *Revitalising the Chamber: The Role of the Backbench Member*, Select Committee on Modernisation of the House of Commons, First Report, Session 2006–07 (London: Stationery Office).

HC 437. (2010) *Parliamentary Voting System and Constituencies Bill*, Political and Constitutional Reform Committee, Third Report, Session 2010–11 (London: Stationery Office).

HC 493. (2009) *e-Petitions: Call for Government Action*, Procedure Committee, Second Report, Session 2008–09 (London: Stationery Office).

HC 513. (2007) *Public Petitions and Early Day Motions*, Procedure Committee, First Report, Session 2006–07 (London: Stationery Office).

HC 600. (1998) *Modernisation of the House of Commons*, Select Committee on Modernisation of the House of Commons, Fourth Report, Session 1997–8 (London: HMSO).

HC 633. (2010) *The EU Bill and Parliamentary Sovereignty*, European Scrutiny Committee, Tenth Report, Session 2010–11 (London: Stationery Office).

HC 697. (2012) *Select Committee Effectiveness, Resources and Powers*, Liaison Committee, Second Report, Session 2012–13 (London: Stationery Office).

HC 1117. (2009) *Rebuilding the House*, House of Commons Reform Committee, First Report, Session 2008–09 (London: Stationery Office).

HC 1706. (2012) *Debates on Government e-Petitions*, Procedure Committee, Seventh Report, Session 2010–12 (London: Stationery Office).

HC 1786-I. (2012) *The Responsibilities of the Secretary of State for Education*, Education Committee, Oral Evidence (London: Stationery Office).

HC 1902. (2012) *Debates on Government e-Petitions: Government Response*, Procedure Committee, Seventh Report, Session 2010–12 (London: Stationery Office).

Heath, A. F., Fisher, S. D., Sanders, D., Rosenblatt, G. and Sobolewska, M. (2013) *The Political Integration of Ethnic Minorities in Britain* (Oxford: Oxford University Press).

Heffernan, R. (2009) 'Political Parties', in M. Flinders, A. Gamble, C. Hay and M. Kenny (eds) *The Oxford Handbook of British Politics* (Oxford: Oxford University Press).

Heffernan, R. (2011) 'Pressure Group Politics', in R. Heffernan, P. Cowley and C. Hay (eds) *Developments in British Politics Nine* (Houndmills: Palgrave Macmillan).

Hefftler, C. and Wessel, W. (2013) *The Democratic Legitimacy of the EU's Economic Governance and National Parliaments*, IAI Working Paper 13/13 (Rome: Istituto Affari Internazionali).

Held, D. (2006) *Models of Democracy* (Cambridge: Polity).

Held, D. and McGrew, A. (2002) *Globalization/Anti-Globalization* (Cambridge: Polity).

Hendriks, F. and Michels, A. (2011) 'Democracy Transformed? Reforms in Britain and the Netherlands (1990–2010)', *International Journal of Public Administration*, vol. 34, no. 5, pp. 307–17.

Henn, M. and Foard, N. (2012) 'Young People, Political Participation and Trust in Britain', *Parliamentary Affairs*, vol. 65, no. 1, pp. 47–67.

Hibbing, J. R. and Theiss Morse, E. (2002) *Stealth Democracy: Americans' Beliefs About How Government Should Work* (Cambridge: Cambridge University Press).

Highton, B. and Wolfinger, R. E. (2001) 'The Political Implications of Higher Turnout', *British Journal of Political Science*, vol. 31, no. 1, pp. 179–92.

HL 86/HC 111. (2010) *Counter-Terrorism Policy and Human Rights (17th Report): Bringing Human Rights Back In*, Joint Committee on Human Rights, Sixteenth Report, Session 2009–10 (London: Stationery Office).

HL 99. (2010) *Referendums in the United Kingdom*, Select Committee on the Constitution, Twelfth Report, Session 2009–10 (London: Stationery Office).

HL 263. (2012) *Referendum on Scottish Independence*, Select Committee on the Constitution, Twenty-Fourth Report, Session 2010–12 (London: Stationery Office).

HM Government (1975) *Britain's New Deal in Europe* (London: Stationery Office).

HM Government/Scottish Government. (2012) *Agreement between the UK and Scottish Governments*, 15 October 2012, http://webarchive.national archives.gov.uk/20130109092234/http://www.number10.gov.uk/wp-content/uploads/2012/10/Agreement-final-for-signing.pdf (accessed 11 August 2013).

HM Treasury (2010) *Spending Challenge*, http://webarchive.nationalarchives.gov.uk/20130129110402/http://www.hm-treasury.gov.uk/spend_spending challenge.htm (accessed 3 March 2013).

Hochschild, J. L. (2010) 'If Democracies Need Informed Voters, How Can They Thrive While Expanding Enfranchisement', *Election Law Journal*, vol. 9, no. 2, pp. 111–23.

Holliday, I. (2000) 'Is the British State Hollowing Out?', *Political Quarterly*, vol. 71, no. 2, pp. 167–76.

Home Office. (2013) *Life in the United Kingdom: A Guide for New Residents* (3rd edn.) (London: Stationery Office).

Hooghe, M. (2011) 'Why There is Basically Only One Form of Political Trust', *British Journal of Politics and International Relations*, vol. 13, no. 2, pp. 269–75.

Hooghe, M., Marien, S. and Pauwels, T. (2011) 'Where Do Distrusting Voters Turn if There is No Viable Exit or Voice Option? The Impact of Political Trust on Electoral Behaviour in the Belgian Regional Elections of June 2009', *Government and Opposition*, vol. 46, no. 2, pp. 245–73.

Hough, R. (2012) 'Do Legislative Petitions Systems Enhance the Relationship between Parliament and Citizen?', *Journal of Legislative Studies*, vol. 18, no. 3–4, pp. 479–95.

House of Commons. (2012) *Corporate Business Plan 2012–13 to 2014–15* (London: House of Commons).

House of Commons Library. (2011) *Free Votes*, Standard Note SN/PC/04793 (London: House of Commons).

Howe, J. (2008) 'Jeff Howe on "Crowdsourcing"', *CNET News*, 27 August, http://news.cnet.com/8301-13772_3-10025730-52.html (accessed 18 February 2013).

Institute of Government. (2011) *Engaging Citizens in Policy Design – The Practicalities*, http://www.instituteforgovernment.org.uk/events/engaging-citizens-policy-design-practicalities (accessed 18 February 2013).

Ipsos MediaCT. (2009) *Social Grade Classification Tool* (London: Ipsos Mori) http://www.ipsos-mori.com/DownloadPublication/1285_MediaCT_thought-piece_Social_Grade_July09_V3_WEB.pdf (accessed 30 September 2012).

Jackson, N. and Lilleker, D. (2009) 'MPs and E-Representation: Me, MySpace and I', *British Politics*, vol. 4, no. 2, pp. 236–64.

Jackson, N. and Lilleker, D. (2011) 'Microblogging, Constituency Service and Impression Management: UK MPs and the Use of Twitter', *Journal of Legislative Studies*, vol. 17, no. 1, pp. 86–105.

James, M. R. (2011) 'The Priority of Racial Constituency over Descriptive Representation', *Journal of Politics*, vol. 73, no. 2, pp. 899–914.

Jessop, B. (2004) 'Multi-Level Governance and Multi-Level Metagovernance – Changes in the European Union as Integral Moments in the Transformation and Reorientation of Contemporary Statehood', in I. Bache and M. Flinders (eds) *Multi-Level Governance* (Oxford: Oxford University Press).

Johal, S., Moran, M. and Williams, K. (2012a) 'The Future Has Been Postponed: The Great Financial Crisis and British Politics', *British Politics*, vol. 7, no. 1, pp. 69–81.

Johal, S., Moran, M. and Williams, K. (2012b) 'Post-Crisis Financial Regulation in Britain', in R. Mayntz (ed.) *Crisis and Control: Institutional Change in Financial Market Regulation* (Frankfurt: Campus).

Johnson, C. and Rosenblatt, G. (2007) 'Do MPs Have the Right Stuff', *Parliamentary Affairs*, vol. 69, no. 1, pp. 164–9.

Johnston, R. and Pattie, C. (2011) 'The British General Election of 2010: A Three-Party Contest – or Three Two-Party Contests?', *The Geographical Journal*, vol. 177, no. 1, pp. 17–26.

Johnston, R., Pattie, C. and Rossiter, D. (2012) 'The Principles and Processes of Redistribution: Issues Raised by Recent UK Legislation', *Commonwealth and Comparative Politics*, vol. 50, no. 1, pp. 3–26.

Jones, G. and Stewart, J. (2010) 'Council Tax Referendums Are Damaging', *Local Government Chronicle*, 5 August.

Jordan, A. G. (1990) 'Policy Community Realism versus "New" Institutionalist Ambiguity', *Political Studies*, vol. 38, no. 3, pp. 470–85.

Jordan, A. G. and Richardson, J. J. (1987) *Government and Pressure Groups in Britain* (Oxford: Clarendon Press).

Jordan, G. and Cairney, P. (2013) 'What is the "Dominant Model" of British Policymaking? Comparing Majoritarian and Policy Community Ideas', *British Politics*, vol. 8, no. 3, pp. 233–59.

Jordan, G. and Maloney, W. (2007) *Democracy and Interest Groups: Enhancing Democracy* (Houndmills: Palgrave Macmillan).

Judge, D. (1978) 'Public Petitions and the House of Commons', *Parliamentary Affairs*, vol. 31, no. 4, pp. 391–405.

Judge, D. (1990) 'Parliament and Interest Representation', in M. Rush (ed.) *Parliament and Pressure Politics* (Oxford: Clarendon Press).

Judge, D. (1993) *The Parliamentary State* (London: Sage).

Judge, D. (1999) *Representation: Theory and Practice in Britain* (London: Routledge).

Judge, D. (2005) *Political Institutions in the United Kingdom* (Oxford: Oxford University Press).

Judge, D. and Earnshaw, D. (2008) *The European Parliament* (Houndmills: Palgrave Macmillan).

Kam, C. J. (2009) *Party Discipline and Parliamentary Politics* (Cambridge: Cambridge University Press).

Kateb, G. (1981) 'The Moral Distinctiveness of Representative Democracy', *Ethics*, vol. 91, no. 3, pp. 357–74.

Katz, R. S. and Mair, P. (1995) 'Changing Models of Party Organization and Party Democracy: The Emergence of the Cartel Party', *Party Politics*, vol. 1, no. 1, pp. 5–28.

Katz, R. S. and Mair, P. (2009) 'The Cartel Party Thesis: A Restatement', *Perspectives on Politics*, vol. 7, no. 4, pp. 753–66.

Katz, R. S. and Mair, P. (2012) 'Parties, Interest Groups and Cartels: A Comment', *Party Politics*, vol. 18, no. 1, pp. 107–11.

Kavanagh, A. (2009) *Constitutional Review Under the UK Human Rights Act* (Cambridge: Cambridge University Press).

Kavanagh, A. (2011) 'Constitutionalism, Counterterrorism, and the Courts: Changes in the British Constitutional Landscape', *International Journal of Constitutional Law*, vol. 9, no. 1, pp. 172–99.

Kavanagh, D. (2009) 'Antecedents', in M. Flinders, A. Gamble, C. Hay and M. Kenny (eds) *The Oxford Handbook of British Politics* (Oxford: Oxford University Press).

Kavanagh, D. and Cowley, P. (2010) *The British General Election 2010* (Houndmills: Palgrave Macmillan).

Keane, J. (2008) 'Hypocrisy and Democracy: The Gap Between Ideals and Perceived Reality is Widening', *WZB-Mitteilungen*, no. 120, June 2008, pp. 30–2, http://bibliothek.wzb.eu/artikel/2008/f-14168.pdf (accessed 15 March 2013).

Keane, J. (2009) *The Life and Death of Democracy* (London: Pocket Books).

Keane, J. (2011) 'Monitory Democracy?', in S. Alonso, J. Keane and W. Merkel (eds) *The Future of Representative Democracy* (Cambridge: Cambridge University Press).

Keating, A., Kerr, D., Benton, T., Mundy, E. and Lopes, J. (2010) *Citizen Education in England 2001–2010: Young People's Practices and Prospects for the Future: The Eighth and Final Report from the Citizenship Education Longitudinal Study* (London: Department for Education).

Keating, M. (2008) 'Culture and Social Science', in D. Della Porta and M. Keating (eds) *Approaches and Methodologies in the Social Sciences* (Cambridge: Cambridge University Press).

Keating, M. (2009) *The Independence of Scotland: Self-government and the Shifting Politics of the Union* (Oxford: Oxford University Press).

Keating, M. (2012) 'Reforging the Nation: Britain, Scotland and the Crisis of Unionism', in M. Seymour and A-G. Gagnon (eds) *Multinational Federalism: Problems and Prospects* (Houndmills: Palgrave Macmillan).

Kellner, P. (2012) *Democracy on Trial: What Voters Really Think of Parliament and Our Politicians* (Oxford: Reuters Institute for the Study of Journalism).

Kelso, A. (2009) *Parliamentary Reform at Westminster* (Manchester: Manchester University Press).

Kickert, W. (2012) 'How the UK Government Responded to the Fiscal Crisis: An Outsider's View', *Public Money and Management*, May, pp. 169–76.

Kitscheldt, H. (2012) 'Parties and Political Intermediation', in E. Amenta, K. Nash and A. Scott (eds) *The Wiley-Blackwell Companion to Political Sociology* (London: John Wiley and Sons).

Kjaer, A. M. (2004) *Governance* (Cambridge: Polity).

Koole, R. (1996) 'Cadre, Catch-All or Cartel? A Comment on the Notion of the Cartel Party', *Party Politics*, vol. 2, no. 4, pp. 507–23.

Korris, M. (2011) *A Year in the Life: From Member of Public to Member of Parliament* (London: Hansard Society).

Kröger, S. and Friedrich, D. (2013) 'Introduction: The Representative Turn in EU Studies', *Journal of European Public Policy*, vol. 20, no. 2, pp. 155–70.

Krook, M. L. (2009) *Quotas for Women in Politics: Gender and Candidate Selection Reform Worldwide* (Oxford: Oxford University Press).

Krook, M. L. (2010) 'Studying Political Representation: A Comparative Gendered Approach', *Perspectives on Politics*, vol. 8. no. 1, pp. 233–40.

Kuper, A. (2004) *Democracy Beyond Borders: Justice and Representation in Global Institutions* (Oxford: Oxford University Press).

Labour Party. (2011) *Refounding Labour to Win: A Party for the New Generation* (London: Labour Party).

Labour Party. (2012) *Refounding Labour: Real Change for Partnership into Power* (London: Labour Party).

Laisney, M. (2012) 'The Initiation of Local Authority Referendums: Participatory Momentum or Political Tactics? The UK Case', *Local Government Studies*, vol. 38, no. 5, pp. 639–59.

Lakin, S. (2008) 'Debating the Idea of Parliamentary Sovereignty: The Controlling Factor of Legality in the British Constitution', *Oxford Journal of Legal Studies*, vol. 28, no. 4. pp. 709–34.

Lakin, S. (2012) 'Why UK Public Lawyers Need to be Legal and Political Theorists', *Durham Law Review*, http://papers.ssrn.com/sol3/papers.cfm?abstract_id=2130593 (accessed 12 November 2012).

Lavenex, S. (2013) 'Globalization and the Vertical Challenge to Democracy', in H. Kriesi, S. Lavenex, F. Esser, J. Matthes, M. Bühlmann and H. D. Bochsler (eds) *Democracy in the Age of Globalization and Mediatization* (Houndmills: Palgrave Macmillan).

Lee, B. J. (2012) 'Window Dressing 2.0: Constituency Level Online Campaigns in the 2010 UK General Election', Paper Presented at the Political Studies Association Annual Conference, Belfast, 3–5 April.

Lees-Marshment, J. (2008) *Political Marketing and British Political Parties* (2nd edn.) (Manchester: Manchester University Press).

Lewis, J. (2004) 'Television, Public Opinion and the War in Iraq: The Case of Britain', *International Journal of Public Opinion Research*, vol. 1, no. 3, pp. 295–310.

Liberal Democrats. (2010) *Liberal Democrat Manifesto 2010* (London: Liberal Democrats).

Lijphart, A. (1984) *Democracies: Patterns of Majoritarian and Consensus Government in Twenty-One Countries* (New Haven: Yale University Press).

Lijphart, A. (1999) *Patterns of Democracy: Government Forms and Performance in Thirty-Six Countries* (New Haven: Yale University Press).

Lijphart, A. (2012) *Patterns of Democracy: Government Forms and Performance in Thirty-Six Countries* (2nd edn.) (New Haven: Yale University Press).

Lilleker, D. G. and Jackson, N. A. (2010) 'Towards a More Participatory Style of Election Campaigning? The Impact of Web 2.0 on the UK 2010 General Election', *Policy & Internet*, vol. 2, no. 3, Article 4, pp. 69–98.

Lilleker, D. G., Pack, M. and Jackson, N. (2010) 'Political Parties and Web 2.0: The Liberal Democrat Perspective', *Politics*, vol. 30, no. 2, pp. 105–12.

Lindner, R. and Riehm, U. (2009) 'Electronic Petitions and Institutional Modernization': International Parliamentary E-Petitions in Comparative Perspective', *Journal of e-Democracy*, vol. 1, no. 1, pp. 1–11.

Lippmann, W. (1922) *Public Opinion* (New York: Free Press).

Local Government Association. (2012) *Neighbourhood Planning (Referendums) Regulations 2012*, Briefing Note, 23 July (London: Local Government Association).

Lodge, M. and Wegrich, K. (2012) *The Californification of Government? Crowdsourcing and the Red Tape Challenge*, Centre for Analysis of Risk and Regulation, Discussion Paper no 72 (London: London School of Economics).

Loomes, G. (2011) 'The Impact of Cartel Strategies in France, Greece, Denmark and Ireland', *Working Paper Series on the Legal Regulation of Political Parties*, No. 13 (Leiden: University of Leiden).

Lord, C. and Pollok, J. (2010) 'The EU's Many Representative Modes: Colliding? Cohering?', *Journal of European Public Policy*, vol. 17, no. 1, pp. 117–36.

Loughlin, M. (2010) *Foundations of Public Law* (Oxford: Oxford University Press).

Louwerse, T. (2011) 'The Spatial Approach to the Party Mandate', *Parliamentary Affairs*, vol. 64, no. 3, pp. 425–47.

Loveland, I. (2012) *Constitutional Law, Administrative Law and Human Rights: A Critical Introduction* (6th edn.) (Oxford: Oxford University Press).

Lovenduski, J. (2005) *Feminizing Politics* (Cambridge: Polity).

Lowe, R. and Rollings, N. (2000) 'Modernising Britain, 1957–64: A Classic Case of Centralisation and Fragmentation?, in R. A. W. Rhodes (ed.) *Transforming British Government: Volume 1 Changing Institutions* (Houndmills: Palgrave Macmillan).

Lynch, M. and Young, E. (2011) *Buckinghamshire Pathfinder Patient Public Engagement Pilot: What Keeps You Well? Citizens Jury*, http://www.networks. nhs.uk/nhs-networks/commissioning-zone/development/working-with-the-public/Buckinghamshire%20PPI%20Pilot%20-%20What%20keeps%20 you%20well%20%20Citizens%20Jury%20v3.pdf (accessed 12 January 2013).

MacCormick, N. (1999) *Questioning Sovereignty. Law, State and Nation in the European Commonwealth* (Oxford: Oxford University Press).

MacCormick, N. (2000) 'Is There a Scottish Path to Constitutional Independence', *Parliamentary Affairs*, vol. 53, no. 4, pp. 721–36.

Macdonald, T. (2008) *Global Stakeholder Democracy: Power and Representation Beyond Liberal States* (Oxford: Oxford University Press).

Macdonald, T. (2010) 'The Ideal of Global Stakeholder Democracy', *New Political Science*, vol. 32, no. 1, pp. 110–16.

Mackay, F. (2008a) 'The State of Women's Movement/s in Britain: Ambiguity, Complexity and Challenges from the Periphery', in S. Grey and M. Sawer (eds) *Women's Movements: Flourishing or in Abeyance?* (London: Routledge).

MacKay, F. (2008b) ' "Thick" Conceptions of Substantive Representation: Women, Gender, and Political Institutions', *Representation*, vol. 44, no. 2, pp. 125–39.

Maer, L. (2007) *Citizens' Juries*, Standard Note SN/PC/O4546 (London: House of Commons Library).

Magnette, P. (2005) *What is the European Union? Nature and Prospects* (Houndmills: Palgrave Macmillan).

Mair, P. (2009) 'Representative Versus Responsible Government', *MPIfG Working Paper 09/8* (Cologne: Max Plank Institute for the Study of Societies).

Majone, G. (2005) *Dilemmas of European Integration: The Ambiguities and Pitfalls of Integration by Stealth* (Oxford: Oxford University Press).

Manin, B. (1997) *The Principle of Representative Government* (Cambridge: Cambridge University Press).

Manning, N. and Edwards, K. (2013) 'Does Civic Education for Young People Increase Political Participation? A Systematic Review', *Educational Review,* Early View, DOI: 10.1080/00131911.2013.763767.

Mansbridge, J. (1999a) 'Should Blacks Represent Blacks and Women Represent Women? A Contingent "Yes" ', *Journal of Politics,* vol. 61, no. 3, pp. 628–57.

Mansbridge. J. (1999b) 'Everyday Talk in the Deliberative System', in S. Macedo (ed.) *Deliberative Politics: Essays on Democracy and Disagreement* (Oxford: Oxford University Press).

Mansbridge, J. (2003) 'Rethinking Representation', *American Political Science Review,* vol. 97, no. 4, pp. 515–28.

Mansbridge, J. (2011) 'Clarifying the Concept of Representation', *American Political Science Review,* vol. 105, no. 3, pp. 621–30.

Mansbridge. J., Bohman, J., Chambers, S., Christiano, T., Fung, A., Parkinson, J., Thompson, D. F. and Warren, M. E. (2012) 'A Systemic Approach to Deliberative Democracy', in J. Parkinson and J. Mansbridge (eds) *Deliberative Systems* (Cambridge: Cambridge University Press).

Margaretten, M. and Gaber, I. (2012) 'The Crisis in Public Communication and the Pursuit of Authenticity: An Analysis of the Twitter Feeds of Scottish MPs 2008–2010', *Parliamentary Affairs,* Advance Access, DOI: 10.1093/pa/gss043.

Marien, S. and Hooghe, M. (2011) 'The Effect of Declining Levels of Political Trust on the Governability of Liberal Democracies', Paper presented at the Annual Conference of the Political Studies Association, London, 19–21 April.

Marini, F. (1967) 'Popular Sovereignty but Representative Government: The Other Rousseau', *Midwest Journal of Political Science,* vol. 11, no. 4, pp. 451–70.

Marquand, D. (1988) *The Unprincipled Society* (London: Fontana).

Marsh, D. (2008) 'Understanding British Government: Analysing Competing Models', *British Journal of Politics and International Relations,* vol. 10, no. 2, pp. 251–68.

Marsh, D. (2011) 'The New Orthodoxy: The Differentiated Polity Model', *Public Administration,* vol. 89, no. 1, pp. 32–48.

Marsh, D. (2012) 'British Politics: A View from Afar', *British Politics,* vol. 7, no. 1, pp. 43–54.

Marsh, D., Richards, D. and Smith, M. (2001) *Changing Patterns of Governance in the United Kingdom: Reinventing Whitehall?* (London: Palgrave Macmillan).

Marsh, D., Richards, D. and Smith, M. (2003) 'Unequal Plurality: Towards an Asymmetric Power Model of British Politics', *Government and Opposition,* vol. 38, no. 3, pp. 306–32.

Marsh, I. (2013) 'The Decline of Democratic Governance: An Analysis and a Modest Proposal', *Political Quarterly,* vol. 84, no. 2, pp. 228–37.

McAllister, I. (1998) 'Civic Education and Political Knowledge in Australia', *Australian Journal of Political Science,* vol. 33, no. 1, pp. 7–24.

McGarry, J. (2012) 'The Principle of Parliamentary Sovereignty', *Legal Studies,* vol. 32, no. 4, pp. 577–99.

McGuiness, F. (2012) *UK Election Statistics: 1918–2012,* Research Paper 12/43 (London: House of Commons Library).

McLaverty, P. (2009) 'Is Deliberative Democracy the Answer to Representative Democracy's Problems? A Consideration of the UK Government's Programme of Citizens' Juries', *Representation,* vol. 45, no. 4, pp. 380–9.

McLean, I. (2010) *What's Wrong with the British Constitution* (Oxford: Oxford University Press).

McLean, I. (2012) '"England Does Not Love Coalitions": The Most Misused Political Quotation in the Book', *Government and Opposition*, vol. 47, no. 1, pp. 3–20.

Mendelsohn, M. and Parkin, A. (2001) 'Introduction: Referendum Democracy', in M. Mendelsohn and A. Parkin (eds) *Referendum Democracy: Citizens, Elites and Deliberation in Referendum Campaigns* (Houndmills: Palgrave Macmillan).

Michels, A. (2011) 'Innovations in Democratic Governance: How Does Citizen Participation Contribute to a Better Democracy?', *International Review of Administrative Sciences*, vol. 77, no. 2, pp. 275–93.

Millard, P., Millard, K., Adams, C. and McMillan, S. (2012) 'Transforming Government Through e-Participation: Challenges for e-Democracy', in M. Gascó (ed.) *Proceedings of the 12th European Conference on e-Government*, vol. 1 (Barcelona: Institute of Public Governance and Management, ESADE).

Miller, L. (2009) 'e-Petitions at Westminster: The Way Forward for Democracy?', *Parliamentary Affairs*, vol. 62, no. 1, pp. 162–77.

Ministry of Justice. (2008) *A National Framework for Greater Citizen Engagement* (London: Stationery Office).

Mitchell, J. (2009) *Devolution in the UK* (Manchester: Manchester University Press).

Modood, T. (2010) 'Ethnicity and Religion', in M. Flinders, A. Gamble, C. Hay and M. Kenny (eds) *The Oxford Handbook of British Politics* (Oxford: Oxford University Press).

Montanaro, L. (2010) *The Democratic Legitimacy of Self-Appointed Representatives* (Vancouver: University of British Columbia).

Moran, M. (2011) *Politics and Governance in the UK* (2nd edn.) (Houndmills: Palgrave Macmillan).

Moss, G. and Coleman, S. (2013) 'Deliberative Manoeuvres in the Digital Darkness: e-Democracy Policy in the UK', *British Journal of Politics and International Relations*, Early View, DOI: 10.1111/1467-856X.12004.

Nabatchi, T. (2010) 'Addressing the Citizenship and Democratic Deficits: The Potential of Deliberative Democracy for Public Administration', *American Review of Public Administration*, vol. 40, no. 4, pp. 376–99.

Näsström, S. (2011) 'Where is the Representative Turn Going?', *European Journal of Political Theory*, vol. 10, no. 4, pp. 501–10.

National Assembly of Wales. (2012) *Petitioning the Assembly: Discover, Debate, Decide* (Cardiff: National Assembly of Wales).

Newton, K. (2001) 'Trust, Social Capital, Civil Society, and Democracy', *International Political Science Review*, vol. 22, no. 2, pp. 201–14.

Newton, K. (2012) 'Curing the Democratic Malaise with Democratic Innovations', in B. Geissel and K. Newton (eds) *Evaluating Democratic Innovations: Curing the Democratic Malaise* (London: Routledge).

Newton, K. and Zmerli, S. (2011) 'Three Forms of Trust and Their Association', *European Political Science Review*, vol. 3, no. 2, pp. 169–200.

Norderval, I. (1985) 'Party and Legislative Participation Among Scandinavian Women', in S. Basekin (ed.) *Women and Politics in Western Europe* (London: Frank Cass).

Norris, P. (1996) 'Women Politicians: Transforming Westminster?', *Parliamentary Affairs*, vol. 49, no. 1, pp. 89–102.

Norris, P. (2011) *Democratic Deficit: Critical Citizens Revisited* (Cambridge: Cambridge University Press).

Norris, P. and Lovenduski, J. (1989) 'Women Candidates for Parliament: Transforming the Agenda', *British Journal of Political Science*, vol. 19, no. 1, pp. 106–15.

Norris, P. and Lovenduski, J. (1995) *Political Representation: Gender, Race and Class in the British Parliament* (Cambridge: Cambridge University Press).

Norton, P. (2012) 'Comparing Leadership Patterns and Dynamics in the Legislative Arena', in L. Helms (ed.) *Comparative Political Leadership* (Houndmills: Palgrave Macmillan).

Norton, P. (2012) 'Parliament and Citizens in the UK', *Journal of Legislative Studies*, vol. 18, no. 3–4, pp. 403–18.

Norton, P. (2013) *Parliament in British Politics* (2nd edn.) (Houndmills: Palgrave Macmillan).

O'Cinneide, C. (2012) *Human Rights and the UK Constitution* (London: British Academy).

Opinion Leader. (2009) *Public Perceptions of Industrial Biotechnology: A Report Prepared for the Department for Business Enterprise and Regulatory Reform (BERR) and Sciencewise*, http://www.berr.gov.uk/files/file51238.pdf (accessed 19 December 2012).

Oppermann, K. (2013) 'The Politics of Discretionary Government Commitments to European Integration Referendums', *Journal of European Public Policy*, vol. 20, no. 5, pp. 684–701.

Ostling, A. (2012) 'Parliamentary Informatics Projects: Who are Their Users and What is Their Impact?', *eJournal of eDemocracy and Open Government*, vol. 4, no. 2, pp. 279–300.

Page, E. (2010) 'Has the Whitehall Model Survived?', *International Review of Administrative Sciences*, vol. 76, no. 3, pp. 407–23.

Panagiotopoulos, P. and Elliman, T. (2012) 'Online Engagement from the Grassroots: Reflecting on over a Decade of e-Petitioning Experience in Europe and the UK', in Y. Charalabidis and S. Koussouris (eds) *Empowering Open and Collaborative Governance* (Berlin: Springer).

Panagiotopoulos, P., Moody C. and Elliman, T. (2011) 'An Overview Assessment of e-Petitioning Tools in the English Local Government', in E. Tambouris, A. Macintosh and H. de Bruijn (eds) *e-Part 2011: IFIP 3rd International Conference on e-Participation* (Berlin: Springer).

Papacharissi, Z. (2009) 'The Virtual Sphere 2.0: The Internet, the Public Sphere, and Beyond', in A. Chadwick and P. N. Howard (eds) *Routledge Handbook of Internet Politics* (London: Routledge).

Parkinson, J. (2006) *Deliberating in the Real World: Problems of Legitimacy in Deliberative Democracy* (Oxford: Oxford University Press).

Parkinson, J. (2010) 'Conceptualising and Mapping the Deliberative Society', Paper Presented at the Political Studies Association Annual Conference, Edinburgh, 29 March – 1 April.

Parkinson, J. (2012) 'Democratizing Deliberative Systems', in J. Parkinson and J. Mansbridge (eds) *Deliberative Systems* (Cambridge: Cambridge University Press).

Parliament Street. (2012) *Parliament: The Failure of MPs to connect on Twitter*, http://www.parliamentstreet.org/wp-content/uploads/2013/04/socialmedia.pdf (accessed 31 May 2013).

Parliament Street. (2013) *Twitter Index 2013*, http://parliamentstreet.org/ (accessed 27 September 2013).

Pateman, C. (2012) 'Participatory Democracy Revisited', *Perspectives on Politics*, vol. 10, no. 1, pp. 7–19.

Pattie, C. J., Johnston R. J. and Stuart, M. (1998) 'Voting Without Party?', in P. Cowley (ed.) *Conscience and Parliament* (London: Frank Cass).

Peele, G. (1998) 'Towards "New Conservatives"? Organisational Reform and the Conservative Party', *Political Quarterly*, vol. 69, no. 2, pp. 141–7.

Pennock, J. R. (1979) *Democratic Political Theory* (Princeton: Princeton University Press).

Peters, B. G. and Pierre, J. (2004) 'Multi-Level Governance and Democracy: A Faustian Bargain', in I. Bache and M. Flinders (eds) *Multi-Level Governance* (Oxford: Oxford University Press).

Phillips, A. (1995) *The Politics of Presence* (Oxford: Clarendon Press).

Phillips Griffiths, A. P. (1960) 'How Can One Person Represent Another?', *Proceedings of the Aristotelian Society*, vol. 34, pp. 187–208.

Phillips, H. (2007) *Strengthening Democracy: Fair and Sustainable Funding of Political Parties*, The Review of the Funding of Political Parties (London: Stationery Office).

Phillips, H. (2012) 'The Funding of Political Parties', *Political Quarterly*, vol. 83, no. 2, pp. 318–24.

Pickles, E. (2010) 'New People Power to End the Era of Soaring Council Tax', Announcement, 30 July (London: Department for Communities and Local Government).

Pierre, J., Svåsand, L. and Widfeldt, A. (2000) 'State Subsidies to Political Parties: Confronting Rhetoric with Reality', *West European Politics*, vol. 23, no. 1, pp. 1–24.

Pitkin, H. F. (1967) *The Concept of Representation* (Berkeley: University of California Press).

Pratchett, L. (2012) 'Local e-Democracy in Five European Countries: Convergence and Divergence in Democratic Development', in I. Snellen, M. Thaens and W. B. H. J. van de Donk (eds) *Public Administration in the Information Age: Revisited* (Amsterdam: IOS Press).

Puntscher Riekmann, S. and Wydra, D. (2013) 'Representation and Democracy in the European State of Emergency: Does One Come at the Expense of the Other', *Journal of European Integration*, vol. 35, no. 5, pp. 565–82.

Putnam, R. D. (1993) *Making Democracy Work: Civic Traditions in Modern Italy* (Princeton: Princeton University Press).

Putnam, R. D. (1995) 'Bowling Alone: America's Declining Social Capital', *Journal of Democracy*, vol. 6, no. 1, pp. 65–78.

Putnam, R. D. (2000) *Bowling Alone: The Collapse and Revival of American Community* (New York: Simon & Schuster).

PwC. (2010) *Dealing With the Deficit: The Citizen's View* (London: PricewaterhouseCoopers) http://www.pwcwebcast.co.uk/dpliv_mu/dealing_with_the_deficit/citizens_review.pdf (accessed 3 February 2013).

PwC. (2011) *Citizens' Jury: One Year On* (London: PricewaterhouseCoopers) http://www.pwc.co.uk/government-public-sector/issues/citizens-jury-one-year-on.jhtml (accessed 3 February 2013).

Pyper, R. and Burnham, J. (2011) 'The British Civil Service: Perspectives on "Decline" and "Modernisation" ', *British Journal of Politics and International Relations*, vol. 13, no. 2, pp. 189–205.

Quinn, T. (2004) *Modernising the Labour Party: Organisational Change Since 1983* (Houndmills: Palgrave Macmillan).

Quinn, T. (2013) 'From Two-Partism to Alternating Predominance: The Changing UK Party System 1950–2010', *Political Studies*, vol. 61, no. 2, pp. 378–400.

Quintelier, E. and Hooghe, M. (2012) 'Political Attitudes and Political Participation: A Panel Study on Socialisation and Self-Selection Effects Among Late Adolescents', *International Political Science Review*, vol. 33, no. 1, pp. 63–81.

Qvortrup, M. (1999) 'A. V. Dicey: The Referendum as the People's Veto', *History of Political Thought*, vol. 20, no. 3, pp. 531–46.

Rallings, C. (1987) 'The Influence of Election Programmes: Britain and Canada, 1945–79', in I. Budge, D. Robertson and D. J. Hearl (eds) *Ideology, Strategy and Party Change: Spatial Analyses of Post-war Election Programmes in 19 Democracies* (Cambridge: Cambridge University Press).

Rallings, C. and Thrasher, M. (2005) 'Not All "Second-Order" Contests are the Same: Turnout and Party Choice at the Concurrent 2004 Local and European Elections in England', *British Journal of Politics and International Relations*, vol. 7, no. 4, pp. 484–597.

Rask, M., Maciukaite-Zviniene, S. and Petrauskiene, J. (2012) 'Innovations in Public Engagement and Participatory Performance of the Nations', *Science and Public Policy*, vol. 39, no. 6, pp. 710–21.

Rasmussen, M. K. (2012) 'The Empowerment of Parliaments in EU Integration: Victims or Victors', in J. Hayward and R. Wurzel (eds) *European Disunion: Between Sovereignty and Solidarity* (Houndmills: Palgrave Macmillan).

Rehfeld, A. (2005) *The Concept of Constituency: Political Representation, Democratic Legitimacy, and Institutional Design* (Cambridge: Cambridge University Press).

Rehfeld, A. (2006) 'Towards a General Theory of Political Representation', *The Journal of Politics*, vol. 68, no. 1, pp. 1–21.

Rehfeld, A. (2009) 'Gyroscopes in the Study of Political Representation and Democracy', *American Political Science Review*, vol. 103, no. 2, pp. 214–30.

Rehfeld, A. (2011) 'The Concepts of Representation', *American Political Science Review*, vol. 105, no. 3, pp. 631–41.

Rhodes. R. A. W. (1994) 'The Hollowing Out of the State: The Changing Nature of the Public Service in Britain', *Political Quarterly*, vol. 65, no. 2, pp. 138–41.

Rhodes, R. A. W. (1997) *Understanding Governance: Policy Networks, Governance, Reflexivity and Accountability* (London: Open University Press).

Rhodes, R. A. W. (2008) 'Understanding Governance: Ten Years On', *Organization Studies*, vol. 28, no. 8, pp. 1243–64.

Rhodes, R. A. W. (2011) *Everyday Life in British Government* (Oxford: Oxford University Press).

Rhodes, R. A. W. and Marsh, D. (1992a) 'Policy Networks in British Politics: A Critique of Existing Approaches', in D. Marsh and R. A. W. Rhodes (eds) *Policy Networks in British Government* (Oxford: Oxford University Press).

Rhodes, R. A. W. and Marsh, D. (1992b) 'Policy Communities and Issue Networks: Beyond Typology', in D. Marsh and R. A. W. Rhodes (eds) *Policy Networks in British Government* (Oxford: Oxford University Press).

Rhodes, R. A. W. and Marsh, D. (1992c) 'New Directions in the Study of Policy Networks', *European Journal of Political Research*, vol. 21, no. 1–2, pp. 181–205.

Rhodes, R. A. W., Wanna, J. and Weller, P. (2009) *Comparing Westminster* (Oxford: Oxford University Press).

Richards, D. (2008) *New Labour and the Civil Service: Reconstituting the Westminster Model* (Houndmills: Palgrave Macmillan).

Richards, D. and Mathers, H. (2010) 'Political Memoirs and New Labour: Interpretations of Power and "Club Rules" ', *British Journal of Politics and International Relations*, vol. 12, no. 4, pp. 498–522.

Richards, D. and Smith, M. J. (2002) *Governance and Public Policy in the UK* (Oxford: Oxford University Press).

Richardson, J. J. (1993) 'Introduction: Pressure Groups and Government', in J. J. Richardson (ed.) *Pressure Groups* (Oxford: Oxford University Press).

Richardson, J. J. (2000) 'Government, Interest Groups and Policy Change', *Political Studies*, vol. 48, no. 5, pp. 1006–25.

Richardson, J. J. and Jordan, A. G. (1979) *Governing Under Pressure: The Policy Process in a Post-Parliamentary Democracy* (Oxford: Martin Robertson).

Riddell, P. (2011) *In Defence of Politicians in Spite of Themselves* (London: Biteback).

Rittberger, B. (2005) *Building Europe's Parliament: Democratic Representation Beyond the Nation-State* (Oxford: Oxford University Press).

Rosanvallon, P. (2008) *Counter-Democracy: Politics in an Age of Distrust* (Cambridge: Cambridge University Press).

Rossiter, D., Johnston, R. and Pattie, C. (2013) 'Representing People and Representing Places: Community, Continuity and the Current Redistribution of Parliamentary Constituencies in the UK', *Parliamentary Affairs*, vol. 66, no. 4, pp. 856–86.

Rothstein, B. (2009) 'Creating Political Legitimacy: Electoral Democracy Versus Quality of Government', *American Behavioral Scientist*, vol. 53, no. 3, pp. 311–20.

Rousseau, J-J. ([1762] 1968) *The Social Contract* (Harmondsworth: Penguin).

Rummens, S. (2012) 'Staging Deliberation: The Role of Representative Institutions in the Deliberative Democratic Process', *The Journal of Political Philosophy*, vol. 20, no. 1, pp. 23–44.

Runciman, D. (2007) 'The Paradox of Political Representation', *The Journal of Political Philosophy*, vol. 15, no. 1, pp. 93–114.

Rush, M. and Giddings, P. (2011) *Parliamentary Socialisation: Learning the Ropes or Determining Behaviour* (Houndmills: Palgrave Macmillan).

Russell, M. (2005) *Building New Labour: The Politics of Party Organisation* (Houndmills: Palgrave Macmillan).

Russell, M. (2012) 'Parliamentary Party Cohesion: Some Explanations from Psychology', *Party Politics*, Advance Access, DOI: 10.1177/1354068812453367.

Ryfe, D. M. (2005) 'Does Deliberative Democracy Work?', *Annual Review of Political Science*, vol. 8, pp. 49–71.

Saffon, M. P. and Urbinati, N. (2013) 'Procedural Democracy, the Bulwark of Equal Liberty', *Political Theory*, vol. 41, no. 3, pp. 441–81.

Saggar, S. (1992) *Race and Politics in Britain* (London: Harvester Wheatsheaf).

Sartori, G. ([1976] 2005) *Parties and Party Systems: A Framework for Analysis* (Colchester: ECPR Press).

Sartori, G. (1987) *The Theory of Democracy Revisited* (Chatham: Chatham House).

Saunders, B. (2012) 'The Democratic Turnout "Problem" ', *Political Studies*, vol. 60, no. 2, pp. 306–20.

Saward, M. (2003) 'Enacting Democracy', *Political Studies*, vol. 51, no. 1, pp. 161–79.

Saward, M. (2010) *The Representative Claim* (Oxford: Oxford University Press).

Saward, M. (2011) 'The Wider Canvas: Representation and Democracy in State and Society', in S. Alonso, J. Keane and W. Merkel (eds) *The Future of Representative Democracy* (Cambridge: Cambridge).

Scharpf, F. W. (2012) *Legitimacy Intermediation in Multilevel European Polity and its Collapse in the Euro Crisis*, MPiFG Discussion Paper, no. 12/6, http://www.econstor.eu/dspace/handle/10419/66580 (accessed 26 June 2013).

Schattsneider, E. E. (1960) *The Semisovereign People: A Realists' View of Democracy in America* (New York: Holt).

Schmidt, V. A. (2013) 'Democracy and Legitimacy in the European Union Revisited: Input, Output and Throughput', *Political Studies*, vol. 61, no. 1, pp. 2–22.

Schumpeter, J. A. ([1943] 1976) *Capitalism, Socialism, and Democracy* (5th edn.) (London: Allen & Unwin).

Schüttemeyer, S. S. (2009) 'Deparliamentarisation: How Severely is the German Bundestag Affected?', *German Politics*, vol. 18, no. 1, pp. 1–11.

Scottish Parliament. (2013) *Petitioning the Scottish Parliament: Making Your Voice Heard* (Edinburgh: Scottish Parliament).

Seaton, J. (2005) 'The Scottish Parliament and e-Democracy', *Aslib Proceedings*, vol. 57, no. 4, pp. 333–7.

Sedley, S. (1995) 'Human Rights: A Twenty-First Century Agenda', *Public Law*, no. 3, pp. 386–400.

Serricchio, F., Tsakatika, M. and Quaglia, L. (2013) 'Euroscepticism and the Global Financial Crisis', *Journal of Common Market Studies*, vol. 51, no. 1, pp. 51–64.

Setälä, M. (2011) 'The Role of Deliberative Mini-Publics in Representative Democracy: Lessons From the Experience of Referendums', *Representation*, vol. 47, no. 2, pp. 201–13.

Severs, E. (2010) 'Representation as Claims-Making. Quid Responsiveness?', *Representation*, vol. 46, no. 4, pp. 411–23.

Severs, E. (2012) 'Substantive Representation Through a Claims-Making Lens: A Strategy for the Identification and Analysis of Substantive Claims', *Representation*, vol. 48, no. 2, pp. 169–81.

Shaw, J. (1999) 'Postnational Constitutionalism in the European Union', *Journal of European Public Policy*, vol. 6, no. 4, pp. 579–97.

Sloam, J. (2012) ' "Reinventing Democracy?" Young People and the "Big Society" Project', *Parliamentary Affairs*, vol. 65, no. 1, pp. 90–114.

Smets, K. and van Ham, C. (2013) 'The Embarrassment of Riches? A Meta-Analysis of Individual-Level Research on Voter Turnout', *Electoral Studies*, vol. 32, no. 2, pp. 344–59.

Smismans, S. (2013) 'Democracy and Legitimacy in the European Union', in M. Cini and N. Pérez-Solórzano Borragán (eds) *European Union Politics* (Oxford: Oxford University Press).

Smith, G (2009) *Democratic Innovations: Designing Institutions for Citizen Participation* (Cambridge: Cambridge University Press).

Smith, G. (2012) 'Deliberative Democracy and Mini-Publics', in B. Geissel and K. Newton (eds) *Evaluating Democratic Innovations: Curing the Democratic Malaise* (London: Routledge).

Smith, M. J. (2008) 'Re-Centring British Government: Beliefs, Traditions and Dilemmas in Political Science', *Political Studies Review*, vol. 6, no. 2, pp. 143–54.

Soroka, S. N. and Wlezien, C. (2010) *Degrees of Democracy: Politics, Public Opinion and Policy* (Cambridge: Cambridge University Press).

Squires, J. (2008) 'The Constitutive Representation of Gender: Extra-Parliamentary Re-presentations of Gender Relations', *Representation*, vol. 44, no. 2, pp. 187–204.

Stark, A. (2011), 'The Tradition of Ministerial Responsibility and its Role in the Bureaucratic Management of Crises', *Public Administration*, vol. 89, no. 3, pp. 1148–63.

Stewart, J. D. (1958) *British Pressure Groups* (Oxford: Clarendon Press).

Stoker, G. (2006) *Democracy Matters. Making Democracy Work* (Houndmills: Palgrave Macmillan).

Stoker, G. (2011) *Building a New Politics: A Report Prepared for the British Academy* (London: British Academy).

Stokes, S. C. (1999) 'Political Parties and Democracy', *Annual Review of Political Science*, vol. 2, pp. 243–67.

Stolle, D. (2007) 'Social Capital', in R. Dalton and H-D. Klingemann (eds) *The Oxford Handbook of Political Behaviour* (Oxford: Oxford University Press).

Stolle, D. and Hooghe, M. (2005) 'Review Article: Inaccurate, Exceptional, One-Sided or Irrelevant? The Debate about the Alleged Decline of Social Capital and Civic Engagement in Western Societies', *British Journal of Political Science*, vol. 35, no. 1, pp. 149–67.

Straw, J. (2010a) 'New Labour, Constitutional Change and Representative Democracy', *Parliamentary Affairs*, vol. 63, no. 2, pp. 356–68.

Straw, J. (2010b) 'The Human Rights Act – Ten Years On', *European Human Rights Law Review*, no. 6, pp. 576–81.

Studlar, D. T. (1986) 'Non-White Policy Preferences, Political Participation and the Political Agenda in Britain', in Z. Layton-Henry and P. B. Rich (eds) *Race, Government and Politics in Britain* (London: Macmillan).

Tant, A. P. (1993) *British Government: The Triumph of Elitism: A Study of the British Political Tradition and its Major Challenges* (London: Dartmouth).

Thomson, R., Royed, T., Naurin, E., Artés, J., Ferguson, M., Kostadinova, P. and Moury, C. (2012) 'The Program-to-Policy Linkage: A Comparative Study of Election Pledges and Government Policies in Ten Countries', Paper Prepared for the 2012 Annual Meeting of the American Political Science Association, New Orleans, 30 August – 2 September.

Thorup Larsen, L., Studlar, D. T. and Green-Pedersen, C. (2012), 'Morality Politics in the United Kingdom: Trapped Between Left and Right', in I. Engeli, C. Green-Pedersen and L. Thorup Larsen (eds) *Morality Politics in Western Europe: Parties, Agendas and Policy Choices* (Houndmills: Palgrave Macmillan).

Tierney, S. (2009) 'Constitutional Referendums: A Theoretical Enquiry', *Modern Law Review*, vol. 72, no. 3, pp. 360–83.

Tierney, S. (2012) *Constitutional Referendums: The Theory and Practice of Republican Deliberation* (Oxford: Oxford University Press).

Tilley, J. and Wlezien, C. (2008) 'Does Political Information Matter? An Experimental Test Relating to Party Positions on Europe', *Political Studies*, vol. 56, no. 1, pp. 192–214.

Torfing, J., Peters, B. G., Pierre, J. and Søressen, E. (2012) *Interactive Governance: Advancing the Paradigm* (Oxford: Oxford University Press).

Turpin, C. and Tomkins, A. (2011) *British Government and the Constitution* (7th edn.) (Oxford: Oxford University Press).

UK Parliament. (2013) *The UK Political System: About Parliament*, http://www.parliament.uk/about/how/role/parliament-government/ (accessed 11 March 2013).

UKHL 56. (2005) *Judgments – Jackson and others (Appellants) v. Her Majesty's Attorney General (Respondent)*, House of Lords Session 2005–06, http://www.publications.parliament.uk/pa/ld200506/ldjudgmt/jd051013/jack-1.htm (accessed 12 November 2012).

Urbinati, N. (2006) *Representative Democracy* (Chicago: University of Chicago Press).

Urbinati, N. (2010) 'Unpolitical Democracy', *Political Theory*, vol. 38, no. 1, pp. 65–92.

Urbinati, N. (2011) 'Representative Democracy and its Critics', in S. Alonso, J. Keane and W. Merkel (eds) *The Future of Representative Democracy* (Cambridge: Cambridge University Press).

Urbinati, N. and Warren, M. E. (2008) 'The Concept of Representation in Democratic Theory', *Annual Review of Political Science*, vol. 11, pp. 387–412.

van Deth, J. W. (2008) 'Introduction: Social Capital and Democratic Politics', in D. Castiglione, J. W. van Deth and G. Wolleb (eds) *The Handbook of Social Capital* (Oxford: Oxford University Press).

van Dorpe, K. and Horton, S. (2011) 'The Public Service Bargain in the United Kingdom: The Whitehall Model in Decline?', *Public Policy and Administration*, vol. 26, no. 2, pp. 233–52.

Vorländer, H. (2013) 'Bringing Democracy Back In? From Local Politics to Global Politics', in J-C. Merle (ed.) *Spheres of Global Justice: Volume 1 Global Challenges to Liberal Democracy. Political Participation, Minorities and Migrations* (Berlin: Springer).

Wahlke, J. C., Eulau, H., Buchanan, W. and Ferguson, L. C. (1962) *The Legislative System* (New York: Wiley).

Walker, N. (2013) 'Sovereignty Frames and Sovereignty Claims', *Research Paper Series*, No 2013/14 (Edinburgh: University of Edinburgh School of Law).

Walzer, M. (1999) 'Deliberation, and What Else?', in S. Macedo (ed.) *Deliberative Politics: Essays on Democracy and Disagreement* (Oxford: Oxford University Press).

Wängnerud, L. (2009) 'Women in Parliaments: Descriptive and Substantive Representation', *Annual Review of Political Science*, vol. 12, pp. 51–69.

Ware, A. (1987) *Citizens, Parties and the State* (Cambridge: Polity).

Ware, A. (1996) *Political Parties and Party Systems* (Oxford: Oxford University Press).

Wauters, B. (2010) 'Bringing Class (Back) In: Methodological Reflections on Social Class and Representation', *Representation*, vol. 46, no. 2, pp. 183–95.

Weale, A. (2007) *Democracy* (2nd edn.) (Houndmills, Palgrave Macmillan).

Webb, P. (1994) 'Party Organizational Change in Britain: The Iron Law of Centralization', in R. S. Katz and P. Mair (eds) *How Parties Organize* (London: Sage).

Webb, P. (2000) *The Modern British Party System* (London: Sage).

Webb, P. (2009) 'The Failings of Political Parties: Reality or Perception?', *Representation*, vol. 45, no. 3, pp. 265–75.

Webb, P. and Childs, S. (2012) 'Gender Politics and Conservatism: The View from the British Conservative Party Grassroots', *Government and Opposition*, vol. 47, no. 1, pp. 21–48.

Weill, R. (2003) 'Dicey was not Diceyan', *Cambridge Law Journal*, vol. 62, no. 2, pp 474–94.

White, I. (2012) *Prisoners' Voting Rights*, House of Commons Standard Note Sn/PC/01764 (London: House of Commons).

Whiteley, P. (2009) 'Participation and Social Capital', in M. Flinders, A. Gamble, C. Hay and M. Kenny (eds) *The Oxford Handbook of British Politics* (Oxford: Oxford University Press).

Whiteley, P. (2012) *Political Participation in Britain: The Decline and Renewal of Civic Culture* (Houndmills: Palgrave Macmillan).

Wilks-Heeg, S. (2011) 'Funding UK Political Parties: A Democratic Dilemma', *Political Insight*, vol. 2, no. 1, pp. 22–5.

Wilks-Heeg, S., Blick, A. and Crone, S. (2012) *How Democratic is the UK? The 2012 Audit* (Liverpool: Democratic Audit) http://demaudituk.wpengine.com/wp-content/uploads/2013/07/auditing-the-uk-democracy-the-framework.pdf (accessed 9 August 2013).

Wilks-Heeg, S. and Crone, S. (2010) *Funding Political Parties in Great Britain: A Pathway to Reform* (Liverpool: Democratic Audit).

Williamson, A. (2009) *MPs online: Connecting with Constituents* (London: Hansard Society).

Williamson, A. (2010) '2010: The Internet Election that Wasn't', *Political Insight*, vol. 1, no. 2, pp. 58–60.

Williamson, A., Miller, L. and Fallon, F. (2010) *Behind the Digital Campaign: An Exploration of the Use, Impact and Regulation of Digital Campaigning* (London: Hansard Society).

Wills, M. (2010) *Accountability Under Democratic Constitutions*, Speech at Wilton Park, February, http://www.opendemocracy.net/ourkingdom/michael-wills/accountability-under-democratic-constitutions (accessed 9 January 2013).

Wright, A. (2010) 'What Are MPs For?', *Political Quarterly*, vol. 81, no. 3, pp. 298–308.

Wright, A. (2012) *Doing Politics* (London: Biteback).

Wright, S. (2009) 'Political Blogs, Representation and the Public Sphere', *Aslib Proceedings*, vol. 61, no. 2, pp. 155–69.

Wright, S. (2011) 'Politics as Usual? Revolution, Normalization and a New Agenda for Online Deliberation', *New Media and Society*, vol. 14, no. 2, pp. 244–61.

Wright, S. (2012) 'From "Third Place" to "Third Space": Everyday Political Talk in Non-Political Online Spaces', *Javnost – The Public*, vol. 19, no. 3, pp. 5–20.

YouGov. (2011a) *YouGov/Sunday Times Survey Results*, Fieldwork: 27–28 October 2011, http://cdn.yougov.com/cumulus_uploads/document/4024/Sunday%20Times%20Results%20111028%20VI%20and%20Trackers%20website.pdf (accessed 30 July 2012).

YouGov. (2011b) *YouGov/Sunday Times Survey Results*, Fieldwork: 3–4 November 2011, http://cdn.yougov.com/cumulus_uploads/document/2011-11-04/YG-Archives-Pol-Sun-results-041111.pdf (accessed 30 July 2012).

Young, A. (2009) *Parliamentary Sovereignty and the Human Rights Act* (Oxford: Hart Publishing).

Index